HIGHER EDUCATION
IN NORTH CAROLINA
BEFORE 1860

D0914870

Other books by William Earle Drake:

The American School in Transition

Co-author of:

Sociological Foundations of Education
Significant Aspects of American Life
and Postwar Education
Teaching World Affairs in American Schools
Reports on European Education

HIGHER EDUCATION IN NORTH CAROLINA BEFORE 1860

by William Earle Drake

A Reflection Book

Carlton Press, New York

PREFACE

The history of higher education in North Carolina before 1860 may be logically divided into the colonial period, with its European traditions and frontier conditions; the influence of eighteenth century rationalism on the founding of the University of North Carolina; the administration of the new institution; the founding and growth of the denominational schools; the college curriculum with a dominant classical interest; the interests, manners, and morals of *ante-bellum* college students and the growth of an interest in the higher education of women.

It is the purpose of this book not only to give the facts concerning the founding and growth of the early colleges of North Carolina but to study life on the campus and in the class room. In the study of the colonial period, the purpose becomes one of seeing what forces prohibited the establishing of an institution of collegiate rank. Throughout this study, attention is devoted to those individuals who stood foremost in the higher education field. William R. Davie, through his leadership, made possible the founding of a state university, but he was not able to keep it in conformity with the ideals which had led him to urge its establishment. David Lowry Swain became president of the University in 1835, with less than one year's college training, but the state institution under his leadership rose to a place of national prominence. Braxton Craven's interest lay primarily in the establishing of a normal college, but the failure of the state to grant him the necessary support for his school forced him to turn to the Methodists for aid. The students' general revolt against the various by-laws passed for

v

the control of their actions as revealed by the faculty minutes of the colleges, the every day interests of the students, their manners and their morals, all throw new light on the *antebellum* college and its work. In the field of the higher education of women, the period proves to be one of controversy and of experimentation among the denominations, with the Moravians making noticeable accomplishments, but with an indifferent attitude continually manifested by the state.

I wish to express my gratitude to all those who have in any way aided in making this work possible. Especially do I wish to thank Miss Mary Thornton of the library of the University of North Carolina who made it possible for me to have access to the manuscript material bearing on the University; Mr. J. P. Breedlove, librarian of Duke University; Miss Cornelia Rebecca Shaw, librarian of Davidson College; Mrs. Ethel T. Crittenden, librarian of Wake Forest College; Miss Adelaide Fries, former librarian of Salem College; Mrs. Reuben A. Alley, librarian of Greensboro Female College, and Dr. Albert Ray Newsome, Secretary of the North Carolina Historical Commission.

Above and beyond all, I wish to express my deep appreciation to the late Professor Edgar W. Knight for his many helpful suggestions and criticism.

CONTENTS

CONTENTS

HIGHER EDUCATION
IN NORTH CAROLINA
BEFORE 1860

I

Introduction

The colonial history of North Carolina was a period of general educational neglect, and few attempts were made to establish any kind of an institution of higher education. The geographic conditions, marked particularly by the absence of good harbors, the widely scattered rural settlements, the absence of urban centers, the general conditions of economic life, all worked against a wholesome intellectual atmosphere. In 1728, after more than half a century of settlement, there were not more than 10,000 people in the colony. In 1790 the 393,-751 inhabitants gave North Carolina the rank of third in population in the Union, but the people were sparsely settled. Bath, the first town, was incorporated in 1704; yet, before 1750 no town west of the line later followed by the Wilmington and Weldon Railroad had a population of 1,000. Newbern, "the metropolis of North Carolina," in 1777 boasted about 150 houses, Hillsboro was only a frontier village, and Wilmington had less than 1000 inhabitants. Most of the early settlers, who came from Virginia, were of English descent, while those who immigrated into the Piedmont section of the colony after 1735 were Scotch, German, and Irish by birth. Of the denominations represented, there were Anglicans, Quakers, Presbyterians, Roman Catholics, Baptists, Anabaptists and, in the latter part of the period, Methodists.

In the eastern part of the colony, living in the scattered settlements along the river banks, most of the people led an isolated life under the influence of frontier conditions which did not encourage educational and intellectual interests. No school existed in the county of Chowan before 1714; there was only one sorry church building, and it was not finished. The inhabitants were poor and unsettled.[1] Little corn was planted, largely because the raising of the crop required too much work, and the abundance of the flora and fauna seems to have encouraged idleness and slip-shod methods of agriculture generally. When Carolina tar was "landed in Europe, the external appearance of the barrel" was "disgusting, but the contents" were "supposed to be worse," containing "sand, chips, leaves and water." "Defects in the barreling of pork" were "also injurious to the North Carolina Planter."[2] "Surely there is no place in the World," wrote Colonel William Byrd, in *The History of the Dividing Line*, in 1728, "where the inhabitants live with less labor than in North Carolina ... by the great felicity of the climate, the easiness of raising provisions, and the slothfulness of the people."[3] The burden of the work seems to have been thrown upon the women. Even the newcomer was forced to adapt himself to the same conditions or be outlawed in the community. Drones were common; plantations were slovenly; Negroes were careless, and a wholesome attitude toward "that damned European stuff" did not exist.[4] Again, if Miss Schaw may be believed, the Sirocco rendered everyone "languid in thought, word, and deed."[5]

Widely scattered settlements, lack of the means of communication, and the perils of traveling made intercourse even among the wealthy almost impossible; while a wide breadth of forest separated the Catawba section from that of the Cape

---

1. *Colonial Records,* Vol. II, p. 119.
2. Williamson, Hugh, *The History of North Carolina,* Vol. II, pp. 213-215.
3. Byrd, William, *The Westover Manuscripts: Containing the History of the Dividing Line Betwixt Virginia and North Carolina,* p. 27.
4. Schaw, Janet, *The Journal of a Lady of Quality,* (ed. E. W. and C. M. Andrews) p. 166.
5. *Ibid.,* p. 183.

Fear for many years after the Revolution. Before 1776 there were no mails at all for the interior of the state. According to the most reliable evidence available, no newspaper was printed in the state before 1751, the first being the *North Carolina Gazette* printed by James Davis at Newbern. Only two other newspapers were printed in the state before the American Revolution. In 1790 the only paper which existed west of Fayetteville was the *North Carolina Gazette* published at Hillsboro by Thomas, the son of James Davis. Not one of these newspapers seems to have attained a wide circulation; and they were often no larger than half of a modern newspaper sheet. "On the whole they were less original, less enterprising, less daring, and less able to influence the thought and action of their readers than those of Boston, New York and Philadelphia."[6]

Little activity was also manifested in the publication of books. Tracks and letters of a political nature were written by such men as Maurice Moore, Herman Husbands, William Hooper and James Iredell. Religious literature in the form of tracks and letters was also published by the Established Church, the Presbyterians, and the Quakers. Educational works were few. The Reverend James Hall wrote a grammar to use in his classes, and the Reverend Henry Patillo composed a *Geographical Catechism* which was intended "to assist those who have neither maps, nor gazetteere, to read newspapers, history, or travel."[7] In 1753 Clement Hall, the first native North Carolina author, published at Newbern a *Collection of Many Christian Experiences*. Probably the first American drama was *The Prince of Parthia*, written by Thomas Godfrey while he was at Wilmington in 1759. There is evidence that there was a theatre in the state in 1768.

Occasionally an excellent library was to be found like that of John Rutherford, who lived near Wilmington, which con-

6. Crittenden, C. C., "North Carolina Newspapers Before 1790" in *The James Sprunt Historical Studies,* Vol. 20, No. 1, p. 10.
7. Weeks, S. B., *Libraries and Literature in North Carolina in the Eighteenth Century,* p. 260.

tained fine globes, mathematical instruments, and a set of telescopes, while in the wills and inventories of the gentry a prominent place was quite often given to books.[8] In 1700 probably the first public library in the colony was established in the town of Bath, but by 1712 it had been "all dispersed and lost by those wretches that do not consider the benefit of so valuable a gift,"[9] supposedly being used for waste paper. Perhaps the most important library of the period was built up successively by Governor Eden, Gabriel Johnston, and Governor Samuel Johnston. This collection contained some 535 volumes by the end of the eighteenth century and included the works of Hume, Rousseau, Locke, Montesquieu, Swift, Addison, Voltaire, Hobbes, Shakespeare, and other eminent authors. Among the most cherished books of Alexander Martin's library were three volumes of "Rousseau upon Education" edited by Titus Ogden.[10] Books, mostly of a religious nature, such as Bibles, prayer books, and tracts on doctrine, were supplied by the representatives of the Society for the Propagation of the Gospel in Foreign Parts. In 1755 the Parish of Saint James received from the Society a gift of Bibles, prayer books and other religious materials, and in 1770 an additional gift of Bibles was made. By the end of the Revolution the total contribution amounted to about 500 volumes. There were a few circulating libraries. The Cape Fear Library at Wilmington was active from 1760 to 1770 and was supported by a society of wealthy gentlemen. The circulating library in Mecklenburg County of this period contained much material "replete with infidel sentiment and infidel philosophy."[11] Libraries were also circulating in Rowan and Irdell counties. "The governors, judges, councillors, lawyers, and clergy furnished evidence enough from their letters and other available documents that

8. Grimes, J. Bryan, *North Carolina Wills and Inventories*, Raleigh, Edwards and Broughton, 1912, is the best source available for information on this matter.
9. Weeks, S. B., *op. cit.*, p. 179.
10. *State Records*, Vol. XXII, p. 885.
11. Weeks, S. B., *op. cit.*, p. 221.

among them there was no deficiency in education,"[12] wrote Hawks, but such a statement is, in the light of the evidence, too sweeping.[13]

Land and slaves comprised most of the wealth in the East, with soap and candle making, spinning, distilling, tanning, and weaving as the chief industries on the plantations. In the West the farms were smaller, there were fewer slaves, and the people were more industrious. People in the towns probably lived more decently than those in the isolated areas and some of the ladies of Wilmington could probably have cut a figure in any part of the world in spite of the fact that the men always reminded one of tar and feathers, or so Janet Schaw believed. Marriages were early and families were large, consisting, quite often, of as many as ten children. On the whole the health of the masses was not good as compared with modern conditions, and they were frequently pestered with many diseases. The doctors of the time were not capable of advancing interest in hygiene and sanitation. Sex relations were extremely lax. People frequently lived together without bothering about the marriage ceremony, and attempts by the General Assembly to check such relations did not improve the conditions. Masters were probably often intimate with their female slaves.[14] Morals in general were probably not at a high level. Colonel Byrd's first impression of the citizens of North Carolina was obtained through his association with

A marooner, that modestly called himself a hermit, though he forfeited that name by suffering a wanton female to cohabit with him. His habitation was a bower, covered with bark after the Indian fashion. . . . Like the

---

12. Hawks, Francis L., *History of North Carolina*, Vol. II, p. 369.
13. "The famous Spelling Book of Thomas Dillworth, was not published in England till 1740, nor was it generally introduced into the colonies, till a much later period. Its merits were certified by Doctors in Divinity, learned professors of colleges, and famous schoolmasters; and even the muse sang in praise of its author." Williamson, W. D., "University of North Carolina" in *Hillsborough Recorder*, February 1, 1844, p. 1.
14. *Ibid.*, p. 201.

ravens he neither plowed nor sowed, but subsisted chiefly upon oysters, which his handmaid made a shift to gather from the adjacent rocks. Sometimes, too, for a change of diet, he sent her to drive up the neighbors' cows, to moisten their mouths with a little milk. But as for raiment, he depended mostly upon his lengthy beard, and she upon her length of hair.... Thus did these dirty wretches live in a dirty state of nature, and were mere Adamites, innocence only excepted.[15]

A look at the *Colonial Records* of the state indicates that the government was interested primarily in the building of roads and bridges, in the regulation of ferries, and weights and measures, in the destruction of vermin in the province, the relief of poor debtors, the punishment of crimes, the protection of game, the establishment of annual fairs, the keeping of town fences in repair, the rites of marriage, the establishment of boundary lines, the regulation of the militia and other affairs of government. Outside of these necessary interests the chief diversions of the people were fishing, fowling, and hunting such animals as deer, bear, racoons, hares, and wild turkeys. Horse racing and cock fighting were prevalent practices and dancing a most popular amusement. Much addicted to gambling at cards and dice, the colonists often had stakes amounting to several hundred pounds.[16] Wrestling, at which gouging was often engaged in, and fighting were also quite common. "It would be difficult, indeed, to overestimate the importance of the place social diversions and sports held in colonial life."[17] Drinking habits were prevalent among the people also. William Attmore of Philadelphia, was much pleased with the drink called *egg nog* furnished him before breakfast on a plantation near Tarboro in 1787. Again, in the words of "the Lady of Quality,"

If they can raise as much corn and pork, as to subsist them in the most slovenly manner, they ask no more; and

---

15. Byrd, William, *op. cit.*, pp. 13-14.
16. Brickell, John, *op. cit.*, p. 39.
17. Connor, R. D. W., *North Carolina*, Vol. I, p. 218.

as a very small proportion of their time serves for that purpose, the rest is spent in sauntering through the woods
with a gun or sitting under a rustick shade, drinking New
England rum made into grog, the most shocking liquor
you imagine.[18]

Brickell, one of the earliest of the Carolina Historians, comments on the weekly sprees of these inhabitants,[19] and Col.
William Byrd, commenting on the North Carolina representatives for running the dividing line between North Carolina
and Virginia in 1728, said that "they stuck by us as long as
our good liquor lasted, and were so kind to us as to drink our
good journey to the mountains in the last bottle we had left."[20]

The philosophy of life generally accepted was that of the
seventeenth century. The ideas of Locke and Rousseau, of
Voltaire and Shaftesbury had hardly permeated widely among
the masses. Government was by the few and for the protection of property. People were to obey, not govern, while order
was to be preserved by keeping the masses ignorant. It appears that the Lords Proprietors cared neither for the spiritual
nor the intellectual man. Children of "Leet men" were con-
demned to be leet men "to all generations."[21] Social distinctions
were carefully drawn. There were the "Gentlemen," the "hus-
bandmen," and the "leet men." Guardians educated their
wards according to "their rank and degrees,"[22] and attempts
were made on the part of the wealthy few to maintain the
customs, traditions, and culture of old England. With dignity
and ceremony at their feasts, and with servants in livery, the

18. Schaw, Janet, *op. cit.*, p. 153.
19. ". . . by the richness of the soil, they live for the most part after
an indolent and luxurious manner; yet some are laborous, and equal-
ize with the negro in hard labor; and others quite the reverse; for
I have frequently seen them come to the towns, and there remain
drinking rum, punch, and other liquors for eight or ten days successively . . . ." Bricknell, *op. cit.*, p. 331.
20. Byrd, William, *op. cit.*, p. 46.
21. Connor, R. D. W., *op. cit.*, Vol. I, p. 165.
22. State Records, Vol. XXIII, p. 70; Knight, E. W., *Public School
Education in North Carolina*, Chapter II.

"grandees" held on to the memories of yesterday. Square-cut coats, stockings of blue or scarlet silk drawn up over the knee, a sword at the side, large hanging cuffs and lace ruffles, lace neck clothes, buckled shoes, and a three cornered hat, made up the dress of the colonial gentry man. Silver plates and other marks of refinement could have been found among the wilds of Albemarle.

In keeping with the seventeenth century philosophy, it was legal to levy taxes for the building of churches and the support of the clergy, but it was not considered a function of government to levy taxes to build schools. Therefore, the little education the masses received came either through the apprenticeship system or religious agencies. Higher education was only for those who would lead, those who would control in the affairs of government, and those who had wealth. Tradition has it that the Cape Fear region was partial to Harvard, and that the northeastern section was most interested in the English institutions. The Presbyterians of the interior and others sent their boys to Princeton, and later to the University of Pennsylvania. Willie and Allen Jones (brothers) were said to have been educated at Eton. Benjamin Smith, Henry E. McCulloch, Gabriel Cathcart, Thomas Child, Enoch Hall, Thomas McGuire, Richard Everard, and William Brimage were in attendance at the English Inns of Court.[23] Maurice Moore of Wilmington was educated in New England where he was supposed to have been imbued with republicanism. Samuel Johnston of Edenton, who was also educated in New England, was said to have received his characteristic bent toward democracy while there.[24] Some of the most prominent of the Princeton graduates were Rev. Hugh McAden, Alexander Martin, Joseph Alexander, Waightstill Avery, Ephrain Brevard, Nathaniel Alexander, David Stone, and William R. Davie. In 1786, A. J. DeRosset entered the University of Pennsylvania

---

23. Jones, E. Alfred, *American Members of the Inns of Court.*
24. *Colonial Records*, Vol. XI, pp. 722-723.

18

where he was graduated in 1790.[25] Whitmel Hall was also a graduate of this institution, and John Rust Eaton also entered the University of Pennsylvania during this period.[26] Probably there were many highly educated citizens scattered throughout the colony.

> There were educated men in the province, some of whom were natives, who had been sent in early life for training in English schools and universities. . . . There were also those who, not natives, had come, in maturer age, with similar tastes and correspondent cultivation.[27]

Hugh Williamson, a graduate of the University of Pennsylvania, who came to North Carolina during this period suggested that

> We cannot account for the general inattention to learning in the province, for such a length of time. Many of the inhabitants had been well educated, and were men of respectable talents. They calculated badly, if they presumed that by sending some of their children to England for instruction the intellects of the community would be sufficiently cultivated.[28]

The absence of an institution of higher education in the colony must have checked its growth intellectually, morally, socially, and economically.

According to the prevailing philosophy of the period, education was a function of the church and of the family, rather than a function of the state. The absence of any strong church in the colony also served to delay the establishment of a college among the people. Competition among the churches in the East was so strong that no church was able to dominate. Differences came up over the question of teaching, and although the law requiring that teachers should be licensed by the Es-

---

25. Battle, K. P., "The DeRosset Papers" in *The James Sprunt Historical Publications*, 1903, No. 4, p. 41.

26. Hamilton, J. G. deR., "Letters of John Rust Eaton" in *The James Sprunt Historical Publications*, Vol. IX, 1910, p. 27.

27. Hawks, Francis, *op. cit.*, Vol. II, p. 572.

28. Williamson, Hugh, *op. cit.*, p. 82.

19

tablished Church was rarely ever enforced, it remained a constant source of irritation. As early as 1731 Governor Burrington was instructed not to let any one teach in the province without first obtaining a license. The purpose of the act, according to the interpretation of the other denominations, was to promote the Established Church, train children in that faith, and strengthen the crown. Dissension was also brought about by the refusal of the king to charter academies and colleges other than those of the Established Church.

After the coming of the Presbyterians, differences arose on the question of the right of marriage by Presbyterian ministers. In the earlier years of the colony, marriages had been performed by the Quakers according to their rights and also by the magistrates when no minister was present; however, following the year 1741, no minister or justice of peace was to celebrate the marriage without a license, and the fee for it was to go to the parish minister. Differences of opinion, following the coming of the Presbyterians, were inevitable. It must also be remembered that the ministers of the Established Church were upholding the action of the crown against the colonists. At Hillsboro, on September 25, 1768, the Reverend George Micklejohn told the colonists, while speaking of their resistance against British rule and authority, "they that resist, shall receive to themselves *Damnation!* not only condemnation in this world, but eternal vengeance in this life to come."[29]

Indeed, the almost united opposition against the Established Church helped to prevent the establishment of an institution of higher education in the colony. In the West, following the coming of the Presbyterians, much was accomplished through classical schools, as will be pointed out later, but educational activity in the East was not wide. Efforts were made by the Lutherans to bring into North Carolina pastors and teachers, some of whom were quite learned, but the influence of this effort was not large. Clergymen, including Nussman, Arends,

---

29. Micklejohn, George, "A Sermon", in *The North Carolina Booklet,* Vol. VIII, 1908, p. 68.

and Roschen, came during the years from 1770 to 1790. The Reverend Samuel Suther, a Swiss, educated in Germany, taught in the counties of Mecklenburg, Cabarrus, and Guilford from 1768 to 1786.[30] The Baptists, perhaps the most aggressive denomination in the eastern part of the state during this period, did not place much emphasis on the value of learning It seems, indeed, that the colonists approved the view of Governor Berkeley who, as a Lord Proprietor of North Carolina in 1671, said, "I thank God there are no free schools, and no printing, and I hope we shall not have them these hundred years, for learning has brought disobedience, heresy, and sects into the world, and printing has divulged them, and libels against the best government."[31]

Statements of the governors and of those representing the religious interests of the colony bear somewhat on the point Governor Arthur Dobbs, writing to the Board of Trade in 1755, pointed out that the lack of clergymen and school-masters to instruct the youth, and the warm climate and the plentifulness of fruit and cattle without labor, accounted for the indolence of the people and their lack of attention to their own good.[32] Governor Dobbs continued the criticism and rebuked the Assembly for its disregard and disrespect for His Majesty's instructions to prepare laws for the education of youth in the province.[33] But Governor Dobbs was not the first of the executives in the colony to urge a reform. The Council of the colony had expressed itself to Governor Johnston in 1736 as lamenting "very much the want of divine publick worship, as well as the general neglect in point of education, the main sources of all disorders and corruptions."[34] Writing to the Board of Trade in October of this same year, Governor Gabriel Johnston said

---

30. *Historical Sketch of the Reformed Church in North Carolina,* (Board of Editions), Philadelphia Reformed Church, 1908, p. 27.
31. Berkeley, William, "An Official Report on Virginia" in *American History Told by Contemporaries* (Ed. A. B. Hart) Vol. I, p. 241.
32. *Colonial Records,* Vol. V., p. 314.
33. *Colonial Records,* Vol. VI, p. 836.
34. *Colonial Records,* Vol. IV, p. 231.

the "ignorance and want of education makes them obstruct everything for the good of the country even so much as the Building of Churches or erecting of schools or endeavoring to maintain a direct trade to great Britain."[35] No copy of the laws of the colony could have been found at this time, and no legislative effort had been made to erect any kind of school. The colony was characterized as "a place where not the least effort had been made to keep up the sense and awe of a Deity; where no care had been taken to inspire the youth with generous sentiments, or the least tincture of literature; where the laws were dispersed in various places, and where even the vilest malefactors could escape from the best of the public prisons."[36]

Statements made by the representatives of the Society for the Propagation of the Gospel in Foreign Parts are quite similar to those of the governors. William Gordon, writing to the Secretary of the Association from Chowan County in 1709, said that "the people indeed are ignorant, there being few that can read, and fewer write, even of their justices of peace and vestrymen."[37] In 1713, John Urmstone wrote General Nicholson: "I believe I need not tell you what a strange mixture of wretched mortals we have here many impatient of all discipline whether spiritual or temporal not a whit better than those St. Paul fought with at Ephes" (sic).[38] Again in 1714 he wrote "They'l neither pay minister nor schoolmaster nay they had need to be hired to go to church or send their children to school."[39] In a letter to the Secretary of the Society for the Propagation of the Gospel in Foreign Parts, dated August 17, 1716, Giles Rainsford said "That poor colony will soon be overrun by Quakerism and infidelity if not timely prevented by your sending over able and sober missionaries as well as school-

---

35. *Ibid.,* p. 178.
36. *Ibid.,* p. 228.
37. *Colonial Records,* Vol. I, p. 712.
38. *Colonial Records,* Vol. II, p. 76.
39. *Ibid.,* p. 126.

masters to reside among them."[40] An even more severe indictment was made by Colonel William Byrd when he said, "The people seem easy without a minister as long as they are exempted from paying him. I believe this is the only metropolis in the Christian or Mohometan world, where there is neither church, chapel, mosque, synagogue, or other place of public worship of any sect or religion whatsoever."[41] "The present state of North Carolina is really curious," remarked a Mr. Quinsey, a lawyer from Massachusetts in 1773. "There are but seven provincial laws in force throughout the colony, and no courts at all in being."[42] Doubtless there are exaggerations in all of these statements, for there must have been a few bright spots in the colony, but, from the best evidence available, North Carolina during the colonial period was not an advanced place. Certainly, there was a dearth of leadership, both in the church and out, due in large part to the lack of facilities for higher education in the colony.

The Established Church and its missionary agency, the Society for the Propagation of the Gospel in Foreign Parts, notwithstanding their ecclesiastical evils, had brought the first libraries and teachers into the colony, but their work in the early years was not extensive. The original grant of the Lords Proprietors provided for a state church, but it was not until 1701 that legal requirement was made that each precinct should be a parish over which a vestry was to be appointed which had the power to employ ministers and to lay a tax of not more than five shillings on the poll for parish purposes, including the care of the poor. In 1711, the province became a member of the crown of England and as such accepted the Church of England as the state church.[43] The bonds were drawn still closer when the colony became royalized in 1729.

Efforts made from time to time to strengthen the interests of the Established Church in the colony received the severe

40. *Ibid.*, p. 245.
41. Byrd, William, *op. cit.*, p. 29.
42. Williamson, Hugh, *op. cit.*, p. 160.
43. Ashe, S. A., *History of North Carolina*, Vol. I, p. 381.

condemnation of the other denominations present. The fact that the Established Church was an agency of the unpopular royalty probably also played a part in antagonizing many toward it, especially after 1760. This attitude did not encourage educational interests by the colonial assembly, as every act passed by it for the education of the people would have advanced the interests of the Established Church. The Quakers were especially bitter toward the Vestry Act of 1741 because of its taxing power, and a bill introduced in 1749 for the advancement of schools failed to pass, probably for the reasons mentioned. The well-known Cary Rebellion has been defined as a protest on the part of the people "against the arrogance, pride, and attempted oppression of the churchmen."[44] A gift of six thousand pounds, which the General Assembly made in 1754, through the efforts of George Vaughan, for the founding and endowing of a public school was used only too willingly in 1755 for war purposes and for the support of the courts. An act was also passed for the erection of a school house in Edenton in 1745 but little immediate action came out of it.

North Carolina was considered as a toilsome and unpromising field for missionaries, and many of those who came proved quite incompetent and unworthy. Coming from the West Indies as a member of the Church of England, a Mr. Griffin opened in Pasquotank County about 1705 what is believed to have been the first school in the colony. It is said that in time he overcame the prejudice of the Quakers to such an extent that "they intrusted him with the education of their children, though they knew that he read prayers twice a day in his school, and required of all his pupils, Quaker children as well as others, to make the responses, and to violate none of the decencies and proprieties of worship."[46] In 1703, the Reverend James Adams took charge of the school and Griffin opened another school in

---

44. Oliver D. D., "The Society for the Propagation of the Gospel in the Province of North Carolina" in *The James Sprunt Historical Publications,* Vol. IX, p. 21.
45. Hawks, Francis, *op. cit.*, Vol. II, p. 347.
46. Hawks, Francis, *op. cit.*, Vol. II, p. 347.

Chowan County. The report coming from a church school conducted by a Mr. Marshburn in Chowan County in 1712 stated that the children under his care could read and write and were all grounded in the principles of the Christian religion.[47] A private school was also conducted in this county at a later date by the Reverend Daniel Earl and his daughter, with such subjects as Mathematics, Latin, and Greek being taught.[48] In keeping with the old English apprenticeship law of 1601, a small number of the boys and girls of the poorer class learned the rudiments of reading and writing.[49] The first bequest for a free school in the state was provided for in the will of James Innes in 1754 near Wilmington, and the sources of support included slaves, a private library, and one hundred pounds sterling, but the school was not chartered until 1783.

The most prominent work of the Established Church in the colony came in the setting up of the two schools at New Bern and Edenton. In 1764, a Vestry act was passed which provided for the levying of a poll tax of ten shillings for the purpose of "building churches and chapels, paying the minister's salary . . . encouraging schools, maintaining the poor . . . and defraying other incident charges of their parish."[50] At the same time an act was passed providing for the building of a school house at New Bern, and for the election and paying of a school master. A tax of one penny per gallon was to be levied on all spirituous liquors imported into the Neuse River district, out of which the school master was to be paid twenty pounds per annum, with the remainder of the proceeds to be devoted to the education of the poor. The act also provided that the teacher should be a member of the Church of England and licensed by the governor. Undoubtedly, this school was to be under the management and control of the church.

In June of 1764, James Reed of New Bern informed the Sec-

47. *Ibid.*, p. 164.
48. Drane, R. B., "Colonial Parishes and Church Schools" in *Sketches of Church History in North Carolina*, (Ed. DeRosset), p. 168.
49. *State Records*, Vol. XVII, p. 266.
50. *State Records*, Vol. XXIII, p. 605.

retary of the Society for the Propagation of the Gospel in Foreign Parts that "we have now a prospect of a very flourishing school in the town of New Bern. In December last, Mr. Tomlinson came here. . . . and, on the first of January he opened a school in this town and immediately got as many scholars as he could instruct."[51] By 1766, the school building provided for by the act of 1764 was completed, and Tomlinson moved into his new quarters. But all was not so bright for the school, for Reed wrote to the Secretary of the Society in 1766, saying, "I have this affair much at heart and the difficulties I have met with have given me much uneasiness." Again he says, "The whole subscription is entirely expended and I have preached and begged in his (Tomlinson) behalf, till the suppliant is entirely weary and charity cold."[52] Tomlinson, in spite of the fact that he is said to have done "excellent work in moulding the characters of the colonial boys,"[53] lost the good will of the parents by the too frequent use of chinquapin and hickory switches.

The academy also seems not to have increased in popularity for in 1771 the poor pupils were withdrawn from the school on the claim of the trustees of insufficient money. Reed wrote to the Secretary on July 2, of the same year, saying, "I'm sorry to inform you that our little academy is not in the most flourishing condition. The scarcity of money and dearness of Board very much disappointed Mr. Tomlinson's expectations, and obliged him to dismiss a very able assistant."[54] The trustees of the academy seem also to have been criticized by Reed for the lack of success with the school for he writes from New Bern on February 15, 1772, to the Secretary of the Society that "the majority of the trustees are wealthy men, but I cannot learn that any of them ever passed thro' a reputable school, or have the least knowledge of the learned languages, or Liberal Sciences, or of

51. Drane R. B., *op. cit.*, p. 168.

52. *Colonial Records*, Vol. VII, p. 241.

53. Cheshire, J. B., "Decay and Revival" in *Sketches of Church History in North Carolina*, p. 157.

54. *Colonial Records*, Vol. IX, p. 6.

the difficulty of governing a school."[55] The school must have closed a short time after the writing of this letter for on June 30, 1775, an advertisement appeared in a local newspaper stating that "By permission and encouragement of the Trustees the public school house of this town is again opened ... "[56]

As early as 1745 a legislative act had been passed which provided for the sale of town lots in the town of Edenton for the purpose of erecting a school house, but no evidence exists that a school house was ever built. Attempts were made in 1767 and in 1768 to set up a school at Edenton similar to that at New Bern, but success did not come until 1770, and then in the face of much opposition, when an act was passed chartering the Edenton Academy. Opposition to the chartering of the school seems to have been due to the hatred of the Assembly for the Schism Act of 1714,[57] which required that all teachers should be members of the Established Church. The act had been enforced in the school at New Bern in 1766, and the provisions under which the Edenton Academy was chartered made it strictly a church school, similar to the New Bern Academy. The provision requiring that the teacher should be a member of the Established Church was not strictly adhered to as Mr. Pettigrew, who took charge of the academy in 1773, was a member of the Presbyterian denomination. Other teachers who followed Pettigrew seem to have belonged to other churches.[58]

Neither of the schools at Edenton and New Bern achieved considerable success, although their work was commendable. The report of the New Bern Academy sent by James Reed to the Secretary of the Society in March of 1772 shows an annual expenditure of 122 pounds including items for the master's salary, the support of poor scholars, the buying of books, paper and firewood, and various repairs on the building.[59] Some thirty scholars or more regularly attended the two schools, mostly

55. *Ibid.*, p. 242.
56. *The North Carolina Gazette*, June 30, 1775.
57. Knight, E. W., *Public School Education in North Carolina*, p. 37.
58. Drane, R. B., *op. cit.*, p. 179.
59. *Ibid.*, p. 175.

children of the inhabitants of the two towns. As to the curriculum, attempts were made to teach such subjects as writing, Latin, English, arithmetic, algebra, trigonometry, astronomy navigation, surveying, geography, bookkeeping, and the like. The study of French seems to have been provided for in 1775.[60]

Educational effort by the Colonial Assembly of North Carolina was not conspicuous, although evidence has recently come to light tending to show that for a few years about the middle of the eighteenth century taxes were levied for schools. Professor William K. Boyd reports[61] that in December, 1768, the assembly authorized John Burgwn, the Clerk of the Court of Chancery and Secretary of the Council, to investigate and report on the condition of the public accounts of North Carolina, the belief being quite prevalent that the local officials were corrupt. A year later this authorization was repeated and in 1770 two reports were filed, one a statement of the sheriffs' accounts, showing that those officers were delinquent, and another which showed "that the taxes levied to retire the currency were greater than the amount of currency issued . . ." A third report which was "made probably at the same time" was in the form of a table which exhibited the number of taxables and the taxes laid for each year from 1748 to 1770. This table shows that a tax for schools was levied from 1755 to 1761, inclusive, but the statutes reveal no provision for the levy, although Governor Dobbs, "writing to the Board of Trade in 1757, mentions the tax as authorized in the aid granted in 1754, and he adds that it yields £900 per annum. The purpose of the tax was undoubtedly to support the £6000 in bills of credit voted in 1754 for a public school in the province. However," continues Professor Boyd, "the money was used for the expenses of the government in the French and Indian War and no reimbursement was granted the colony by the British authorities in settling the accounts at the end of that conflict. Hence the pub-

---

60. *The North Carolina Gazette,* June 30, 1775.
61. See his *Some Eighteenth Century Tracts Concerning North Carolina,* pp. 415, 416, published by the North Carolina Historical Commission, Raleigh, 1927.

lic school was never established." Copies of the first and second reports are in the *Colonial Records* but the third report is not in those documents. The only copy known to exist is in collections of the Massachusetts Historical Society.

That denomination which appeared to believe most in the value of education seems to have been the Presbyterian. Its followers, the Scotch Irish, the Irish, and the Germans, emigrating into the colony in the second and third quarters of the eighteenth century, soon became influential in the Piedmont section of the state. Boldly, they defied the Schism Act of 1714. Trained ministers they needed and trained ministers they would have, educated and instructed in the Presbyterian faith. Souls must be saved. The Bible should be read, for in that, they thought, rested one's only hope of salvation.

In spite of the opposition of the crown, the Presbyterians early established schools which represented the best educational interests of the colony. "It is to the Presbyterian Church that North Carolina owes the establishment of her first classical schools, and during the second half of the Eighteenth Century the history of education in this state is inseparably connected with that of this denomination."[62] Libraries of value were also collected by such leaders of the denomination as Waightstill Avery, the Reverend Henry Patillo, Reverend James Hall, and the Reverend David Caldwell. Missionaries were sent out by the New York and Pennsylvania Presbyterian Synods, the most representative of whom was the Reverend Hugh McAden, a leader in the founding of the Presbyterian Church in the South. Moreover, Princeton University served as the guiding intellectual life and interest of these peoples.

Perhaps the first of these classical schools to be set up in North Carolina was Tate's Academy, which was founded at Wilmington in 1760 by the Reverend James Tate and which continued in operation until 1768. Crowfield Academy, located in Mecklenburg County and also founded in 1760, seems to have gained an extensive influence. Still higher ambitions were

---

62. Smith, C. L., *History of Education in North Carolina*, p. 23.

held by the founders of Queen's Museum, which was opened in Charlotte in 1767 under the supervision of the Reverend James Alexander, a graduate of Princeton University. On January 10, 1771, the General Assembly of the colony passed an act to incorporate the school as Queen's College, and apparently without much serious objection, although all the fourteen trustees of the school, except two, were Presbyterians. The trustees of the institution had reported that several grammar schools had already been established in the western part of the colony, but not any of them offered a finished education. They reluctantly submitted to the provision in the charter which stated that the president of Queen's should be a member of the Established Church and licensed by the governor; yet, they realized the necessity of the hated requirement and probably thought to get around it in some way. According to the charter, the trustees included, among others, Edmund Fanning, Waightstill Avery, Henry Patillo, and Abner Nash. These men were to appoint "some learned, pious, exemplary, and discreet person to be president of the said college."[63] The right of perpetual succession was also granted to the board of trustees. The president of the institution was granted the power to confer the degrees of Bachelor and Master of Arts and to grant the appropriate diplomas. The curriculum was to consist principally of the Greek, Hebrew, and Latin languages. In general, the rules of the college were to "correspond and be as near as may be agreeable to the Laws and customs of the University of Oxford and Cambridge or those of the Colleges of America."[64] Further provision in financing the college was made by the levying of "a duty of six pence per gallon on all rum and spirituous liquors brought into and disposed of in Mecklenburg County."[65]

The Charter of Queen's College, after being granted by the colonial Assembly, had to be first referred to the Board of Trade and later to the King in Council. Governor Tryon, in writing

63. *Colonial Records*, Vol. VIII, p. 488.
64. *Colonial Records*, Vol. VIII, p. 488.
65. *Ibid.*, p. 490.

to the Board of Trade on the Act, expressed himself by saying "that it is but an outline of a foundation for the education of youth,"[66] and that the necessity for such an institution was obvious. The Board of Trade, however, in a letter written from Whitehall on February 26, 1772, to the King, took the stand that although the president of the institution was "to be of the Established Church and licensed by the governor yet the Fellows, Trustees, and Tutors were to be Presbyterians; and that if the college were permitted to be incorporated, it would "in effect operate as a Seminary for the Education and Instruction of Youth in the Principles of the Presbyterian Church." The advice offered to the King was that the royal assent be not given "to an establishment which in its consequences promises with great and permanent advantages to a sect of Dissenters from the Established Church who have already extended themselves over that province in considerable numbers." Objection was also made to the rum levy on the ground that it would check the British rum trade, and that spirits manufactured in Mecklenburg County might be exempted. Objection was also made to the levying of the tax only on Mecklenburg County on the grounds "That a Foundation professedly for general uses, ought not in regularity to be supported by a tax partially imposed upon any one County in particular;"[67] and criticisms were offered because the act contained no clause of suspension. Perhaps there was another reason for the opposition to the charter as Edmund Fanning, who was elected nominal president of the institution, was "described by many writers as being an abandoned extortionist and libertine . . .",[68] a man who received degrees from Yale, Harvard, King's College (Columbia), Dartmouth, and Oxford. The Act was vetoed by the King in Council on April 22, 1772. Thus, the only real attempt to establish an institution for higher education in the colony of North Caro-

66. *Colonial Records*, Vol. IX, p. 249.
67. *Ibid.*, p. 250.
68. Haywood, M. D., "The Story of Queen's College or Liberty Hall in the Province of North Carolina" in *The North Carolina Booklet*, Vol. XI, No. 3, p. 173.

lina before 1776 failed largely because of religious differences. Failure to secure the imperial charter did not completely destroy the institution but checked its possibilities for growth.

On May 9, 1777, Queen's Museum was rechartered by the North Carolina Legislature as Liberty Hall Academy. This charter, although granted on the basis that the education of youth was highly useful to the state, provided that this academy was not to be considered as "one of those Seminaries, mentioned in the Constitution."[69] Perpetual succession was also granted to the board of trustees who were authorized to confer degrees. The board met for the first time in 1778 and among other things decided to pay the president 195 pounds annual salary, to build a new frame house, and to pay 920 pounds to Colonel Thomas Pope for the old property and equipment. By an amendment passed by the state legislature in this same year money which was secured from the sale of eighty lots, in and about the town of Charlotte, should go to the academy. But the Revolutionary War was now in progress and in 1780, following the approach of Cornwallis' troops on Charlotte, the institution was closed. Efforts to revive it in 1784, by changing the name to Salisbury Academy and by moving it to Salisbury, seem not to have materialized. A final comment on the academy was written by George Washington in his diary on May 28, 1791, when he said, "Charlotte is a trifling place, though the Court of Mecklenburg is held in it. There is a School (called a College) in which, at times, there has been 50 or 60 boys."[70] In 1842, the Reverend John Robinson, pastor of a church at Popular Tent, and a former graduate of the institution, wrote, "The Instruction given by the President and two professors embraced a complete literary course, and as much of the mathematics and natural philosophy, as was customary in any college in America."[71]

One of the most prominent of all the educational institutions

---

69. *State Records,* Vol. XXIV, p. 32.
70. Haywood, M. D., *op. cit.,* p. 173.
71. Viator, "The First College in North Carolina" in *Hillsborough Recorder,* February 24, 1842, p. 1.

in the colony was that of the Reverend David Caldwell, a graduate of Princeton who had entered North Carolina as a Missionary in 1763. In 1766 or 1767, he founded near Greensboro a school which became known as Caldwell's Log College. Quite early after the opening of his school, he built a two-storied log building in order that he might do his work more effectively. The school had only the founder for its teacher but it served as a theological seminary, academy, and college, and had an annual average attendance of fifty until 1800. Most of the Presbyterian ministers of the South and Southwest for many years were trained in Caldwell's Log College, and many lawyers, doctors, and statesmen boasted of having received their training there. Students came to the school from every state south of the Potomac. Measured by the standards of the time, the standard set by Caldwell in his College seems to have been quite high. Many of his students were admitted into the junior class at Princeton and after 1795 into the junior class of the University of North Carolina.

The curriculum of the Log College was set up after the entrance requirements of Princeton, and was centered around the classics. In the absence of an adequate library, students were supplied with a few of the Greek and Latin classics, Euclid's "Elements of Mathematics" and Martin's "Natural Philosophy." Caldwell also had studied medicine under the noted Philadelphia physician, Benjamin Rush, and this he taught at times. John Motley Morehead, the *ante-bellum* railroad builder of North Carolina, attended Caldwell's school and later wrote that the "course of studies in the language, Latin, Greek, and Hebrew, as well as in the sciences, was extensive for his day . . ."[72] An interesting sidelight was thrown on Caldwell's teaching by Morehead when he said that "often has he made me recite from four to six hours a day, parsing every difficult word, and scanning nearly every line when the recitation happened to be in any of the Latin poets. Indeed you could not get along with

---

72. Konkle, B. A., *John Motley Morehead and the Development of North Carolina*, p. 16.

33

him, with any comfort, without knowing accurately and thoroughly everything you passed over."[73] Never using the rod, never expelling a student from his school, Caldwell proved an inspiration to the boys who came under his care.

Caldwell continued in his educational work until he was ninety-five years of age. He died in August, 1824, in his hundredth year. From 1766 until 1822, the school was in regular session except for a brief period following the year 1781, when Cornwallis burned Caldwell's home and his library.[74] It has been said that after the establishment of the State University he was offered its presidency, but declined, and in 1810 he was awarded the honorary degree of Doctor of Divinity by the institution. David Caldwell was instrumental in creating a desire for higher education in his state and ranks among the great teachers.

The efforts to build up an institution of higher education in North Carolina during the colonial period were not large. Libraries of value were to be found in only a few hands and the circulation of newspapers was small. The philosophy of life was that of the seventeenth century. The support and control of schools was a problem of the church and of the family. There were a few educated men in the colony, but the education of the masses was neglected. The Established Church and the Presbyterian Church were active, but because of denominational differences, geographic conditions, social conditions and unfavorable economic conditions no permanent institution of higher education was established. The most prominent efforts made toward the establishment of such an institution appeared in the academies at New Bern and Edenton, Queen's Museum, and the work of David Caldwell.

---

73. *Ibid.*, pp. 15-16.
74. Orr, J. L., "A Log College and Its President," in *North Carolina University Magazine,* March, 1912, p. 7.

II

The Founding of the State University

The forty-first article of the North Carolina constitution of December, 1776, provided:

> That a school or schools be established by the Legislature, for the convenient Instruction of youth, with such Salaries to the Masters, paid by the Public as may enable them to instruct at low prices; and all Useful Learning shall be duly encouraged and promoted in one or more Universities.[1]

Such an advanced educational provision seems a bit out of character in a constitution whose larger purpose appears to have been class protection.[2] The educational provision is the expression of an advanced ideal, one which seems to hold that government exists for the protection and betterment of individuals rather than the protection of property, and reflected the philosophy of the American Revolution as set forth in Thomas Paine's *Common Sense*, education as a function of the state and not of the church or family.

The eighteenth century voiced the doctrine of nature and reason against that of superstition and faith, a doctrine that "the inner forces of life could be trusted."[3] Milton, Bacon, Locke,

---

1. *Colonial Records*, Vol. X, p. 1012.
2. Articles XXXI and XXXIV provided for the separation of church and state but not for religious freedom. Article XXXII denied religious freedom, and articles V, VI, VII, and XV specified property qualifications for voting and for holding office.
3. Hansen, A. O., *Liberalism in American Education*, p. 12.

Newton, Hume, and Bolinbroke helped to lead the way in England for the enlightened age. Carried over into France, English liberalism turned to French radicalism in the hands of Rousseau, Voltaire, Volney, Helevetius and Diderot, all driving in the same direction. French radicalism advocated sweeping "away the long accumulated mass of prescriptive rights, the dead hand of the past," and encouraged "free men to create a new society that should have as its sole end and justification, the common well-being."[4] Rousseau, the great exponent of nature, in his *Social Contract* maintained "that the richest possible living came through society . . . that man could move most creatively through social organizations . . . and that man could determine the destiny of the race by means of educational and other institutional controls."[5] With a high power of sarcasm and ridicule, Voltaire made all the old systems appear absurd. Theology should be natural, he said, based on a natural moral law, since all knowledge appeared to be man-made. "The great object of human endeavor was to discover what in every field was natural and reasonable, and to brush aside the accretions of irrational tradition that Reason and Nature might the more easily be free to display its harmonious order."[6]

The deification of reason first came through religious ideas. An attack was made on the old theology as represented by Catholics and Protestants because it did not seem to promote good citizenship or social utility, and was not acting in reason according to things as they are. The followers of the idea of a natural religion came to be known as Deists, who said that religion must be either natural, superstitious, or revealed. To the Deist it was easier to believe that there is a God than there is not, but he attacked the doctrine of revelation and considered miracles, prophecy, religious rites and traditional beliefs as mere superstitions. Thomas Paine's *The Age of Reason*, which appears to have been an attack not so much upon the Chris-

4. Parrington, V. L., *The Colonial Mind, 1620-1800*, p. 272.
5. Hansen, A. O., *op. cit.*, pp. 7-8.
6. Randall, J. H., *The Making of the Modern Mind*, p. 276.

tian Epic as upon false interpretations, organized force, and theology best expressed the Deist's belief. Paine pleaded for an open-minded, reasoned attitude toward the Scriptures and God. The Newtonian world which embodied the order of nature and which led men to believe there was an order of natural moral law as well as natural physical law, meant that the science of ethics was independent of any theological or supernatural foundation, and in this sense was striking at the roots of Christianity. Moral principles were to be retained only as they seemed reasonable and natural and promoted the order of good living. To the Deist, nature was the face of God and it was only through the study of nature that man could hope to attain perfection. It was thus that religious interests came to be subservient to an interest in science.

Science was the divine force in human life for it placed man above the brutes. It advocated free play to the activities of every man, for people were happy only when they were scientific. Men should be free from the strings of tradition so that they could act and think clearly as individuals without the fear of being molested by organized power. To Bacon, who first set forth his ideas in the *Advancement of Learning* in 1605, experimental philosophy was "the multiplying of human enjoyments and the mitigating of human sufferings."[7] To Newton, the value of experimental philosophy was based on its being a stepping stone to the true cause, and though Newton fought bitterly against breaking with the doctrine of revelation, he felt that true religion would come as a culmination of science.[8] To Priestley, science was the power of God which would raise man from the dead past, and upon such a basis science demanded reform in the thinking of the Church. As all people live in their society for their mutual advantage, the goodness and happiness of the majority of the members, "of any state, in the great stand-

---

7. Macauley, Lord, "Lord Bacon" in Critical and Historical Essays, Vol. II, p. 366.
8. Snow, A. J., *Matter and Gravity in Newton's Physical Philosophy*, pp. 225-226.

ard by which everything relating to that state must finally be determined."[9] In France, Descartes and Lavoisier also exemplified a similar activity and interest. Rousseau said that man had corrupted himself and advocated going back to nature, and Voltaire would subject everything to a basis of reason. "Out of this attitude of faith in nature and in what reason approved grew the great ideals of the age of enlightenment, humanitarianism, toleration, pacifism, cosmopolitianism,"[10] through which was to be developed the ideal society of man.

Science for the first time now captured the mind of the educated man and entered into every field of human interest. The eighteenth century is marked by a change in beliefs, habits, and thoughts which laid the foundations for our present belief in every field. With Condorcet it is no longer back to nature, but onward to the ideal. Here was a doctrine of the science of man expressing the dignity and worth of man's life upon earth through harmony in nature. All social facts were now tied up with the laws of nature. Human society, according to the Physiocrats, was to be taken out of its confusion and adjusted to the harmonious order of nature. Property, security, and liberty were the necessary laws of human society. Lest the laws be misinterpreted and corruptly used, those in office "should in turn be restrained by an educated public opinion, educated primarily in *political economy*. Hence the Physiocrats wanted the government, when not protecting private property, to promote universal education . . ."[11] It was asserted that "the only adequate means of freeing men from the limitations of superstition and archaic institutions would be through a system of education that would make inevitable a scientific, objective, experimental attitude that would lead to creative innovation and that would energize reconstruction of everything related to the progress of man. The lines of progress could in this way be scientifically determined."[12]

---

9. Huxley, Thomas Henry, *Science and Culture*, p. 126.
10. Randall, J. H., *op. cit.*, p. 370.
11. Randall, J. H., *op. cit.*, pp. 324-325.
12. Hansen, A. O., *op. cit.*, p. 21.

Sir Isaac Newton was a bitter critic of the Universities of Cambridge and Oxford, feeling that students failed "to acquire the knowledge and habits which are requisite to the performance of the duties which the individual's profession or employment renders necessary."[13] Daniel Defoe, in 1745, saw these two institutions as places for drinking, and suggested the establishment of a university at London, to become "the scene of science."[14] In a little book on *Dialogues Concerning Education;*, published at London in 1745, David Fordyce wondered how it came about that the education of his time was "so little adapted to qualify men for the world," and asked the question: "Will the Dialectics, Metaphysics, or Theological and moral systems that are now so generally taught, qualify the students for the cabinet or camp, for being men of business or fine Gentlemen?"[15] Joseph Priestly in "An Essay on a Course in Liberal Education," first published in 1764, suggested that "the studies of youth should tend to fit them for the business of manhood; and that the object of their attention, and turn of thinking in younger life should not be too remote from the destined employment for their riper years."[16] He felt that there should be a system of public education, "provided for gentlemen who are designed to fill the principal stations of active life, distinct from those which are adapted to the learned professions."[17] The learned languages were considered desirable but not necessary, and the striving for purity of Latin style was considered a futile pursuit. In general, he said that the curriculum should be based on a study of the modern languages, science, law and government, economics and history.

The application of this new doctrine of science in education appeared first in France. In 1666, following the chartering of

13. Knox, Vicesimus, *Liberal Education,* p. 24.
14. Defoe, Daniel, "Augusta Triumphans" in *The Complete English Tradesman,* vol. II, p. 4.
15. Fordyce, David, *Dialogues Concerning Education,* vol. II, pp. 249-251.
16. Priestley, Joseph, *Lectures on History and General Policy,* p. 5.
17. *Ibid.,* p. 1.

the French Academy in 1635, the "Old Academy of Science" was chartered, from which came men like Descartes, Pascal, and even Sir Isaac Newton, who was a foreign associate of the organization. Roemer, the Danish astronomer, and Tschirnhausen, German physician and geometer, were members of the organization. Great emphasis was laid on the study of mathematics, chemistry, and physics, and the funds for instruments and experiments were provided by the Royalty. Monroe says in his article on the "Academy," in *A Cyclopedia of Education,* that England never had such an academy, and that it was not until 1672 that a scientific academy was founded in Germany. With the coming of the French radicals, Rousseau in particular, there came the demand for the application of scientific principles and practices to the school. Helvetius, Diderot, and Condorcet, all advocated the doctrine of the omnipotence of education.

Coming at a time when the colonies were breaking with the mother country, the ideas of the French philosophers were widely accepted by the American people. The fact that many of these ideas were extremely radical rather appealed to the American Revolutionists. "Throughout this great political battle the participants never ceased to think of France, to feel the influence of her philosophers, and to seek to realize the ideal that France had set for the United States."[18] Many French

18. Fay, Bernard, *The Revolutionary Spirit in France and America,* p. 228.

books were translated and scattered throughout the American colonies, by Rousseau, Voltaire, Helvetius, and others, and many of the French soldiers who came to fight the English remained in the colonies after the war. Paine rejoiced that the American Revolution had come violently. Now there should be intellectual independence in America as well as political independence. Government should be in harmony with the law of nature, and, for a just and permanent government, there was only one basis, that of "the natural constitution of man."[19]

19. Hansen, A. O., *op. cit.,* p. 27.

State education, the comprehensive force of perpetuating the republic, a theory worthy of consideration, was a power in which men's thoughts and actions could be restrained. The people representing the source of power were to be educated for self-protection and in order that from them might come their leaders. In the new commonwealth, no form of ecclesiasticism had the breadth and power to secure the desired result.[20] "France was considered as the best school — in art and in all higher education."[21] "Following the victory at Yorktown, another foreign collegiate influence entered. The French academic influence was, in a sense, the rescript of the French political power. French influence in literature and philosophy as well as in government became pervasive."[22] E. E. Slosson, in his book on *The American Spirit of Education,* says that "The germ of the state university came from France, ... The revolution that severed the political bonds connecting America with the mother country also broke the thread of educational traditions, and American educators turned from their English enemies to their French friends."[23] He suggests that the institution rose out of the work of Abelard in the eleventh century, and helped to mark the downfall of religious zeal.

Leading in the acceptance of the revolutionary ideas for education in America was Benjamin Franklin, who served as a connecting link between France and America. His philosophy may be termed as "an amalgam of English and French Liberalism, supplemented by the conscious influence of the American frontier."[24] Franklin was charmed by the physiocratic philosophy headed by Dupont de Nemours which emphasized the study of agriculture, the doctrine of *produit net,* and the principle of *laissez-faire* as a social concern. Franklin was "the first American to abandon the traditional mercantile school — a generation before other American thinkers had repudiated it; and

20. Thwing, C. F., *A History of Higher Education in America,* p. 193.
21. Fay, Bernard, *op. cit.,* p. 212.
22. Thwing, C. F., *The American and the German Universities,* p. 4.
23. Slosson, E. E., *The American Spirit in Education,* p. 169.
24. Parrington, V. L., *op. cit.,* p. 344.

41

he was the first to ally himself with the rising school of *laissez-faire*."[25] He was the first writer to assert "that labor is the measure of value,"[26] an ideal which Adam Smith later capitalized in his *The Wealth of Nations*. Franklin was a devout Deist in his religious beliefs; while his activities and interests in experimental science, including agriculture and architecture, are too well-known and need not be commented on here. Bernard Fay states in a recent book called *The Revolutionary Spirit in France and America* that the French influence almost marked a downfall in religious zeal and "that the whole movement had been started by Franklin, who had the gift of circulating every kind of knowledge and of stirring intellectual activity in all those who came in contact with him."[27] In Paris he was received with the honors of a demi-god — "Eripuit coelo fulmen, sceptrum que tyrannis."[28]

As early as 1727, Franklin organized the famous Junto Club, the first of its kind in America, for the purpose of creating a wider interest in literature and science and in the development of a better citizenry. The following questions were asked every prospective member: "Do you sincerely declare that you love mankind in general of whatsoever profession or religion? Do you think any person ought to be harmed in his body, name, or goods for mere speculative opinions or external way of workship? Do you love truth for truth's sake and will you endeavor impartially to find and receive it yourself and communicate it to others."[29] Following in the line of his French interests, Franklin led in the organization of the American Philosophical Society in 1743, which was modeled after the French Academy. After the close of the revolution, the American Philosophical Society for Promoting Useful Knowledge, of which Franklin was president, offered a prize for "the best system of liberal education and literary instruction, adapted to the genius of the

25. *Ibid.*, p. 170.
26. *Ibid.*, p. 171.
27. Fay, Barnard, *op. cit.*, p. 214.
28. Hooper William, *Fifty Years Since*, p. 27.
29. Knight, E. W., *Education in the United States*, p. 390.

government of the United States."[30] Several plans were presented, and of the two selected for the prize, both followed Franklin's suggestions in his *Proposals Relating to the Education of Youth in Pennsylvania,* first proposed in 1743, but not published until 1749. Here Franklin set forth many of the educational ideals which were later accepted by the founders of the University of North Carolina, that all students "should not be compell'd to learn Latin, Greek, or the modern foreign languages; yet none that have an ardent Desire to learn them should be refused; their English, Arithematick, and other studies absolutely necessary, being at the same time not neglected."[31] History would show "the wonderful effects of oratory," and "the advantages of civil orders and constitutions;" it would offer an opportunity for the discussion of questions of right and wrong, justice and injustice; it would "give a connected idea of human affairs;" and it would offer a way of introducing "all kinds of useful knowledge" with advantage, and to the "pleasure of the student."[32] The best histories of nature were to be read "not only to be delightful to youth," but to be useful to them, and "while they are reading Natural History, might not a little Gardening, Planting, Grafting, Innoculating, etc., be taught and practiced; and now and then Excursions made to the best Farmers, their Methods observ'd and reason'd upon for the information of youth. The Improvement of Agriculture being useful to all and Skill in it no Disparagement to any."[33] The plan had "an extensive circulation and was widely read,"[34] and out of it came Franklin's Academy which later grew into the University of Pennsylvania.[35] In

30. Hansen, A. O., *op. cit.*, p. 110.
31. Franklin, Benjamin, *Proposals for the Education of Youth in Pennsylvania,* p. 27.
32. *Ibid.*, pp. 21-27.
33. *Ibid.*, pp. 28-30.
34. Knight, E. W., *op. cit.*, p. 373.
35. In 1787, twenty-one of the fifty-five members of the board of trustees of the Philadelphia Academy were Frenchmen, and every year the academy received the best scientific works published in France. — Fay, Barnard, *op. cit.*, p. 214.

July of 1776, following a trip to France where he was in regular attendance at the French Academy, Franklin aided in drawing up (he was president of the Constitutional Convention) and supervised the final writing of the Pennsylvania Constitution in which first appeared the educational clause already quoted from the North Carolina Constitution of this same year.[36] The clause was thus at least in part, if not wholly so, the work of Franklin. The words "low prices" almost mark it as his work."[37]

There is no reason to believe that the people of North Carolina accepted the idea that education was the function of the state. The fact that the king of England refused to grant the charter for a college to the Scotch-Irish of Mecklenburg County seems to have been in part responsible for placing the educational clause in the constitution; but as schools were not made mandatory in the state until 1868, and as taxation as a policy for financing the University was accepted at no time during the *ante-bellum* period, it is evident that the principle of public education was not widely accepted. From the interpretation

---

36. It was not uncommon in those days for one colonial assembly to adopt acts and parts of acts passed by other colonial assemblies.

37. This is not to say that there were not many other men in the colonies who were advocating similar ideas. William Livingston in a series of fifty-two articles published in the *Independent Reflector*, New York, during the year 1752-1753, advocated and laid out a plan for a state university, but smacking of Protestant flavor. His statement that "societies have an indisputable right to direct the education of their youthful members", sounds much like the utterances of La Chalotais in his *Essai d'Education Nationale* written ten years later, "but the idea was already abroad in France; and it is possible that Mr. Livingston, who read French, may have been familiar with the advanced French thought of the time upon this subject. — Brown, E. E., "The Origin of the State University" in *University of California Publications,* Vol. 3, April, 1903, p. 23. Thomas Jefferson also was following in the steps of his teacher, Franklin. In 1779, Jefferson introduced a plan of education into the legislature of Virginia, and in the same year, as governor, he modernized the curriculum of the College of William and Mary. In 1818, he founded the University of Virginia.

given to the article, however, there is evidence of French and Franklin influence, chiefly in the establishment of academies.

It was stated in Chapter I that the Presbyterians were the most active of all agencies in the colony for the establishment of schools and academies. This activity was continued after 1776, but in many cases in a modified form, for the doctrine of the French radicals had now permeated the state. The Reverend Henry Patillo, a devout Presbyterian who had established a school in Orange County about 1765, wrote of this period: "I would just observe that this seems to be the versatile season of America; and a change of religious profession has become almost as common and as little noted as the variations of the weather in this most changeable climate."[38] The Reverend Francis Asbury, an itinerant Methodist preacher, said of a sermon which he preached at Hillsboro on March 7, 1783: "Preached to some Calvinistic professors, and sinners. The people are very careless, and professors are unfaithful: what have I suffered on account of these things."[39] Writing on February 13, 1788, he reported that "we had many dead souls at the quarterly meeting at Lee's."[40] In Mecklenburg County, where there was a circulating library "replete with infidel philosophy and infidel sentiments on religion and mortality," an "Infidel Debating Society" was organized, backed by much "wealth and talent."[41] N. Blunt writing from Beaufort County, on January 23, 1802, to the Reverend John Pettigrew felt that

Perhaps not in any part of the United States where infant Baptism was once so generally approved of and used, is at this time in a greater state of the indifferency, or rather entire coldness about the matter, than in the eastern part of this state; — where there has been so few preach-

---

38. Ashe, S. A., "Social Conditions in North Carolina in 1783" in *The North Carolina Booklet,* Vol. X, April, 1911, p. 207.
39. Asbury, Francis, *The Journal of the Reverend Francis Asbury,* Vol. I, p. 355.
40. *Ibid.,* Vol. II, p. 27.
41. Foote, W. H., *Sketches of North Carolina Historical and Biographical,* p. 248.

ers (except Methodists) but have endeavored to set the people against it. Charity teaches me to hope that many of them have not been aware of the evil they may have done, by getting people into this state of neutrality to all religions — which seems to have so great a tendency towards bringing them forward in that lamentable situation (the now so prevalent opinions of Deism). Your observations on the Deistical and detestable T. Paine and his adherents are weighty. What a dareing (sic)' and presumptuous man he must have been...."[42]

This description is quite similar to that given by Robert Heron in his text on *A New and Complete System of Universal Geography,* published in 1796, in which he says of Edenton: "It has a brick church for Episcopalians, which for many years has been neglected, and serves only to show that the people once had a regard, at least for the externals of religion."[43] "The works of Voltaire and his royal patron, Frederick of Prussia, of Rousseau, Helvetius, Bolinbroke, Hume, Gibbon, and Paine, were found in the libraries of our principal families however small these libraries."[44] The spirit of the times is further shown by William R. Davie and Major Pleasant Henderson naming their sons Hyder Ally and Tippo Saib, in honor of two Hindu despots.[45]

As a contrast to the waning interest in denominationalism there was a growing interest in education, particularly from the state point of view. During the period from 1776 to 1789 an average of more than one academy for each year was chartered. Between 1776 and 1778 the Reverend James Hall, a graduate of Princeton, opened in Iredell County what he called "Clio's Nursery and the Academy of the Sciences," the first scientific school in the state. In 1778, Science Hall, at Hillsboro, was incorporated with William Hooper. James Hogg and Alexander Martin numbered among the trustees. In 1784, the charter was amended so as to provide funds by way of lottery pro-

42. *Pettigrew Letters, 1772-1803,* Vol. I p. 102.
43. Heron, Robert, *A New and Complete System of Universal Geography,* p. 469.
44. Hooper, William, *op. cit.,* p. 28.
45. *Ibid.,* p. 9.

vided the sum should not exceed 500 pounds. For a recitation hall the legislature also gave to the school the old Episcopal Church, the funds for which had been raised by taxation in colonial times.[46] This academy began its work August 1, 1786, under the control of W. Perkins[47] and an assistant Mr. Pinto, and was open to boys who could read the English language in "Spectators" or some other standard English work. Such subjects as English, geography, penmanship, arithmetic, merchants' accounts, and other branches of mathematics were taught. Hours of work were from seven to nine, ten to twelve-thirty in the forenoon, and from three to five in the afternoon. William Hopper, writing from Edenton November 6, 1786, to John Witherspoon in an effort to get a teacher for the academy at Hillsboro said that "a knowledge of the French language would make him an important acquisition to us."[48] Other academies incorporated were Granville Hall, Granville County, 1779; Smith's Academy, Edenton, 1782; Morgan Academy, Burke County, 1783; Innis Academy, Wilmington, 1782; Salisbury Academy, Salisbury, 1784; Newbern Academy, Newbern, 1784; Davidson Academy, Davidson County, 1785; Kinston Academy, Dobbs County, 1785; Grove Academy, Duplin County, 1785; Warrenton Academy, Warren County, 1786; Franklin Academy, Franklin County, 1786; Pitt Academy, Pitt County, 1786; Pittsborough Academy, Chatham County, 1786; Richmond Academy, Richmond County, 1788; Currituck Seminary, Currituck County, 1789.[49]

In general, the chartering of these academies showed a pro-

---

46. *State Records*, Vol. XXIV, pp. 606-607.
47. His salary was 89 pounds, 17 shillings for three months. Students paid 3 pounds, 6 shillings and 8 pence on entrance — *Accompts For the Hillsboro Academy, Begun 1784*, (Manuscript)
48. Nash, Francis, "The History of Orange County," in *The North Carolina Booklet*, Vol. X, October, 1910, p. 11.
49. Most of these academies are listed in Knight, E. W., *Public School Education in North Carolina*; Raper, C. L., *Church and Private Schools of North Carolina*; Smith, C. L. *History of Education in North Carolina*; an original source is Martin, F. X., *Collection of Private Law*.

gressive state interest. The lottery and church building grant to the Hillsboro Academy may be considered as partial state support. In the case of Smith's Academy, the governor was granted the right to attend the meetings of the board of trustees as an ex-officio member. Teachers were exempted from military duty. Students were to be fitted "for an honorable discharge of the social duties of life."[50] Buildings to be erected could be named after those making the largest donations within six months. The property of Davidson Academy was, by the charter, to be exempted from taxation for ninety-nine years, and that part of the state's land "most remote from the salt springs near Nashville" was to be invested in the hands of the trustees for the use of the seminary.[51] In 1786, an act was passed granting lands in the town of Newbern to the Newbern Academy; while in this same year a charter issued for Warrenton Academy granted the right of conducting a lottery for a partial financial support to that institution.[52]

Not one of these academies may be considered as a state project, however, for they were local in appeal and were sponsored only by a few enterprising citizens of a particular locality. In most cases, the charters of the incorporated academies provided a clause which implied that they were not to be construed as those schools "mentioned in and intended by the constitution."[53] Governor Martin, in an address before the Legislature in 1784, showed, however, the continued development of a state interest when he said: "Let me call your attention to the education of youth; may seminaries of learning be revived and encouraged, where the understanding may be enlightened,

---

50. Martin, F. X., *op. cit.*, p. 102; *State Records*, Vol. XXIV, p. 454.
51. Martin, F. X., *op. cit.*, p. 156.
52. Although not an incorporated academy, the classical school, conducted by Samuel E. McCorkle near Salisbury in 1785, which he called "Zion Parnassus," showed a liberalizing tendency. In addition to the classical department, there was a department for the preparation and training of teachers, and free tuition was granted to poor worthy young men. — Knight, E. W., *op. cit.*, p. 40.
53. Martin, F. X., *op. cit.*, p. 172; *State Records*, Vol. XXIV, p. 692.

the heart mended, and genius cherished; *where the state may draw forth men of abilities to direct her councils and support her government.*[54] Again, in 1785, he said: "Your schools of learning . . . *are objects of legislative attention,* which cannot be too often repeated and held up to your view; that the mist of ignorance be dissipated and good morals cultivated . . ."[55]

Most active in the development of an interest in a state university was William R. Davie. An Englishmen by birth, a graduate of Princeton in 1776,[56] and a major in the American Revolution, Davie soon revealed high qualities of statesmanship in the new democracy. He was an excellent scholar of active mind; he was brave and courageous in war; he was fearless and daring in public life. Although looked upon as a Presbyterian, he accepted the liberal doctrine of the enlightened age, and like Franklin became a professed Deist. "Davie took Lord Bolingbroke for his model . . . and . . . applied himself with so much diligence to the study of his model, that literary men could easily recognize in the eloquence of Davie the loftly flowing style of Bolingbroke."[57] He like Franklin and Jefferson was interested in scientific agricultural pursuits and in 1784 organized a company to drain the Scuppernong Lake hoping that the uncovered land would prove valuable for the cultivation of rice and hemp.[58] His first active interest in education was shown when he obtained the charter for Warrenton Academy; and he became president of the board of trustees of that institution. Following his return from the National Constitutional Convention, meeting at Philadelphia in 1787, he was elected a member of the North Carolina Convention for the ratification of the Federal Constitution which was meeting at the same time.

54. *State Records,* Vol. XIX, p. 498.
55. *State Records,* Vol. XVII, p. 533.
56. *Colonial Records,* Vol. X. p. 870.
57. Hoyt, W. H., *The Papers of Archibald D. Murphey,* Vol. II, p. 349.
58. Sparks, Jared, "Lives of William Richardson Davie and Samuel Kirkland" in *The Library of American Biography,* Vol. XV, p. 103. An excellent brief sketch of Davie's life, written by Walter Clark, is to be found in the *Magazine of American History,* December, 1892.

At the meeting of the Legislature at Fayetteville in 1789 Davie, who had been appointed to the committee on public bills, introduced into the House November 12, "A Bill to Establish an University in this State."[59] The bill met much opposition, for the hard pressure of the public burdens during the "Critical Period" gave many men grounds for an objection. Others raised the cry of "economy," pretended a peculiar regard for the poor, raised the cry of "aristocracy," and feared to lose public favor. Advocates of the bill spoke of the need for the state to educate its leaders, of advancing the power of the state, of the prevailing method of sending boys out of the state to be educated, and of the need for an institution which would provide an education for every phase of life. What they advocated was a "Social Contract." "Tact, logic, satire, eloquence, were needed and employed to carry the measure through the assembly, and were at length successful."[60] Luckily for the bill, it had the two best orators of the Assembly behind it, Davie and Alfred Moore, later an associate judge of the United States Supreme Court, as well as the influence of such men as Hugh Williamson, Benjamin Smith, James Iredell, Samuel Johnston, Richard Dobbs Spaight, William Blunt, Samuel Ashe, Thomas Person, James Hogg, William Barry Grove, Alexander Martin, Willie Jones, and others. After being amended, a sufficient number of the original opponents were secured for the bill to pass its third reading in the Senate December 11, 1789.[61]

The preamble to the charter reads:

Whereas, in all well regulated governments it is the indispensable duty of every Legislature to consult the happiness of a rising generation, and endeavor to fit them for an honourable discharge of the social duties of life, by paying the strictest attention to their education: And whereas, an university supported by permanent funds and well endowed, would have the most direct tendency to answer the above purpose:

---

59. *State Records*, Vol. XXI, p. 228.
60. Sparks, Jared, *op. cit.*, p. 107.
61. *State Records*, Vol. XXI, p. 673.

I. Be it therefore enacted—[62]

Most of the trustees, numbering forty, had already been active as trustees of the academies and were members of the Legislature at this time.[63] "The Trustees of the University of North Carolina," having perpetual succession and a common seal, were to handle all the funds and properties of the university in "special trust and confidence," and to bargain and sell for the institution as they saw fit. It was ordered that the board of trustees should meet at "Fayetteville on the third Monday in the session of the next General Assembly" to choose a president and secretary, and to select a place for the next annual meeting. A treasurer was to be elected for a term of two years who should receive "all monies, donations, gifts, bequests and charities whatsoever that may belong or accrue to the said university during his office...." Funds collected were to be published annually in the *State Gazette*, "under the penalty of one hundred pounds, to be received in suit by the Attorney General, in the name of the Governor...." All monies collected for the University were to be paid into the State Treasury for which the University would receive from the state notes of the same amount bearing six per cent interest. Such payments were to

---

63. *State Records,* Vol. XXV, pp. 21-22.

63. Hugh Williamson, William Blount, and Richard Dobbs Spaight were signers of the Constitution of the United States.

Samuel Ashe, Benjamin Williams, Benjamin Smith and William R. Davie became governors of the State.

Joseph Graham and Thomas Person were Generals in the Revolutionary War.

Samuel Spencer, John Williams, and Samuel Ashe were judges under the court of law of 1777.

Samuel Johnston and Benjamin Hawkins were United States senators.

Charles Johnson, James Holland, Alexander Mobene, Joseph Winston, and William Barry Grove were or became members of the Lower House of Congress.

James Hogg was an enlightened merchant of Hillsboro; Samuel E. McCorkle was a minister and leading educator in the State; and John Hay was an eminent lawyer from Fayetteville.

Other members of the Board included members of the state legislature and men active in public life.

constitute a permanent fund, only the interest being used for financing the institution. As soon as the fund was considered sufficient by the trustees, they were to direct a meeting "for the purpose of fixing on and purchasing a healthy and convenient situation, which shall not be situated within five miles of the permanent seats of government, or any of the places of holding the courts of law or equity . . ."[64]

The trustees were given the power to elect a president of the University, professors, and tutors, whom they could remove "for misbehavior, inability, or neglect of duty." They were also to have the power to make all laws for regulating and governing the institution, but these laws could not be contrary "to the inalienable liberty of a citizen, or to the laws of the state." The power of conferring degrees and honors was invested in the faculty. Any person who within five years should subscribe ten pounds to the University, payable within five years, was entitled to have one student educated free at the University; while the "public hall of the library, and four of the colleges'" were to be named after "one or another of the six persons" who within four years contributed the largest sums to the University. A book was ordered to be kept in the library in which to record the name and place of every donor and benefactor of the institution. Hugh Williamson, liberal follower of Frank lin and spoken of by Jefferson as a man of acute mind and a high degree of erudition, graduate and ex-professor of the University of Pennsylvania, doctor of medicine from the University of Edinburgh, and a representative of North Carolina to the National Congress from 1789 to 1793, later wrote that this charter was granted for the purpose of promoting civic liberty. "Ignorance in the subjects and despotism in rulers go hand in hand," he said, and then added, "that there never has been a nation, who preserved the semblance of freedom, without being enlightened by the rays of science." Convinced of these truths, many were determined to "provide a proper seminary within the state; for they knew that children, who are sent abroad for their education, are apt to form sentiments concern-

64. *State Records,* Vol. XXV, p. 24.

ing their native soil, which do not consist with the degree of patriotism or love of country that is necessary to its prosperity ...."[65] The doctrine of eighteenth century enlightment was permeating the state.

Following the passing of the charter a bill was introduced for "Raising a Fund for Erecting the Buildings and for the Support of the University of North Carolina."[66] An even more bitter struggle developed over this bill than had developed over the charter. Thomas Tyson, of Moore County, led the opposition on the grounds that "He believed it to be repugnant to the constitution of the state to grant any exclusive emoluments to any man or set of men except for services rendered," and that "applying public revenue to the above-mentioned purpose must augment the Tax on the citizens who can by no means be in any measure benefited thereby."[67] In spite of the opposition a modified bill again went through under the leadership of Davie. It provided that all the monies (arrearages) due the State of North Carolina up to January 1, 1783, should be used for the construction of buildings, employing professors and tutors, and carrying into "complete effect the act before recited."[68] All property which had escheated to the state or would escheat to the state was vested in the hands of the trustees, and all lands or property belonging to the University was declared exempt from taxation.

The trustees were hopeful. A state university offered the needs to unify the work of the religious schools, and would serve as a cure for those who had no denominational tendencies. North Carolina was in her infancy as a state, and it was the hope of the founders of the University of North Carolina that this newly created institution would guide her in the right direction. The most serious problem facing the board of trustees was the question of finance. While the legislature was still in

65. Williamson, Hugh, *The History of North Carolina*, Vol. II, pp. 83-84.
66. *State Records*, Vol. XXV, p. 24.
67. *State Records*, Vol. XXI, p. 430.
68. *State Records*, Vol. XXV, pp. 24-25.

session, Benjamin Smith had made the first donation to the University, a grant of twenty thousand acres of land in Tennessee. In reply to the thanks which he received for the gift he regretted that it was "not more immediately productive," but hoped that in the future it would become a more beneficial fund to the institution. "In all enlightened countries the encouragement of learning is acknowledged to be one of the wisest measures a State can pursue", said he, and "In this sentiment I sincerely wish for the prosperity of our University, and shall be happy in every opportunity of promoting its encouragement."[69] Following the first meeting of the board of trustees on December 18, 1789, at which seventeen of the forty trustees appointed were present, it was decided that an effort should be made to secure a loan from the state as the attempt to secure direct appropriations had failed in the previous Legislature. It was their sincere wishes that the University of North Carolina should grow into existence and become more than a name. But their zeal for the welfare of the institution caused them to be distressed when they reflected "how extremely illy the resources of the trustees" were "proportioned to their necessities: of the arrearages voted them by the Assembly of 1789."[70] On November 1, 1790, Davie addressed a letter to Governor Martin asking him to give the University every assistance in his power, realizing "the importance of education in a country just forming its manners and government."[71] In accordance with Davie's wishes, Governor Martin appealed to the Legislature for the desired aid, saying:

This institution which hath been stamped with importance and *erected for the cause of humanity*, might do honour to this and the Southern states, had it a proper support, where youth might be nurtured in *true religion,*

---

69. *State Records,* Vol. XXII, pp. 802-803.

For the thanks of the Board see *The North Carolina Chronicle;* or *Fayetteville Gazette,* December 6, 1790, p. 3.

70. *Minutes of the Board of Trustees of the University of North Carolina,* November 15, 1790, to December 6, 1796, p. 41.

71. *State Records,* Vol. XXII, p. 801.

sound policy and science, and men of abilities draw forth to fill the different departments of government with reputation, or be formed for useful and ornamental members of society in private or professional life. To your further notice permit me to recommend this infant establishment, which without your fostering care must fall or rise slow into consequence. That a loan be granted from the treasury on the security of the present funds, and future to be established, to the commissioners, to enable them to proceed in erecting the buildings and give it a more essential than a paper being.[72]

The Governor's message was referred to the committee on public bills which failed to report favorably on the petition. This was no doubt due to the absence of Davie. An attempt made, however, to exclude the university trustees from holding seats in the General Assembly failed.[73]

Although the situation seemed gloomy when the second meeting of the board of trustees was held at Fayetteville on November 15, 1790, the leaders were not discouraged. Some of the trustees resigned but their places were immediately filled Governor Martin was added to the board and was immediately elected to the presidency on the resignation of William Lenoir A vote of acceptance of the grants provided in the act for raising funds for buildings and for the support of the University was ordered to be transmitted to the General Assembly. No amendments were considered necessary to the charter and the fund act. It was decided that the board should meet at Hillsboro on July 3, 1791, "to fix on the place where the buildings of the University" should be erected.[74] The appeal to the Legislature for the loan was to be continued, and the Treasurer was ordered to advertise for and to endeavor to collect the escheats and arrearages due the University. During these early years the most pressing problem continued to be that of finance.

On December 2, 1790, the situation looked somewhat bright

72. *State Records*, Vol. XXI, p. 878.
73. *Ibid.*, p. 983.
74. *Minutes of the Board of Trustees of the University of North Carolina*, November 15, 1790 to December 6, 1796, p. 19.

er with the payment of $2,706.41 by the clerk of Perquiman's County Court which had been recovered from a delinquent "Commissioner of Specifics." This was ordered, according to the provisions of the grant, to be invested in United States Bank stock. By December of 1791, the sum of $301.24 additional had been collected and there was hope of collecting $300.00 more. But with such meager funds it was necessary that a loan be secured from the state if any building were to be erected in the near future. William R. Davie, again in the Legislature as a borough member for Halifax, led the appeal before that body. Supporting Davie were Benjamin Smith, John Lanier, John Williams, David Stone, Thomas Person, Joseph McDowell, Joel Lane, and Governor Alexander Martin. Leading the opposition were Thomas Tyson, Joseph Graham, Thomas Wynne, David Caldwell and Thomas Wade. No sectional opposition or support was noted. A. D. Murphey, in an oration delivered at Chapel Hill on June 27, 1827, said: "I was present in the House of Commons, when Davie addressed that body upon the bill granting a loan of money to the trustees for erecting the buildings of the university; and although more than thirty years have since elapsed, I have the most vidid recollections of the greatness of his manner and the powers of his eloquence upon that occasion."[75] The loan, calling for an appropriation of $10,000, was secured, but only on the close vote of fifty-seven to fifty-three in the House and twenty-eight to twenty-one in the Senate.

With the funds now available, it was possible to go ahead with the selection of a site and other plans for the establishment of the institution. On August 2, 1792, the trustees decided that ballots should "be taken for a given point, with a latitude of erecting the buildings within fifteen miles of said point,"[76] and on the following day Cipritz(sic) Bridge or New Hope in Chatham County was chosen, it being approximately near the center of the state. A committee was appointed which was to meet in Pittsboro on November 1, 1792, to visit all the places thought

75. Hoyt, W. H.,. op. cit., Vol. II, p. 350.
76. Minutes of the Board of Trustees of the University of North Carolina 1790-1796, p. 62.

to be eligible. On November 7, 8, and 9, this committee while in session received among other offers lands totaling 1180 acres on Chapel Hill in return for an agreement to make that place the seat of the University.[77] Other gifts, totaling $1,596.00 were later contributed. It is said that the committee, stopping at the foot of the great poplar which still stands on the University campus, greatly admired the place, which lay at the intersection of the highways runnnng from Raleigh to Greensboro and from Pittsboro to Petersburg, Virginia, and had an elevation of 500 feet. It was a retired and beautiful spot, amidst rolling hills, and well situated for the whole state. The soil, of Laurentian granite, a wealth of springs, the oak forests, the mountain rhododendron, all made the proposed location appear attractive as well as useful. Davie seems to have been pleased with the selection, "elevated above the surrounding country as to furnish an extensive and beautiful landscape, composed of the heights in the vicinity of Eno, Flat and Little Rivers."[78]

With a site purchased, the trustees proceeded with more definite arrangements. As a seal for the University, they chose the face of Apollo, the God of Eloquence, and his emblem, the rising sun, expressive of the dawn of higher education in the state. In compliance with the order of December 8, 1792, a committee, appointed by the board of trustees, and including Davie, had laid off a town of thirty lots. The main street they called Franklin in honor of "the first civilized American."[79] The committee in reporting the affair said, "Before the sale it became necessary to give each street a name, by which the lots might be distinguished. Your Commissioners therefore called them as in the plan."[80] The town was already known as Chapel Hill, be-

77. *Ibid.*, p. 82.
78. Battle, K. P., *History of the University of North Carolina*, Vol. I, p. 26.
79. *History of the University of North Carolina*, (manuscript) p. 25.
80. A large number of the bretheren of the Masonic order from Hillsborough, Chatham, Granville and Warren, attended to assist at the ceremony of the placing the cornerstone; and the procession for his purpose moved from Patterson's at 12 o'clock in the following order:

ing named after an old chapel of the Church of England which stood at the crossroads. In April, 1793, a contract was let to James Patterson for erecting a building 96 feet, 7 inches long by 40 feet, 1 1/2 inches wide, and to contain 16 rooms and 4 passages. The building was to cost $5,000.00 in addition to the brick, sash weights, locks, hooks, fastenings, and paint, to be furnished by the trustees, and was to be completed by November 1, 1794. On October 12, 1793, the cornerstone of the first university building, "Old East," was laid.

From the records, it appears to have been a very impressive occasion. Many people were present from all over the state, and some brought donations to the new institution.

The Masonic Brethren in their usual order of procession, the Commissioners, the Trustees not Commissioners, the Hon. Judge Macay and other public officers, then followed the gentlemen of the vicinity. On approaching the south end of the building, the Masons opened to the right and left, and the Commissioners, etc., passed through and took their place. The Masonic procession then moved on round the foundation of the building, and halted with their usual ceremonies opposite to the south east corner, where *William Richardson Davie*, Grandmaster of the fraternity, etc., in this state, assisted by two Masters of the Lodges and four other officers, laid the cornerstone, enclosing a plate to commemorate the transaction.

81. *The North Carolina Journal*, October 30, 1793, p. 2. Masonry was quite prevalent among the leading, thinking, liberal men of the time. It seems to have been connected with the deistic movement in religion. In 1832, when the national political circles were stirred by the rise of the Anti-Masonic party, Free Masonry was accused of being "a system of deism in its first degrees, and of Atheism in the end." The writer asserted that on the question of revealed religion, the Grand Master Mason said to a candidate for a higher degree: "Behold my dear brother, what you must fight against and destroy, before you can come to the knowledge of the true good and sovereign happiness." — Thacher, Moses,

The plate of the cornerstone, it is thought, was stolen during the years 1865 to 1875. In September, 1916, it was found by T. B. Foust in the Foundry and Machine Works of Clarksville, Tennessee, where it had been purchased from a junk dealer. It is a plate of bronze, one eighth of an inch thick, five and one quarter inches wide, and seven and a half inches long, and carries the following inscription:

Dr. Samuel E. McCorkle gave the address of the day in which he said that science and learning were the great means of ensuring the happiness of mankind as they would bring power and wealth to the state. Liberty and laws called "for general knowledge in the people, and extensive knowledge in the ministers of the state, and these in fine demand public places of education." Franklin of America was made to compare with Newton of England as the doctrine of the eighteenth century humanitarianism was proclaimed:

Britons glory in the name of a Newton . . . . Americans glory in the name of a Franklin, and every nation boasts of her great men who has them. Savages cannot have them *rather cannot educate them,* though many a Newton has been born and buried among them. Knowledge is liberty and law. When the clouds of ignorance are dispelled by the radiance of knowledge, power trembles, but the authority of laws remain inviolable. And how this knowledge, productive of so many advantages to mankind, can be acquired without public places of education, I know not.[82]

Plans had already been under way for drawing up a plan of

The Right Worshipful
William Richardson Davie
Grand Master of
The Most Ancient and Honorable Fraternity
of Free Masons in the State of North
Carolina
One of the Trustees of the University
of the Said State
and a Commoner of the Same
Assisted by
The Other Commissioners and the Bretheren
Of the Eagle and Independence Lodges,
On the 12th day of October
In the Year of Masonry 5793
And in the 18th Year of American Independence
Laid the Cornerstone of this Edifice.

R. Huntington Sculp. - - - - -

"The Presentation of the Plate" in *The Alumni Register,* November, 1916, pp. 39-41.
82. *The North Carolina Journal,* October 30, 1793, p. 2.

education. At the meeting of the board of trustees in July, 1791, Hugh Williamson, Samuel E. McCorkle, and Benjamin Hawkins were appointed as a committee to secure information on the laws, regulations, revenues, expenditures and buildings of the Colleges of the United States and elsewhere, and other members seem to have been added to the committee from time to time. Available to these men were the courses of study in the colleges of America, all of which, except one, were under the control of some denominational agency and which accepted the classical studies as a basis for work.[83] There were the incorporated academies dating from 1776, in which most of the men had participated as trustees. Various plans of education had also been published, the most popular of which was that of Benjamin Franklin. Davie was familiar with Rollin's *Belles Lettres*, a book used quite extensively by Franklin in his plan of education, for he suggested this book for use in the University. He was also familiar with Priestley's *Lectures on History and General Policy*, and appears to have been familiar with Sheridan's *A Plan of Education . . .*, published in London in 1769 as an attack on the classics which it said "made only good Latin and Greek scholars, and minute philosophers; whereas the true ends of education in all Christian countries ought to be to make good men, and good citizens."[84] The book also shows a strong French influence. In a preliminary report made on December 8, 1792, the committee reported that due to the uncertainty as to the time when the university buildings would be completed and to the meager financial conditions "the pursuits of Literature and Science should on the first institution be confined to the following objects:

the study of the languages particularly the English. The acquirement of Historical Knowledge ancient and modern. The study of the Belles Lettres-Mathematics and Natural

---

83. The exception mentioned refers to the University of Pennsylvania. It is also stated in Chapter V that Jefferson had modified the curriculum of the College of William and Mary while he was governor of Virginia in 1779.
84. Sheridan, Thomas, *A Plan of Education . . .*, p. 42.

Philosophy the improvement of the intellectual powers including a rational system of logic and moral philosophy. Information in Botany to which should be added a competent knowledge in the theory and practice of agriculture best suited to the soils of the State. The principles of Architecture.[85]

In closing their report, the committee urged "that steps be taken to procure an apparatus for experimental Philosophy and Astronomy. In this they would include a set of Globes, Barometers, Thermometers, Miscroscope, Telescope, Quadrant, Primatic Glass, Air pumps and an Electrical Machine."[86] A library should also be secured but the choice of the books was to be left to the faculty. It will be noticed that Greek and Latin, although implied, are not mentioned. K. P. Battle in writing the *History of the University of North Carolina* expressed great surprise at the liberality of the plan: "The report is remarkable as being far ahead of the times, notwithstanding that the chairman and the second on the list, Stone, were graduates of Princeton, a seat of the old curriculum. . . . It is probable however, that as the University of Pennsylvania, the alma mater of Dr. Hugh Williamson, was conspicuous in exalting scientific studies, his influence had weight in the report of the committee."[87]

On December 1, 1795, Davie laid before the trustees a more detailed plan which was accepted as the curriculum for the University. It divided the work into two departments, a preparatory school and five professorships. In the preparatory school, the basis for work "was reading and pronouncing the select English passages from the present English Authors," and "Copying in a fair and correct manner select English Essays."[88] Geography, French, Latin, and Greek were to be taught, and any of the languages (English excepted) could be omitted if the Par

---

85. *Minutes of the Board of Trustees of the University of North Carolina 1790-1796*, pp. 88-89.
86. *Ibid.*, pp. 89-90.
87. Battle, K. P., *op. cit.*, pp. 49-50.
88. *Minutes of the Board of Trustees of the University of North Carolina 1790-1796*, p. 203.

ent or Guardian of the Student should so direct.[89] The five professorships included a professor of moral and political philosophy and history; of natural philosophy, astronomy and geography; of mathematics; of chemistry and the philosophy of medicine, agriculture and mechanics; and of languages. Any candidate was acceptable to the University under the first three of the professorships who could pass an approved examination upon the English language, the first four rules of arithmetic and the rules of three. No specific qualifications were required under the fourth professorship. Any one was eligible to the fifth who could pass an examination on English and explain the government and connection of words. The scientific interest and the liberality of the curriculum appear to be even more advanced than the plan proposed by Franklin or any other man of the time. Science, English, and History were to be the core of the University curriculum. The classics, although offered, were to be electives.

Now the principal task of the trustees was to secure teachers. As early as December 12, 1792, professors had been advertised for in *The North Carolina Journal* who knew the "languages, particularly the English, History, ancient and modern- the Belles Lettres- Logic and Moral Philosophy"- and "Mathematics, and Natural Philosophy- Agriculture and Botany, with the principles of Architecture."[90] But the professors were slow to apply and the trustees made other efforts to find some. It seemed that the condition of the University's funds would not justify the salary of a man whose experience and reputation for learning earned him the position of the presidency, and an acting president, styled "The Professor of Humanities," was to be elected at a salary of $300.00 annually, plus two thirds of the tuition fees. He, in turn, was to select a tutor at a salary of $200.00 annually, plus one third of the tuition fees, subject to the approval of the board of trustees.[91] On December 13,

---

89. *Ibid.*, p. 204.
90. *The North Carolina Journal*, December 12, 1792, p. 3.
91. *Minutes of the Board of Trustees of the University of North Carolina, 1790-1796*, p. 129.

1798, the names of the Reverend John Brown, a former pupil of Dr. Samuel E. McCorkle and later President of the University of Georgia; Dr. Samuel E. McCorkle; the Reverend George Micklejohn, one time Tory and minister of the Church of England; the Reverend James Tate, of New Hanover, and the Reverend David Ker were suggested. It was generally believed that Dr. McCorkle would secure the position. But Davie, a dominant leader in the deliberations, believed that McCorkle lacked executive ability and was too strong a believer in the doctrine of revelation.[92] At a later date, Davie, writing of some criticisms against the University, seems to have explained his attitude toward McCorkle: "Bishop Pettigrew has said it is a very dissipated and debauched place. Some priests have also been doing us the same good office to the westward. Nothing it seems goes well that these *men of God* have not some hand in."[93] On January 10, 1794, David Ker was elected the first acting president of the University. He was an able, liberal scholar, had been educated at Trinity College, Dublin, and at the time of his election was thirty-six years of age.

The trustees now proceeded to lay out the final plans for opening the University. It was decided that students should be divided into four literary classes, that the prices for tuition should be $8.00 a year for reading, writing, arithmetic and bookkeeping; $12.50 for the languages, geography, history, and the Belles Lettres; and $15.00 for the sciences, including astronomy, natural philosophy, moral philosophy, chemistry, geometry, and agriculture. These fees were to be paid over to the acting pres-

---

92. On numerous occasions, McCorkle found an opportunity to preach sermons against Deism. McCorkle, S. E., *A Discourse on the General First Principles of Deism and Revelation Contrasted*, Salisbury, Coupee, 1797.

93. Battle, K. P., *op. cit.*, p. 60.

For such an attitude toward Dr. McCorkle, Davie was bitterly criticized by General John Steele, one time member of the National Congress. In 1789, he wrote: "I have no sons to educate, and my nephew (son of Dr. McCorkle) is relieved of the humiliation of acquiring his education at an institution whose outset was characterized by acts of ingratitude and insults toward his father." — *Ibid.*, p. 100.

ident, who was also the Professor of Humanities. It was ordered that a steward's house be built and ready for occupancy by the opening of the University. John Taylor, of Raleigh, selected as steward for the first year, was ordered to see that the floors, staircases and passages were washed once every two weeks, that the boys' rooms were swept and cleaned once a day, and that fresh water was brought from the spring four times a day and "placed in such a situation as the professor shall think proper."[94]

A committee, reporting on the quantity and quality of the meats and drink to be furnished to the students, believed that only a simple diet should be provided and that "no *Drink* other than water" should be furnished.[95] Students were allowed, but not compelled, to live in the University buildings and board at Commons.

For the beginning of the library, books were donated by James Reid, twenty-one volumes; Judge Williams, three volumes; William R. Davie, six volumes; David Ker, three volumes; Abraham Hodge, ten volumes; and F. W. N. Burton, two volumes. For a beginning on text books, Hugh Williamson was given the sum of $200.00 with which he purchased, among other books, forty-eight Webster's Grammars at $1.00 each, forty-eight Ruddiman's Rudiments at twenty-eights cents each, twenty-four Erasmus at $1.33 each, six Young's Dictionaries at $2.25 each, and six Greek Testaments at $1.67.[96] Due to the scarcity of books, it was planned that these texts should be rented to the pupils at prices determined by the faculty. Probably the first piece of scientific equipment owned by the University was a compass given by the State Legislature on December 21, 1789.[97] Other early gifts included an ostrich egg, the tooth of a young mammoth, a piece of asbestos, a pine limb and a piece of

---

94. *Minutes of the Board of Trustees of the University of North Carolina, 1790-1796*, p. 144.

95. *Ibid.*, p. 140.

96. For the original list see *History of the University of North Carolina* (manuscript), p. 27.

97. *State Records*, Vol. XXI, p. 720.

resin petrified, a piece of cloth made of bark, incisors of a beaver, a porcupine skin, petrified beech nut, a testaceous bracelet taken from an Indian grave, and various stones and specimens of Indian clothing. The ladies of Newbern, after the University had been open a few years, donated a quadrant and the ladies of Raleigh a pair of globes.[98] According to the minutes of the trustees for July 11, 1795, William B. Grove had been sent to Philadelphia for the purchase of scientific apparatus for the University. With these preparations, announcement was made in *The North Carolina Journal* January 5, 1795, that the University of North Carolina would open on January 15 of that year, and that the first Monday after June 10 was to be commencement day at which there should be public examinations, exhibitions, and public visitations.[99]

The institution opened on the date announced but with no students. Newspapers, in reporting the opening, stated that the unfavorable condition of the weather kept many visitors and friends away, but that the "Governor of the State, and President of the Board, accompanied by several Members of the Corporation, and many other gentlemen, Members of the General Assembly, made a visit... to the seat of the University ... in order to be present at the beginning of the exercises of that institution." The officials, after viewing the buildings and grounds, reported that the exercises of the institution had begun and that students disposed to enter "may come forward with an assurance of being received."[100]

Chapel Hill must have been a rather lonesome place to Professor David Ker after his guests departed. Three weeks passed and still no students. Finally, Hinton James, of Wilmington, arrived on February 12, 1795, the "precursor of a long line of seekers after knowledge."[101] Two weeks later other students arrived: Maurice and Alfred Moore of Brunswick County, Richard Eagles of New Hanover, John Taylor of Orange, William Sneed

---

98. *History of the University of North Carolina* (manuscript) p. 179.
99. *The North Carolina Journal,* January 5, 1795, p. 3.
100. *The North Carolina Journal,* February 25, 1795, p. 2.
101. Battle, K. P., *op. cit.,* p. 63.

and Hutchins, Francis, and Robert Burton of Granville.[102] By the end of the term, the enrollment had reached forty-one and by the end of the collegiate year more than a hundred students were in attendance. Charles W. Harris, a first honor graduate from Princeton who had been added to the faculty of the University as a tutor in mathematics, wrote from Chapel Hill to Dr. Charles Harris, Cabarrus County, on April 10, 1795:

> We have begun to introduce, by degrees the regulations of the University, and as yet have not been disappointed. There is one class in Natural Philosophy and Geography and four in the Languages —
>
> The Constitution of this college is on a more liberal plan than any in America, and by the amendments which I think it will receive at the next meeting of the trustees, its usefulness will probably be much promoted. The notion that true learning consists rather in exercising the reasoning faculties, and laying up a store of useful knowledge, than in overloading the memory with words of a dead language, is becoming daily more prevalent. It appears hard to deny a young Gentleman the honour of a College, after he has with much labor acquired a competent knowledge of the sciences.[103]

In July of the following year, Harris wrote to Joseph Caldwell, tutor at Princeton: "Our education at Princeton was shamefully neglected and inexcusably Deficient in experimental Philosophy, a circumstance which I have often reflected upon with concern." He advised Caldwell to go by Philadelphia and get acquainted with various apparatus, and asserted that he would feel ridiculous if he had "not gotten a smattering of experimental Philosophy by visiting Williamsburg College in Virginia."[104]

A spirit of optimism pervaded the meetings of the board of trustees. Davie, in a letter to John Haywood, treasurer of the

---

102. For a complete list of the *ante-bellum* students at the University see Grant, Daniel L., *Alumni History of the University of North Carolina.*

103. Wagstaff, H. M., "The Harris Letters" in *The James Sprunt Historical Studies*, Vol. XIV, p. 13.

104. *Ibid.*, pp. 32-33.

University, dated July 22, 1795, said he was well pleased with the first final examinations of the students. There was a feeling that the students would soon be suffering "for want of rooms" said Davie, and because of this the trustees had ordered "a grammar school built with three or four lodging rooms."[105] In their society meetings[106] and commencement orations the students spoke on the advantages of science and public education.[107] John Henry Hobart, a tutor at Princeton, wrote in November, 1796, to Joseph Caldwell, who was at this time a member of the University Faculty:

> It is to be hoped, however, that the rays of light from your University the sun of Science, will illuminate the darkness of society, and chase away ignorance and vice. ... With all due respects to the Faculty of the University of North Carolina. ... they seem to constitute as motley a group as I have lately hard of. Presbyterians and Arians, infidels and Roman Catholics. Bless me what a collection. The age of Reason has surely come. Superstitition and bigotry are buried in one common grave. Philosophy and charity begin to bless the earth. Transporting thought. What a glory to the University of North Carolina that in her sacred seats they have first appeared.[108]

Davie, it seems, was author of an article which appeared in *The North Carolina Journal,* on August 1, 1796, which stated: "It was said with great truth by the French Convention 'That as in every free government, the law emanates from the people, it is necessary that the people should receive an education to enable them to direct the law, and the political part of this education should be consonant to the principles of the constitution under which they live.' The plan of education established by the Board appears to be predicated upon this principle. ... "[109]

105. Hamilton, J. G. deR., "William Richardson Davie; A Memoir" in *The James Sprunt Historical Studies,* Vol. VII, p. 30.
106. *Minutes of the Philanthropic Society, 1795-1797,* p. 62.
107. *Journal of the Examination Committee of the University of North Carolina, 1795-1809,* pp. 77-76.
108. *Letters, University of North Carolina, 1796-1835,* manuscript.
109. *North Carolina Journal,* August 1, 1796, p. 2.

But the spirit of optimism soon began to wane and the years from 1795 to 1805 turned out to be years of experiment rather than years of progress. Professor Ker had not only the enmity of the old religious group, which was always present in the Board of Trustees, and led by Dr. McCorkle, but by mixing himself up in the political thought of the time secured the ill will of Davie. He was thus forced to resign in July, 1796. Mr. Harris, tutor in mathematics and liberal in his religious views, was considered for Ker's place, but he seems to have been displeased with his work, and sent in his resignation shortly after Ker withdrew from the University. Samuel A. Holmes, first a tutor and later professor of languages, carried his liberalism to the extreme, became an outspoken atheist, and horrified the ecclesiastics to such an extent that he too was forced to withdraw. Nicholas Delevaux, a French Catholic and for a short time teacher in the preparatory school, resigned because he could not get along with William Richards, a fellow teacher. He also had the ill will of Caldwell, although Davie had a high opinion of the Frenchman's "grammatical accuracy."[110] Richards, a well educated Englishman and one time sailor and stroller player, seems to have done creditable work, but he died in 1798. For a time, Dr. Smith, president of Princeton, was considered for the presidency of the young University at Chapel Hill and he seriously considered accepting the position. But one condition was that he be given complete control and this Davie refused.[111] Samuel E. McCorkle was offered the professorship of moral and political philosophy but he refused because Davie was not willing to grant him a salary equal to that of the acting president. Hugh Williamson, writing from Philadelphia to John Haywood in November, 1796, spoke of the difficulty of securing teachers: "The allowance mentioned was so small as to preclude the chance of inducing any respectable man of learning to remove to a southern state where, as they all believe, the chances of health are greatly diminished. Men of moderate talents and considerable learning commonly expect to be able to

---

110. Hamilton, J. G. deR., *op. cit.*, p. 35.
111. *History of the University of North Carolina*, (manuscript) p. 25.

make more money by some other business than they can by teaching, hence it is that men capable of teaching can hardly be found except in the ministry."[112] The attempt to secure liberal scientific men who were not identified with the ministry seemed doomed to failure, which marked in part the failure of Davie's plan of education.

The election of Joseph Caldwell as professor of mathematics on December 9, 1796, was the beginning of the downfall of Davie's ideals for a higher educational institution based on the enlightened and humanitarian thought of the eighteenth century. Apparently there were two groups of thinkers interested in the University. One was headed by McCorkle and the other by Davie. The question was whether the classics or science should become the core of the curriculum, whether the old collegiate curriculum should give way to the ideas so strongly urged by Franklin in 1749, by Jefferson in 1779, and by Davie in 1795. Caldwell cast his lot with the former, although in his later years of life he showed a strong scientific interest. In 1803, he wrote: "The University early excited expectations which were unfortunately too sanguine and premature to be realized. Though the attainment of knowledge may be rendered comparatively easy, it is chimerical to propose that it shall be universal, or totally without expense."[113] He considered the idea of free mass education, a principle upon which the University was founded, impossible if not wrong. Early after his arrival in Chapel Hill, Caldwell had entered into a conversation with Davie on the question of Deism,[114] and Davie, it seems, was losing faith in the eighteenth century ideals of "Nature" and "Reason." Deism, he believed was leading to atheism[115] and had already connected itself with the Jeffersonian party. As the excesses of the French Revolution came on in full strength, oth-

---

112. *Letters, University of North Carolina, 1796-1835,* (manuscript) p. 7.
113. Battle, D. P., *op. cit.,* p. 132.
114. *Letters, University of North Carolina,* 1796-1835, p. 7.
115. For a good discussion of this question see Randall, J. H. Jr., *The Making of the Modern Mind,* p. 304.

ers began to lose faith in the doctrine of Rousseau and Voltaire. In 1795, students of the University literary societies had been talking about an alliance with France and in 1798 about war. Students were also complaining about their meat being too fat and the faculty was receiving replies from the steward that the "information was false as Hell."[116] Ideals of freedom among the students had led to many controversies with the faculty, in spite of the fact that a group of students had drawn up a petition in 1799 declaring to stand by the laws of the University as good government "must necessarily be a government of sentiment, not of force."[117] The elective system had led students into "the capricious disposition" to change from one study to another before "obtaining a competent knowledge of the books in the class in which they were placed."[118] The discipline of the classics, it seemed, was probably better than student freedom and initiative demanded by Science." Thus in 1800 Latin became a required subject for all University students, and, in 1804, Greek was put on the required list. The following year Davie moved to South Carolina. The University had returned to the classical fold.

In sum, the philosophy upon which the University was founded went back into the work of the English liberals of the seventeenth century, but was more particularly expressed in the eighteenth century radicalism of Voltaire and Rousseau. The application of the ideals of "Nature" and "Reason" to schoolroom practices in America seems to have been first accepted and promulgated by Benjamin Franklin with wide influence. The first appearance of the humanitarian ideal in North Carolina was in the Constitution of 1776, but no staunch supporter advanced its cause until 1789 when William R. Davie introduced a bill for chartering the University. In the plan of education first set up for the state institution, the eighteenth cen-

---

116. *Letters, University of North Carolina, 1796-1838*, p. 37.
117. *Faculty Record of the University of North Carolina, 1795-1815*, p. 61.
118. *Minutes of the Board of Trustees of the University of North Carolina, 1790-1796*, p. 236.

tury doctrine of humanitarianism was further expressed with the study of science and English taking foremost positions. But the excesses of the French Revolution, the superstitions of the time, the revival of an interest in theology, the apparent connection of Deism with the Jeffersonian party, the unpopularity of the French government during Adam's administration, disciplinary problems arising out of the new curriculum, and the influence of Caldwell, all led to a return to the classics in 1800 and 1804.

III

Administering the New Institution

1. Support

One of the most stubborn problems that faced those charged with the responsibility of administering the affairs of the University was that of finances. By the "Act for Raising a Fund for Erecting the Buildings and for the Support of the University of North Carolina," passed in December, 1789, the institution had been granted all the arrearages due the state prior to January 1, 1783. These arrearages were due the state from sixty-eight officials, sheriffs and other officers, and in some cases these were men of high character and included such men as Governor Burke and General Hogan. The monies due totaled approximately $11,410 and ranged in amounts from $2,660 against one person to $3 against another. They included fees from lawyer's license, bonds, notes, certificates, old dollar money, hire of Negroes, a public horse, and fifteen head of cattle.[1] Exceptions in the grant included the sales of confiscated lands, which the state hoped to collect, and all arrearages due by Robert Lanier, Treasurer of the district of Salisbury, and the sheriffs of that district. If these latter funds were not settled within two years, however, the University was to have the residue. In general, the arrearages granted the University were funds which the state never hoped to collect. Of those which were due the state

1. *Journal of the University of North Carolina* (Treasurer's Reports), 1789-1859, pp. 1-5.

from colonial days, no evidence seems to exist except a report of balances made out by a committee of the Assembly in 1783. During the years from 1776 to 1783 the revenue business of the state was under a treasurer of each district. Many of these treasurers had kept inadequate records; others had fled the state, taking their books with them, and still others had died. Yet, in face of these conditions, attorneys who had been appointed by the University succeeded in wresting an unexpected total of $7,362 out of the arrearages. This was invested in United States and State bank stock as a working fund for the University, the interest only being used. In 1809, an additional act was passed granting to the University all debts due the state up to December 31, 1799.[2] From this act, which involved derelict personal estates amounting to 74,976 pounds, 2 shillings and 11 pence, less than a third was realized.

Even more valuable to the University as a financial aid were the escheated lands, first granted in the act of 1789. Most of these lands came as a result of unclaimed land warrants granted to North Carolina soldiers as salaries during the Revolution, and were located in the wilds of Tennessee. Lands of those of foreign birth who died without relatives as North Carolina citizens also escheated to the University until 1831. In 1794, an additional act was passed by the state, granting to the University all escheated lands within its borders. The act provided, however, that all monies above $20,000 should be paid to the state, that only the interest should be used, and that after ten years the principal should become subject to the disposition of the state. The lands especially mentioned were those bought and sold by Henry Eustace McCulloch on a mortgage in Mecklenburg County, which had become confiscated to the state. This act and the escheated property act were repealed in 1800, as a result of a series of complaints against the University, but the escheated property act was restored in 1805.[3] In 1809, an

2. *Statutes Relative to the University of North Carolina*, p. 29.
3. This act was repealed by an act of the Legislature in 1850, but was later restored after the constitutionality of the act had been determined in the case of the University *vs* Maultsby in 1853.

additional grant was made of "all sums of money, or other estate of whatsoever kind, that may be in the hands of such executor" after a period of seven years.[4]

Although it appeared to the university trustees that these escheats were of doubtful value, these officials immediately laid plans for their collection. On July 20, 1791, the trustees made arrangements for the appointment of an attorney in each district of the state who should look after the interests of the University and should render an account of his collections at each meeting of the board.[5] Each member of the board of trustees was given a similar power. The plan followed is shown in an advertisement which appeared in the *State Gazette of North Carolina*, December 17, 1797:

> Will be sold, at public sale,
> As coming by escheat to the Trustees of the University of North Carolina
> On Saturday the 19*th* of December, next, On the premises.
> A tract of land in Chowan county, containing about sixty acres, late the property of James White, of the said county, deceased.
> This land lies near Deshon's Ferry, on Chowan River.
>
> David Stone, Attorney for
> Edenton District.

The treasurer's report of the University for December, 1793, showed that William Hill of the Wilmington District and Adalai Osborne of the Salisbury District had been paid commissions of $60 for the sale of escheated property.[6] On July 6, 1793, John Whitaker, Attorney of the Halifax District, sold a tract of land escheated to the University for the sum of $200 and William R. Davie purchased property in Chatham county, escheat-

---

4. In the case of the McCulloch grants the University lost the principal in 1804 when it was decided in the cases of Ray's Executors *vs* McCulloch and Trustees *vs* Rice that McCulloch's claims were made good by the Peace Treaty of 1783.
5. *Minutes of the Board of Trustees of the University of North Carolina, 1790-1796*, p. 26.
6. *Journal of the University of North Carolina* (Treasurer's Reports) 1789-1859, p. 6.

ed to the University in October, 1795, for the sum of $1600. In June, 1796, the value of the property escheated to the University from the districts of Morgan and Salisbury, Halifax, Newbern, Wilmington, and Edenton totaled about $6,500. From June, 1795 to July, 1798, Adalai Osborne reported sales amounting to $14,946, principally from the McCulloch lands. The escheated lands were thus proving a substantial aid to the University when the state passed the repealing act of 1800.

With the repeal of the repealing act in 1805, the trustees again proceeded with the collection of the escheats in a business-like way. The state was divided into ten districts (1809) and the attorneys were urged to be diligent in searching out any property that seemed to be available. Questions were decided on the basis of the laws of the state, but care was taken not to involve the University in useless controversies. On December 5, 1816, the trustees concluded in the case of Margaret McRay that they would not in any way oppose the "Court of the Supreme jurisdiction in the state," but that they did not deem it to be their duty to relinquish voluntarily so extensive a claim.[7] Consideration was shown when necessary. John R. Donnell, a graduate of the University in 1807, but born in Ireland, fell heir to a plantation previously owned by his uncle in Lenoir county. As the law stood, he could not inherit the land, but in 1810 the University relinquished its claims on this property, first, however, securing the approval of the General Assembly. Liberality was also shown in the case of Mrs. Jasper Cummings, a widow of Iredell county, who was allowed to retain the lands of her late husband during her life, free of rent. As a result of the efforts of the trustees more than $47,000 were realized from the sale of escheats in the state during the years from 1810 to 1820. A general decrease in these funds came after 1831, due in part to the granting to widows by law "the surplus of the personal estate of their deceased husbands."[8]

7. *Minutes of the Board of Trustees of the University of North Carolina, 1811-1822*, p. 127.
8. *Laws of North Carolina*, 1831, p. 16.

During the years from 1840 to 1850 less than $20,000 were realized.[9] The decrease in proceeds was accompanied by the difficulty in enforcing the escheats acts, which had increased to such an extent that a committee was appointed to investigate the question as to whether it was advisable to return to the state its franchise or not. The committee reported back that the terms "escheat" and "confiscated property" did embrace all real estate "which public policy had directed should be returned to the sovereign," that the franchise be held, and that a more adequate system of collecting the monies be provided.[10] In 1851, and as a result of this report, a redistribution of the districts was made and a principal escheator was appointed for the state as a whole with the various local escheators working under him. Special attention was now to be given to wills and inventories and ten per cent was to be allowed for each attorney's services.[11] Proceeds, however, did not materially increase and the difficulties of collection persisted. In 1852, the sale of an escheat on a school house for one dollar created some local excitement and opposition was voiced on the grounds that some poor boy was being cheated out of his right to become a prominent member of society. In 1861, a group of claims against the property of more than 330 Cherokee Indians failed to prove of any value to the University.

The escheated western lands of Tennessee proved almost as difficult to handle as the state escheats. Lands comprising more than 150,000 acres were involved in the transaction which included, in addition to the escheated state lands, the gifts of Governor Benjamin Smith and Major Charles Gerrard.[12] In

---

9. *Journal of the University of North Carolina* (Treasurer's Reports) 1789-1859.

10. Moore, B. F., *Report on Escheats to the Trustees of the University of North Carolina*, p. 7.

11. *Minutes of the Executive Committee of the University of North Carolina, 1835-1873*, pp. 160-161.

12. Major Charles Gerrard was a Revolutionary officer and had received as his share from the state a grant of 2,560 acres of Tennessee land. In 1798, he donated this land to the University along with 11,354 additional acres which he had purchased.

1789, North Carolina had ceded all of its territory in Tennessee to the United States, with the reservation, however, that the lands already granted by the General Assembly should go to the benefit of the owners, heirs, and assigns, respectively.[13] Following the admission of Tennessee as a state in 1796, a controversy arose over the question of these reserved lands. The State of Tennessee contended that the North Carolina rights expired in 1792, for the General Assembly of North Carolina had limited the time of procuring the grants to that date. The General Assembly of North Carolina, maintaining that it had a right to make extensions if it so desired, disregarded this claim and continued to make grants from time to time until 1824 when the books were ordered closed and the balance of the unclaimed lands were made out to the University. In 1819, a board was created, composed of the governor, comptroller, and treasurer, for the discussion and settlement of problems arising over the western lands,[14] and it was before this board that the University made its appeal.

Difficulties between the University and the State of Tennessee had appeared quite early. In 1798, the legislature of Tennessee levied a tax on all lands claimed by the University, but the trustees refused to pay the tax and, in a letter to the Tennessee legislative body, stated that all the University's lands were exempt from taxation. In a reply received from that body on December 15, 1801, it was stated that they had "not yet arrived to that period to enable them to patronize learning in their own state, and therefore," could not consistently exempt from taxation the lands in that state belonging to the University of North Carolina.[15] The university trustees still refused to pay the tax in spite of the threats of seizure by the State of Tennessee. In 1806, an act passed by the National Congress ceding to Tennessee sixteen or seventeen million acres, subject to North Carolina claims and certain Indian titles, somewhat

13. *State Records,* Vol. XXV, p. 4.
14. *Laws of North Carolina,* 1819, p. 12.
15. *Minutes of the Board of Trustees of the University of North Carolina, 1801-1810,* p. 8.

relieved the tension. But in 1811, following an attempt on the part of North Carolina to survey these lands, the Tennessee legislature passed an act prohibiting any outside surveying and threatened to disbar and fine any lawyer who would bring suit on such a claim. An appeal was then made by North Carolina to the National Congress which, in an act passed on March 26, 1818, authorized the state of Tennessee "to issue grants and perfect titles" on all lands described in the act of 1806.[16] As a result of this act, Tennessee was forced to open a land office in 1819, and the University was soon able to keep some of the benefits of its western lands. One other difficulty over Governor Smith's grant was removed in 1818 by a treaty between the United States and the Chickasaw Indians, by which the Chickasaws ceded all their lands east of the Mississippi River.

The most serious difficulties were now removed and the trustees proceeded to make secure their land grants in Tennessee. Judge Archibald D. Murphey journeyed to Nashville to study the problem first-hand and in this mission seems to have rendered his best services to the cause of higher education in North Carolina. By private conferences and discussions with the attorneys who had been appointed to look after the University's interests, and by speaking before the Legislature of Tennessee on two occasions, Murphey was able to secure the appointment of a commission to settle the differences between the University and the State of Tennessee. On August 26, 1822, an agreement was reached under which all the lands owned and acquired by the University in Tennessee were declared exempt from taxation until January 1, 1850. In return for this privilege, the University agents agreed to transfer to East Tennessee College, now the University of Tennessee, 20,000 acres of land, and to Cumberland College, now the University of Nashville, 40,000 acres. The University agents also guaranteed three-fourths of these lands at $1.50 per acre against the lawful

---

16. *Annals of the Congress of the United States, 1817-1818,* 1st Session, Vol. I, p. 293.

claim of any other person up to January 1, 1831. The agreement was duly ratified by the university trustees and the Legislature of Tennessee.[17]

But many difficulties still remained in the way of an efficient disposal of these lands. Frauds perpetrated by James Glasgow, Secretary of the State of North Carolina, and John and Martin Armstrong, registrars of the land office in Tennessee, had aroused hostility and the suspicion of false entries against the University's claims. The continual grant of the old soldiers' warrants by the North Carolina Legislature made them appear inexhaustible to the people of Tennessee and raised such a clamor that North Carolina closed its books on the question in 1824. An attempt by Murphey to secure a recognition of additional military warrants was opposed by Tennessee in 1823, but two years later an act was passed under which the University received $15,000 in cash for some of its land claims. The magnitude of the University's claims was enough to arouse ill feeling Probably the most annoying of these difficulties was the public speculator who was continually working up prejudice over the military warrants. Claimants as heirs of the old soldiers appeared on all sides, ready to grab whatever the law would give them. Hugh Moore, a preacher who had prepared to bring numerous suits against the University, was found to have been committing frauds on the United States Treasury for some time.[18] So many spurious witnesses appeared in fraudulent cases that the University was forced to hire special agents and attorneys to fight for its interests which, as the opposition increased, the trustees found it necessary to defend vigorously. In a report written by George E. Badger, a former superior court judge, and published in 1826, it was stated that most of the adversaries in the University's claims were not the brave men who fought for their country, nor their children, but

17. *Minutes of the Board of Trustees of the University of North Carolina, 1811-1822*, pp. 248-259.
18. Battle, K. P., *History of the University of North Carolina*, Vol I, p. 393.

greedy, cunning speculators.[19] Due to the efficiency with which the university agents handled the situation, however, the opposition gradually died, and by 1830, the University was able to proceed in patience and peace with the final sale of its lands.

A report of November 24, 1830, shows that the sale of the western lands had, up to that date, totaled $71,081.28, and that the value of the unsold lands totaled $240,642.00, of which not more than half was expected to be realized.[20] A report of December, 1832, showed that $52,436.71 of the $131,415.10 due the University on lands sold had been collected and that there were still 112,602 acres unsold. By this time, it had been decided that all the western lands should be sold in spite of the expressed wish in Major Charles Gerrard's will that his gift be retained by the University. The need of funds by the University and the revival of speculation in western lands had probably made this course seem advisable. On January 2, 1835, the management of all the affairs of the University was placed in the hands of an executive committee of seven members, the Governor being a member ex-officio and the others being elected annually. At a meeting of this committee, on March 5, 1835, Charles Manly was appointed to go to Tennessee and make a final settlement of the University's lands with Samuel Dickens, agent for the University in Tennessee. In a report returned to the executive committee on November 21, 1835, Manly stated that Dickens had sold 59,319 acres for $160,147.95, of which $94,339.98 had been collected. He had himself collected $1,500, a good work horse and two mules.[21] The report also included the sale of the remainder of the lands, totaling 62,345 acres, to

---

19. Badger, G. E., A View of the Question in Controversy Between the University of North Carolina and the Claimants of Her Western Lands, p. 9.
20. Minutes of the Board of Trustees of the University of North Carolina, 1823-1840, p. 187.
21. Minutes of the Executive Committee of the University of North Carolina, 1835-1873, p. 25.

Orme and Gifford of Boston for $56,345.83, the money payable by drafts on New York and Philadelphia banks.[22] The total amount of money collected by the University from its western lands finally amounted to $195,294.82 1/2.[23]

The other sources of funds for financing the *ante-bellum* University were private gifts, the lottery grant of 1801, and the tuition fees from the students.[24] Following the chartering of the University, a call was sent out soliciting gifts to the University and payable to agents appointed for each judicial district. The appeal sent out by William R. Davie and Willie Jones for the Halifax District illustrates the kind of appeal that was made.

> The gentlemen of the county of Orange have already subscribed near one thousand pounds towards the endowment of this important institution; and we flatter ourselves that the Gentlemen of Halifax county will not, on this occasion, so interesting to the rising generation, suffer any county in the state to exceed it in making efforts to promote an institution of such vast and general utility.
>
> We have opened a subscription for donations to the University, and either of us, on behalf of the institution, will thankfully receive subscriptions, however small, at any time.

The form of the subscription blank was as follows:

> Each subscriber promises for himself, his heirs, executors and administrators, to pay to the President and Trustees of the University of North Carolina, the sum annexed to his name, for the use and benefit of the said University,

22. Due credit was given by Manly in his report to "Murphey's Book," a work done by Murphey in 1823 which set forth and described each tract of land owned by the Trustees.

23. As a result of these sales, the University was able to purchase 1000 shares ($100,000) of North Carolina Bank stock. In 1859, another 1000 shares of bank stock were purchased but only the initial payment of $10,000 was made. As a result of the war, this stock was made worthless and the University found itself $90,000 in debt.

24. This is an exception to the state loan of $10,000 made in 1792 and which was later turned into a gift. The land grants around Chapel Hill were mentioned in Chapter II.

81

at the periods expressed by each individual at the time of the signing. In witness whereof the several Subscribers have hereto set their hands and seals.[25]

The contributions received, although never large, were surprising. During the year 1793 and 1794, those made by the several districts totaled $6,723.30 — Hillsborough ($1,614.80), Halifax ($1,608.00), Wilmington ($2,222.00), Newbern ($950.-00), Fayetteville ($170.00), and Salisbury ($158.50). The contributors numbered more than 200 and the gifts ranged from five dollars to $200.00. Especially to be noted were the gifts of Dr. McCorkle's congregation ($42.00), that of the Central Benevolent Society of Iredell County ($100.00) and William Bingham ($20.00).[26] Other subscriptions were received under the charter which granted each donor a four years' free scholarship to the University, but this privilege was cancelled in 1796. The largest gift to the University during this period ($1,025) was made by General Thomas Person in 1796 for the completion of the old chapel, which had been begun in 1795. In recognition of his gift, this building became known as Person Hall, the first building on the University campus to be named for an individual.[27] From 1803 to 1806 subscriptions amounting to $808.37 were collected from sixteen counties, the gifts ranging from $100 by Samuel Johnston of Chowan to twenty-five cents by Archibald McAlop of Jones county. Thomas D. Bennehan made a delivery of fifty bushels of oyster shells as his gift. These latter gifts came as a result of a special appeal sent out for subscriptions to the completion of the main building (South) which had been begun in 1798, but which had been only partly finished because of lack of funds.[28] Other funds collected made a total of $1,664.00. Subscriptions were again called for from 1809 to 1811 for the completion of South Building, and this time, largely due to the efforts of Caldwell, the necessary

---

25. *The North Carolina Journal*, January 9, 1793, p. 3.
26. *Journal of the University of North Carolina, 1795-1859, pp.* 8-19.
27. Battle, K. P., *op. cit.*, pp. 121-122.
28. *Minutes of the Board of Trustees of the University of North Carolina, 1801-1810*, pp. 35-38.

funds, which amounted to $10,535, were subscribed for and collected.[29] The largest contributions came from Wilmington, Hillsboro, Raleigh, and Newbern. A subscription of $100 was received from Andrew Flinn, of Charleston, South Carolina.

The first attempts, however, to secure funds for the completion of South Building had been by lottery. Following the repeal of the escheats act in 1800, the Legislature passed an act granting the right to the university trustees "to raise annually, by one or more lotteries, a sum of money not exceeding two thousand pounds. . . ."[30] The Trustees hoped to use this fund, not only for the purpose of completing the South Building but also to aid in "defraying the annual expenditures of the institution."[31] During the years 1801 and 1802, two lotteries were provided in accordance with the state law. The first called for a sale of 1,500 tickets at $5.00 each, and included 1864 blanks and 964 prizes, the prizes ranging from $10 to $1,000. State officials who had charge of the drawing asserted that it was to the interest of the University and the cause of science and learning in the state and urged an immediate sale. In order to inspire further confidence, it was arranged that the proceeds of the sale should be handled by the governor of the state. The result of the sale of the two lotteries showed that the University had secured a net profit of $5,081.81 out of its sales.

Another source of revenue for the *ante-bellum* University was the tuition fees and room rent. Prior to 1804, the records for these fees were kept by the faculty. As these records have been lost, nothing definite as to the sums collected for this period is known. Probably the collections never amounted to more than $600 a year. In 1804, Professor William Bingham showed, in his report to the trustees, a collection of $247 for the first term and $359 for the second, a total of $606 for the year. Tuition

---

29. *Reports from the Faculty to the Trustees of the University of North Carolina, 1809-1829*, pp. 1-8.
30. *Statutes Relative to the University of North Carolina*, p. 17.
31. *Minutes of the Board of Trustees of the Universiy of North Carolina, 1801-1810*, p. 10.

fees at this time were $5.00 per student each session and room rent was $1.00. In 1815, the collections for an average of eighty students amounted to $1,795.50, the tuition fee being $10, double that of 1804, the room rent remaining at $1.00. The increase in students during this period was only one-fourth but the increase in expense doubled, and the increase in collections trebled. For the year 1830 no such progressive tendency was evident. During that year, the sum of $2,400 was collected for room rent and tuition fees. The report of 1845, however, showed increased prosperity with collections aggregating $7,146 for the year. Tuition fees had been raised to $50 per session, and room rent to $2.00. The increase in enrollment to 156 students was also double that of 1830. Collections over the period of fifteen years had trebled and the increase in the individual tuition fee was five-fold. The year 1859 showed a similar increase — $22,070 was collected. At this time, the tuition fee was $60 per session and the room rent was $10. From 1804 to 1859, the tuition fee increased from $5.00 per session to $60, and the room rent from $1 to $10. The boy of less wealth, however, was not eliminated by this increase in fees, as the University admitted after 1836 as many of such students as desired to enter free of tuition fee and room rent. In 1857, twenty-two students made use of this free grant.[32]

It appears that the funds collected by the University during the *ante-bellum* period must have been in excess of $800,000 A report made by Governor Edward B. Dudley before the state Legislature in 1840 showed the following collections up to that time:

---

32. *Bursar's Ledger, University of North Carolina*, 1857-1880, p. 11. Board for students showed an increase from $36 in 1804 (per year) to $140 in 1859.

Sales of Tennessee lands $195,294.82 1/2
Sales of lands in North Carolina ... 13,520.00
Profits on two lotteries 5,080.89
Donation from the State 10,000.00
Subscriptions 7,684.40
Caldwell Subscriptions 10,535.00
Tuition fees since July, 1804 .... 111,581.91
Dividends on bank stocks 33,028.50
All other sources, escheats in
   North Carolina, etc. 134,066.99
          Total ....$520,782.42 1/2[33]

In 1860, the funds of the University consisted of
  2000 shares in Bank of North
      Carolina — par value $200,000.00
  7 North Carolina State Bonds 9,000.00
  1 Virginia State Bond 10,000.00
  55 Wilmington Coupon Bonds 5,500.00
  Bonds of sundry individuals 27,556.00
  Cash on hand 1,772.30
    Carolina — par value ....$253,828.30[34]

Expenditures for the most part during the *ante-bellum* period
were for buildings and teachers' salaries. For buildings, including repairs on professors' houses, the sum of approximately $166,857.57 was spent. The five main buildings erected were
Old East, in 1796; Person Hall, in 1799 (these buildings, Steward's Hall and the President's Home — $12,180.00); South
Building, in 1814 (begun in 1799 and erected at a cost of $16,-
889.00); Old West, 1823; third story to Old East, in 1824; Gerrard Hall, in 1827 (expenditures for these projects — $48,605.-
42); Smith Hall, in 1852 (expenditures approximately $10,303.-
63); New West and New East, in 1857-1861 ($54,798.62, in-
cluding also the erection of a belfry on South Building and re-

33. *Legislative Documents, Senate, 1840-1841,* Doc. No. 24, p. 6.
34. *Minutes of the Board of Trustees of the University of North
Carolina, 1841-1868,* p. 279.

pairs on professors' houses). Other expenditures, amounting to $24,080.90, were for repairs and for enlarging Old East and Old West (1845). From 1836 to 1863, the sum of approximately $12,000 was expended on beautifying the campus and $10,000 for library and scientific equipment (This includes $1,400 for a cabinet of minerals and $4,500 for Mitchell's library and apparatus.)

The expenditures for salaries of officers and faculty varied and, throughout the whole period, were made in part to depend upon the tuition fees. Tutors in the preparatory school in 1798 received $200 a year plus board at Commons. Regular tutors in the University received $300 at this time. On June 19, 1804, Reverend David Caldwell was elected to the presidency of the University at a salary of $1,000. A professor's salary at this time was $800. In 1818, the salaries provided were as follows:

President ....$	1,440.00
Professor of Rhetoric and Logic	1,240.00
Professor of Chemistry and Mineralogy ...	1,240.00
Professor of Math. & Natural Philosophy ..	1,240.00
Professor of Languages	1,240.00
Two tutors at $400 each	800.00
	$7,200.00[35]

However, this is not the correct scale. By a previous order of the board of trustees, the dividends from the bank stock and one half of the tuition fees were to be paid to the officers of the University and the remainder of the tuition fees to increasing the salaries of the faculty. Fire wood was also furnished free to the faculty. In an ordinance adopted by the board of trustees on June 27, 1827, it was provided that a superintendent of property and financial concerns should be hired at a salary of $500 annually. In 1837, with the appointment of Professor Mitchell as bursar for the University, it was provided that his salary, which was supplemented by a commission from the

35. *Minutes of the Board of Trustees of the University of North Carolina, 1811-1822*, p. 184.

tuition receipts, should never equal or exceed that of the president. The establishment of the professorships of Greek, Latin, and French in 1838 was made to depend on the tuition fees, which the trustees said must equal $7,000.00.[36] At this time, a professorship of rhetoric and belles lettres was established at a salary of $1,000, and $100 was set aside as the annual salary of the librarian. In 1842, Thomas Marshall was hired by the trustees as instructor in French at a salary of $500 annually, but he taught only a few months and resigned. By a resolution of November 5, 1855, it was determined by the trustees that the salaries of the faculty should be as follows, provided that the tuition fees should exceed $12,0000.00 (which they did):

President	$2,200.00
Professor of Chemistry	1,250.00
Professors of Mathematics, Natural philosophy, Greek, Latin & Literature (each)	1,650.00
Professor of History	1,550.00
Professor of Rhetoric & Logic	1,350.00
Professor of Civil Engineering	1,400.00
Professor of Agriculture	1,400.00
Adjunct Professor of Latin & Greek	1,200.00
Tutor	800.00
Tutor	700.00[37]

Average salaries for the year 1859 were $2,500 for the president and $1,700 for each professor. The faculty pay roll increased from appropximately $1,000 in 1795 to $14,000 in 1859 with an average of $7,000 for each year during the period. An increase in the president's salary from $1,000 to $2,200 was made, as well as an average increase of $800 on professors' salaries, or double the original amount. The total expenditures for salaries for the period were probably about $450,000.

36. *Minutes of the Executive Committee of the University of North Carolina, 1835-1873*, p. 70.
37. *Ibid.*, pp. 183-184.

2. *Internal Control*

In the act for the establishment of the University, passed by the state Legislature in 1789, it was provided that the trustees should

have the power to make all such laws and regulations for the government of the University and preservation of order and good morals therein, as are usually made in such seminaries, and as to them may appear necessary; provided the same are not contrary to the unalienable liberty of a citizen, or to the laws of the state.[38]

In keeping with this order Samuel E. McCorkle, as a member of the board of trustees, drew up the first by-laws and regulations for the University which, after being referred to a committee, were amended and adopted by the board on February 6, 1795.[39] These regulations, added to from time to time, were the basis for the control of the affairs of the University before 1860. For the sake of convenience, they will be discussed under the heads of faculty regulations, collegiate duties and restriction, deportment of students, punishments, and miscellaneous matters.

According to the by-laws, as drawn up in 1795, it was the president's duty to superintend all the studies of the college, and particularly those of the senior class. It was also his duty, or that of some other member of the faculty, to conduct morning and evening prayers and to examine the students each Sunday evening on "questions previously given them, on the general principles of morality and religion."[40] Morning prayers, by the laws of 1822, were to follow after the reading of a chapter in the Old or New Testament, by the professors and tutors in their turn. Until a professor or some other officer was appointed in his place, the president was to deliver a lecture once during the week on the principles of agriculture, botany, zoology,

---

38. *State Records,* Vol. XXV, p. 24.
39. *Minutes of the Board of Trustees of the University of North Carolina, 1790-1796,* pp. 162-171.
40. *Ibid.,* p. 163.

mineralogy, architecture, and commerce. Only temporary regulations were to be made by the faculty and those were to be during the recess of the board. No president or other officer of the University could be removed from his place without a hearing before the authority from whom he received his appointment. A very peculiar provision inserted in the laws after 1799, requiring that no member of the faculty could be a sitting member of either society, came as a result of controversies arising between the faculty and students over the attendence of faculty members at the meetings of those organizations.

Requirements on the tutors were extremely heavy. In addition to their teaching duties, they were required to reside in the dormitories of the University for the purpose of maintaining order among the students, to ask the blessing at the dining table, to pay particular attention to the manners and habits of the students, and to report twice each session on the condition of the locks, doors, windows, and cupboards of each student's room. Professors and tutors were in succession required to examine the rooms of the students at least once a week to see that order and neatness were preserved. Professors were also to visit the rooms of the students at night "as often as convenient," and to spend as much of their time as possible in college.

Most of the duties assigned to faculty members, however, were similar to those of the present day. Aside from their regular teaching work, teachers were required to hold monthly meetings on the call of the president and, with a majority of the members present, they could transact business. Records of the meetings were ordered to be kept and placed before the trustees at each meeting and no act which was not recorded was considered valid. No vote or opinion of any member of the faculty was to be revealed to the students except by the unanimous vote of the faculty. It was the president's duty to report to the board of trustees, annually, or oftener if called upon, on the state of the affairs of the University, and to make those recommendations considered necessary. By the by-laws of 1859, the president was considered as a trustee and as the mediator between the faculty and the board of trustees. Faculty members were ordered to see that the by-laws of the University were enforced and to report any infractions thereof to the president or body assembled for the purpose of punishing the guilty ones. They were to be punctual in the discharge of their duties, always on time at their class meetings, and never to dismiss a class until the bell rang for the expiration of the period. The power of awarding degrees was vested in the faculty; however, no student was to receive the A.B. degree who had not been enrolled at least one year. The rank of a professor was determined by the date of his appointment.

The restrictions and duties of the student were probably even more carefully specified. After being examined and admitted into the University, a student was required to turn over all his money to the bursar who used it in disbursing the student's expenses, returning to the student from time to time whatever was considered necessary. A copy of the laws of the institution was also required to be purchased by each student and this document, bearing the president's signature, was considered sufficient testimony that he was a student of the University. Every student was required to bind himself by promise in the presence of his fellow members, that he would obey the laws of the University. The order of procedure was: "Question — Have you read and understood the laws? Answer — I have. Question — Do you solemnly pledge your truth and honor to obey them? Answer — I do."[41] After these questions and answers, the student signed a form which was kept by the faculty. A student was expected to be punctual at recitations and at prayers; if late at any time, he could be called to account before his classmates for the offense. If good reason were not shown for his lateness, he could be called before the faculty. A student was neither to receive visitors in his room nor visit others in the time of study without permission from a member of the faculty.[42] When the bell rang a student was supposed to move whether the signal was for prayers, class, dinner, or bed. A student was not to make any noise, such as whistling, dancing, or anything of a

41. *Laws of the University of North Carolina*, 1822, p. 7.
42. *Laws of the University of North Carolina*, 1859, p. 27.

boisterous nature, in his room or in the passages. No student was to go beyond the sound of the bell without permission of the president. There was to be no congregating of students during study hours, and any student seen on the campus after the ringing of the bell at night (8 o'clock) was to be held to account therefor, and if found there in time of a disturbance, was to be looked upon as a participator. Absence from an examination subjected a student to an examination in the presence of the faculty before he could rejoin his class, and absence from any other duty subjected the student to punishment according to the degree of the offense. Any student found deficient at final examinations was publicly mentioned as a bad scholar by the faculty or trustees. A student was not to hang around any recitation room door, or be in the recitation room until the bell gave him permission. The laws of 1798 provided that each class should have a monitor appointed by the teacher who was to note down those absent without leave and those engaged in riotous or disorderly conduct, such as profane swearing, gross or vulgar language, eating, and lounging upon the benches. A by-law, passed in 1798 and retained in the catalogue throughout the whole period, provided that no student should absent himself from the University without first obtaining permission from the president or the presiding professor;[43] however, permission for absence from a recitation could be granted by the student's professor or tutor. In public speaking, which was required of each student as a part of the curriculum, nothing indecent, profane, immoral, or of a political nature was to be alluded to under penalty of severe censure to the guilty one. Plainness in dress was recommended and neatness and cleanliness were required. The officers of the University were ordered to admonish any negligent student and see that he preserved a decent ap-

---

43. In the University catalogue of 1928-1929 a similar regulation reads: "No student is allowed to absent himself from the University without written permission from the Registrar or his representative. This permission may, at the discretion of the executive officer, be granted only upon the formal request of the parent or guardian." — *The University of North Carolina Catalogue*, 1938-1929, p. 74.

pearance. They were also to see that no student wore his hat while in the college buildings, and that he cleaned the bed bugs out of his room once every two weeks. A student was neither to bring in the college filth of any kind, nor to "throw on the outside of the college, against the walls, or within twenty yards thereof, any sort of dirt or filth under the penalty, besides removing the same, of such censure as the offense may deserve."[44]

Full and complete religious freedom was denied to the student. The by-law in part stated: "If any student shall deny the being of a God, or the divine authority of the Holy Scriptures, or shall assert, and endeavor to propagate among the students, any principle subverting the foundation of the Christian Religion, and shall persist therein after admonition, he shall be dismissed."[45] In addition to being required to attend prayers twice daily and two Sunday services, the student was required to attend any other religious exercises designated by the faculty. While attending these meetings, he was to maintain a solemn and reverent countenance; he was not to laugh, whisper, talk, or behave in any indecent manner. On Sundays, the student was to refrain from ordinary exercises and diversions. He was not to fish, swim, or "walk abroad," but was to observe a quiet and orderly behavior. A student was not to use ardent spirits, or to go to a tavern, beer house, or any such place without the permission of the faculty. He was not to keep company with persons of bad character under penalty of severe punishment. Betting and attendance at horse races and cock fights were strongly forbidden. A student was not to engage in any kind of a game of hazard such as raffling, playing at cards, or shooting dice, or to make a bet of any kind. All swearing, profane, and indecent language was to be utterly excluded from the University. A student was neither to possess nor expose to another any book or picture which was impious or obscene. He was not to make any indecent gesture or to use any indecent language to

44. *Laws of the University of North Carolina*, 1799, p. 14.
45. *Laws of the University of North Carolina*, 1813, p. 10.

This regulation does not appear in the University laws before 1800 and probably not before 1805.

any other person. He was not to lie or strike any one in a fit of anger. A student was to be careful in his deportment to the people of the village, refraining from any kind of insulting language or treatment, and from trespassing on private property. He was not to own any kind of fire arms, gun powder, sword cane, sword, dirk, or weapon of any kind, and the purchase of merchandise of any kind from a local merchant was forbidden. Participation in a duel in any way, either by sending a challenge, carrying a message, acting as a second, or accepting a challenge, subjected the student to expulsion.

There were other regulations of a miscellaneous nature. Students living in the college during vacation had to pledge themselves not to damage their rooms or the buildings on the campus without making reparation. The faculty and students were ordered to wear neat, black gowns at public worship on Sunday and on all public occasions. According to the by-laws of 1825, a uniform dress, the coats of dark gray mixture, chiefly cotton, with white pantaloons and waist coat for summer, and a dark blue suit for winter, was prescribed. In the conduct of the University dining hall, students were to go peaceably to the door and there arrange themselves in classes, each class giving precedence to the one above it. If necessary, they were to wait in this manner at least five minutes for the arrival of a professor or tutor. Students coming into the hall after the asking of the blessing were not to take their seats without special permission from the presiding officer, and no students were to leave the hall without permission. In case students were not satisfied with the food on their plates they could send them to one of the professors or tutors present for an examination. If the food was found satisfactory, the students were to be reprimanded and required to eat without further complaint. When the presiding professor arose for the dismissal, all students were to stop eating, rise, and after the return of thanks, march out of the hall in a quiet, orderly manner. A few brief by-laws were passed for the regulation of the library. The library was to be kept open one hour each week for the purpose of securing books. No student was to take a book from the shelves on the penalty of being fined ten cents, and no book was to be kept for more than two weeks. The librarian was ordered to keep a catalogue of the library books, to make a record of every book loaned out, and to levy a fee (from fifty cents to two dollars a session) on each student for the use of the library. Students who lost or defaced a book were required to pay a price set by the faculty for such loss or destruction.[46]

Methods of trials and punishments were graduated according to the seriousness of the offense. The by-laws of February 6, 1795, required that "the students charged shall have timely notice and Testimony taken on the most solemn assurance shall by the Faculty or Trustees be deemed valid without calling on a magistrate to administer an oath in legal form."[47] During the first decade of the University an attempt was made to try students for offenses in the same procedure followed by a court of law. The system created so much controversy between the faculty and students that after 1805 punishments were inflicted, in most cases, by a majority vote of the faculty. Students, however, could testify for themselves and other witnesses were often called. The mildest form of punishment was private admonition by a member of the faculty and was inflicted for such a petty offense as reclining at prayers. If the offense was of a more serious nature the student could be admonished by the president before the faculty, or by the president before the student body. For still more serious offenses, such as being intoxicated, or stealing, the penalty was suspension for six months and perhaps admonition before the trustees. Expulsion was permitted with the approbation of five members of the board of trustees, and corporeal punishment was inflicted in the preparatory school with the consent of the president. In case of suspension or expulsion, the president was authorized to notify the parent or guardian of the guilty student and explain the action of the faculty. A student suspended or expelled from the

46. The curriculum outlined for the University is discussed in Chapters II and V.
47. *Minutes of the Board of Trustees of the University of North Carolina, 1790-1796*, pp. 169-170.

University was to leave the campus within forty-eight hours and not to reside within two miles of the University unless he were already living in the local neighborhood. If a student persisted in neglecting his college duties or continued to engage in petty offenses, it was the duty of the president to address a letter to his parent or guardian advising a withdrawal of the student from the institution. A student caught destroying property of another individual was ordered to pay for the damage, the price being determined by a committee of three selected by the student, the defendant, and the faculty.

In an effort to aid the trustees and faculty to administer the regulations of the University, the Legislature passed several laws. By an act of 1794, no person was allowed to set up or keep any billiard table "or any other table or device for playing at any game of hazard within five miles of the said University" on penalty of the sum of fifty pounds, one half to the informer and one half to the state.[48] In 1823, an act was passed forbidding horse races or cock fights within five miles of the University on penalty of a fine of one hundred dollars. Holding elections for congressmen and members of the General Assembly at Chapel Hill were also forbidden. In 1824, it was decreed:

Whereas the exhibition of strolling players in the vicinity of the University without any tendency to improve either the genius or the morals, are often calculated to lead youth into dangerous associations, while their parents and friends rely on the Faculty of the institution for their protection from the seduction of vice under the names of pleasure and amusement. . . .

"it shall not be lawful for any person or persons to exhibit any theatrical performance or dramatic recitations, at Chapel Hill, nor within five miles thereof without the special permission in writing of Three Members of the Faculty of the University."[49] Offenders were to be fined at the discretion of the court. In 1836, the theatrical act of 1824 was extended to sleights of hand or equestrian performances, rope or wire dancing, or natural or

---

48. *Statutes Relative to the University of North Carolina,* p. 12.
49. *Ibid.,* p. 40.

artificial curiosities. At this time, it was made unlawful for any merchant, shopkeeper, or other person at Chapel Hill, or within two miles thereof, to sell to any student "goods, wares, merchandise, spirituous liquors or wines" without the written consent of the faculty and any contract made for the sale of such articles was declared null and void. An act passed in 1842 made it a misdemeanor for any person to erect or conduct within two miles of Chapel Hill "any tippling house or houses."[50] In 1855, an act was passed appointing five commissioners, including two members of the University faculty, for the government of the town of Chapel Hill. They were to see that the proper taxes were levied and collected, that the laws of the state were enforced, and that all the white males of the village, faculty and students excepted, did patrol duty. The commissioners were given the power to adopt such ordinances as seemed necessary for the suppression of nuisances, the regulation of shop-keepers, and the exclusion of venders of spirituous liquors and other articles not licensed by the laws of the state.[51]

3. *The Faculty and Its Work*

The University of North Carolina from the time of its inception was a state institution and was so intended.[52] Although the charter in 1789 granted perpetual succession to the Board of Trustees, more than three-fourths of its members were either members of the State Legislature at that time or of the state constitutional convention of 1789. In 1804, the charter was so modified as to make the appointment of members subject to the will of the Legislature. The amendment stated that "it would tend to render the institution more conformable to the wishes

50. *Act of the General Assembly and Ordinances of the Trustees of the University of North Carolina*, 1852, p. 5.
51. *The Acts of the General Assembly for the Better Regulation of Chapel Hill*, 1855, pp. 3-5.
52. Elmer E. Brown says in his article on "The Origin of the American State University" that "this institution . . . . did not come under direct state control till 1821". — See *University of California Publications in Education*, 1903, Vol. 3, No. 1, p. 35.

of the people, if the power of filling up such vacancy or vacancies and making such new appointment or appointments should be vested in the Legislature."[53] The governor of the state in these early years was recognized as the chairman of the trustees and by an act of 1805 was made chairman. Direct appropriations from the state to the University were small ($10,000). This paucity was deeply regretted by the founders, but the escheats grants, which appeared so small and useless in 1789, proved to be the means of sustaining the institution, totaling about half of the *ante-bellum* income. The fact that the State Legislature could make or break the University was shown in its withdrawal of the escheats grants in 1800, which act President Caldwell declared to be unconstitutional on the ground that it was a law taking away the property of a corporation.[54] The escheats were restored in 1804. On November 24, 1830, when the proceeds from the escheats had reached a low ebb, an appeal was made to the Legislature for a loan of $25,000 and this was granted, but only on the basis of a lien on all the University property and the right to modify the University charter as the Legislature saw fit. The loan was rejected with determination and anger. The realization of this attitude of the Legislature made the trustees so careful, however, in the administration of the affairs of the University, particularly in its first decade of existence, as to hamper the work of the faculty. The failure of the trustees to control the malicious tendencies of the student body made necessary the appointment of a president of the institution. Joseph Caldwell came into that position in 1804.

Joseph Caldwell was born two days after the death of his father at Lamington, New Jersey, April 21, 1773,[55] of Huguenot and Scotch-Irish parents. He soon came to exhibit some of the best traits of these two races. Through energy and effort, his

---

53. *Statutes Relative to the University of North Carolina*, p. 18.
54. *Reports from the Faculty to the Board of Trustees of the University of North Carolina 1809-1929*, p. 118.
55. *Autobiography and Biography of Rev. Joseph Caldwell, D.D., LL.D.*, p. 10.

mother, Mrs. Rachel Caldwell, was able, in spite of the Revolutionary times, to secure educational advantages for her son who was graduated from Princeton in 1791. Five years' teaching apprenticeship, first as a teacher of young children, then an assistant in a classical academy at Elizabethtown, New Jersey, and finally for one year a tutor at Princeton, laid the basis for his work in North Carolina. Upon his arrival at Chapel Hill, Caldwell was amazed at the little religious interest which he found in the state and said that the condition afforded no little temptation to undertake its cause. Especially was he struck by the leadership of General Davie who, in the Legislature, seemed "like a parent struggling for the happiness of his children."[56] From the first, he was not pleased with his situation, the lack of classical interest at the University, the infidel faculty, and the too idealistic, yet likeable Davie, worried him. And yet, in spite of frequent threats to resign as Professor of Mathematics, he was persuaded to remain at his job. Because of his ability, the changing conditions of the time, and the scarcity of good teachers, he became president of the University.

From 1804 to the day of his death, January 27, 1835, Caldwell labored for the University. He realized that the institution could hardly hope to prosper until a good working faculty was secured, and no doubt his dislike for his early faculty associates was still retained when Andrew Rhea, a Virginian, was elected as professor of ancient languages in 1806. Rhea, a good-natured widower and apparently a man of some ability,[57] proved indolent[58] and made no reputation for learning and scholarship. He resigned in 1814. A change of tutors once a year during this period was the rule, probably the most able being Abner W. Clopton, a Virginian, who served during the year 1809, Williamson Henderson, of Chapel Hill (1812), and Lewis Williams, later a member of Congress (1810-1812). A good reason for the frequent changes was expressed by Clopton who said, when

---

56. Battle, K. P., *op. cit.*, p. 113.
57. Hamilton, J. G. deR., "William R. Davie: A Memoir" in *James Sprunt Historical Studies*, Vol. VII, p. 39.
58. Hooper, William, *Fifty Years Since*, p. 12.

he sent in his resignation in 1809, that he found it utterly inconvenient to receive no more than $250 a year, but that he was willing to serve for $500 a year, and was richly worth it.[59] There were also the facts that the college tutor was forbidden to marry, that he was forced to live in the dormitories with the boys, that he was a jack of all teaching, and because of his youth usually found his disciplinary problems vexing. In the meantime, Caldwell had made his threats of resignation good and had resigned the presidency to Robert Hall Chapman on December 16, 1812.[60] Caldwell, however, who had agreed to remain at the University as professor of mathematics, was not to be relieved of his burdens so easily, for Chapman, who was strongly pro-English, early incurred the ill will of the students and resigned, November 23, 1813, disgusted with the teaching profession and ready to go back to the ministry.[61] The trustees, accepting his resignation, seemed more pleased than chagrined.

With the resignation of Chapman, Caldwell again took up the presidency on December 14, 1816, and this time served faithfully until his death. During the second half of the term ending June, 1817, the University was without a professor, and was run by the president and three tutors — William Hooper, William D. Moseley, and Robert Rufus King. Efforts, however, to secure able teachers proved more successful. Hooper, who had shown himself an able tutor since 1810, was made professor of ancient languages in 1817. Resigning in 1822, he returned to the University again in 1825 to serve as professor of rhetoric and logic until 1828 and from then until 1837 as professor of ancient languages. With the eyes of the trustees now turned toward Yale, on December 5, 1817, it was reported that Elisha Mitchell had been elected to the professorship of mathematics,

59. *Reports from the Faculty to the Board of Trustees of the University of North Carolina, 1809-1829*, p. 66. Clopton, however, accepted the principalship of the grammar school which was run by the University until 1819.
60. *Minutes of the Board of Trustees of the University of North Carolina, 1811-1822*, p. 48.
61. *Ibid.*, p. 122.

"a gentleman every way qualified ... to perform the duties of that appointment in a manner creditable to himself and beneficial to all."[62] At the same time, the trustees also elected W. Denison Olmsted as professor of chemistry, particularly for the benefit of "the agriculturalist of our county."[63] Both of these men were natives of Connecticut. Scholarly and of fine personality, they soon proved to be probably the most able men of the *ante-bellum* University faculty. The trustees, feeling that the financial situation of the University was to be much improved by the proceeds from the western lands, and largely through the influence of Caldwell, elected the Reverend Shepard K. Kollock, of New Jersey, as professor of rhetoric. He served until 1825 and then returned to the ministry. From 1821 to 1828, Ethan A. Andrews served as professor of ancient languages, an appointment also due to the influence of Caldwell. On December 13, 1825, following the resignation of Olmsted, who returned to the services of his alma mater, Mitchell, by his own request, was transferred to the professorship of chemistry, and here he served during the rest of Caldwell's presidency. As a successor to Mitchell for the professorship of mathematics, the trustees selected James Phillips, a staunch, able, and well educated old Englishman.[64] He, too, was to serve at the University until his death, April 14, 1867. On December 15, 1825, a professorship of modern languages was established and N. M. Hentz was elected to fill the position,[65] but upon his withdrawal in 1831 the professorship remained vacant until after Caldwell's death. The creation by the trustees December 19, 1833, of an adjunct professorship of natural philosophy and astronomy, as an aid to Caldwell who was failing in health, led to the election of Walker Anderson as a member of the faculty.[66] In 1836, after Caldwell's death, Anderson resigned and emigrated to Florida

62. *Ibid.*, p. 145.
63. *Ibid.*, p. 146.
64. *Minutes of the Board of Trustees of the University of North Carolina, 1823-1840*, p. 80.
65. *Ibid.*, p. 53.
66. *Ibid.*, p. 254.

100

where he became the first chief justice of that state. These men, added to by a number of tutors, made up the University faculty under Caldwell.

The laws and regulations passed by the Legislature and the board of trustees were accepted in good faith by the members of the faculty and it seems that their administration was attempted with a deep seriousness of purpose. The University was considered somewhat of a monastic institution in which young men should separate themselves from the other affairs and interests of the state in the preparation for manhood. Students were supposed to disassociate themselves from the habits and customs of the time in a sheltered preparation for a future life. The fact that the classical training offered them had little practical application to their later activities seems not to have worried the faculty. The prevailing educational theory was disciplinary. It was the common belief that a good foundation was the principal requirement in the proper education of the individual. It was the policy of Caldwell's faculty, therefore, to give every student close, scrutinizing care, watching and critically judging his every activity outside as well as inside the classroom. It is true that after the coming of Mitchell and Olmsted there was an attempt to connect the University more closely with the life of the state and that Mitchell, in the face of the threats of the trustees to make deductions from the salaries of the faculty for leaving the campus,[67] roamed the state in an attempt to learn something of its soil and its products. It is also true that President Caldwell came to apply himself to similar interests, in an effort to make the University useful to the people outside the campus as well as to the students inside it. But the general purpose of the University during the years of Caldwell's presidency seems to have been discipline of mind and body of the student through memorization of material in books and a close application of a strict code of laws and regulation.

To Caldwell and to every member of his faculty the situation

67. *Minutes of the Executive Committee of the University of North Carolina,* 1835-1873, p. 10.

proved difficult and trying. The financial condition of the University was not satisfactory and members of the faculty were continually worried about the uncertainty of receiving their pay checks. It was poverty that drove Caldwell out into the state for two years to beg charity for his institution and it was because of the uncertainty of salaries for the teachers that objection was raised by the faculty to the erection of any new buildings on the University campus in 1822. Books and materials for work were also scarce until Caldwell visited Europe in 1824 and not too plentiful afterwards. The years from 1825 to 1835 must have been trying to the faculty: Caldwell in his old age, the bank stocks unproductive, the University on the decline, with a student body of only eighty and the institutions to the North and South drawing students away.[68] Some members of the faculty believed that the location of the University hampered its growth and urged a removal; and in 1835, the board of trustees resolved: "That the University be removed to such place as the Trustees thereof may select. . . ."[69] Criticism and interference by members of the board of trustees had appeared early, and as early as 1805 Caldwell had tried to check it when he said: "Whenever the trustees of an institution invade the public eye, it is impossible that the business of it should not be impaired."[70] In 1809, the trustees had asked for the removal of a suspension of student William Long, and in spite of the charter the governing body had continued to confer degrees until 1811. Bitter criticism from various factions in the State also had to be met. The religious faction, although not strong in the early years, had been so strong as to make Charles Pettigrew write to Caldwell from Edenton in November, 1797, that he was afraid to send his son to the University because of "the danger of having all fear of the Almighty eradicated from his mind."[71] This

68. *Minutes of the Board of Trustees of the University of North Carolina, 1823-1840*, p. 195.

69. *Ibid.*, p. 290.

70. *Letters, University of North Carolina, 1796-1835* (manuscript), p. 47.

71. *Ibid.*, p. 20.

opinion seems to have been generally held in the northeastern section of the state.[72] Bartlett Yancey's mother at this same time objected to his entering the University because she had "never known a young man to enter that institution who was ever of any account afterwards."[73] Caldwell said that there were many people in the State who believed that the University was a "parcel of inveterate demons from among the damned."[74] By 1818, although there were four Presbyterians and only one Episcopalian, but with Baptist leanings, on the faculty, the University was generally accused of being under the control of the Presbyterians,[75] but Caldwell firmly denied the charges. In the earlier years, the University had been charged with Federalistic tendencies and there is some evidence to show that this criticism caused the escheats to be withdrawn in 1800.[76] The bitter attack of "X," published in the *Raleigh Register* for November 9, 1829, against schools and the University in particular, seems to have come from some members of the Legislature who were afraid of losing their positions in their counties to men of better education.[77] To the faculty, however, the political question was brought nearer home on election days in Chapel Hill, concerning which Caldwell wrote: "We tremble at such times for the dissipation, the excess, and the misunderstandings between the students and the people from the country."[78] There were those who bitterly criticized the University as an institution of the aristocracy. Others said it was monastic in its outlook, and should be removed to a place where boys could be taught man-

72. Hamilton, J. G. deR., *op. cit.*, p. 35.
73. Hamilton, J. G. deR., "The Political and Professional Career of Bartlett Yancey" in *James Sprunt Historical Studies*, Vol. X, No. 2, p. 9.
74. *Letters, University of North Carolina, 1796-1835,* (manuscript), p. 207.
75. *State Records,* Vol. V, p. 1184.
76. *Letters, University of North Carolina, 1796-1835,* (manuscript), p. 210.
77. *Ibid.,* p. 185.
78. *Reports from the Faculty of the Board of Trustees of the University of North Carolina, 1809-1829,* p. 245.

ners as well as books.[79] Still others criticized the curriculum and laughed at the puzzled alumnus who could not translate the language of his own diploma.

The most difficult of all faculty problems was the rebellion of the student against the laws and regulations which both the faculty and the student had sworn to observe. The refusal of the student to adapt himself to a monastic life and to accept the professors as standing *in loco parentis* was often not understood by those in authority in the campus. They considered the student "rather fond of low amusements; and forgetful of the laws of decency, too pertinacious in his own opinion, and unwilling to admit to the justice of a reproof,"[80] as the faculty minutes of the period reveal. Riots at the University in 1799 led to the adoption of a new set of laws for the institution, which were to be rigidly enforced. The wholesale destruction of property brought about the passage of an act, July 10, 1805, which inflicted a public punishment of not less than five nor more than ten stripes on any student under sixteen caught damaging any University property. Students over sixteen were to be suspended for such depredations. Two monitors were to be selected by lot from each class who were to take an oath to report all offenses on the penalty of indefinite suspension. Forty-five students retaliated by agreeing never to take the prescribed oath, and any student who violated his promise was to be rejected from all company where decency and respectability had any place. The refusal of the trustees to withdraw the act also led to the withdrawal of all the larger boys as soon as they could get horses. "The crisis is awful," said Judge Cameron at the time of the incident.[81] In 1809, President Caldwell sent in his resignation, saying, "I can on no terms consent to act longer, than till

79. *Proceedings and Debates of the Convention of North Carolina of 1835*, p. 43.
80. *Journal of the Faculty of the University of North Carolina, 1800-1809*, p. 59.
81. *Faculty Record of the University of North Carolina, 1795-1815*, pp. 129-137; *Minutes of the Board of Trustees of the University of North Carolina, 1801-1810*, pp. 77-78.

the expiration of six months from the present date."[82] The result of such controversies between the faculty and students was evident in 1811 when there were no graduates present for the commencement. President Robert H. Chapman, in making his report to the trustees in 1814, spoke of the faculty as having passed through troublous times, but that they were able "to stand at their posts and maintain the authority of the institution."[83] In fact, the riotous spirit of the students continued unabated throughout the whole *ante-bellum* period. Professor Phillips probably expressed the sentiments of Caldwell's faculty when he said in 1834 that he had completely failed, as the small number of successful students showed, and that the failure was in part due to students spending their time "wading through trashy productions or consuming it in enervating indolence."[84]

Measured on the basis of broad aim and purpose, little seems to have been accomplished by Caldwell's faculty, for the students apparently never fully accepted the aims and purpose of those in control. Looked at in another way, however, much was accomplished and many students profited considerably by their attendance at the University. The lowest attendance for any one year was in 1809 when thirty-six were enrolled and the high mark during the presidency of Caldwell was reached in 1823 when there were 173 students. The largest number of graduates was thirty-nine, in 1825. The total enrollment for the period was 2594, with 560 graduates. Probably the most prominent class was that of 1818 which had fourteen members, most of whom became more or less distinguished. Among these were James K. Polk, later governor of Tennessee and president of the United States; William W. Green, later chancellor of the University of the South; and Robert H. Morrison, who became the first president of Davidson College. The class also produced a reporter of the Supreme Court, a president of the State Senate,

---

82. *Letters, University of North Carolina, 1796-1835* (manuscript), p. 83.
83. *Reports from the Faculty to the Board of Trustees of the University of North Carolina, 1830-1839*, p. 222.
84. *Reports from the Faculty to the Board of Trustees of the University of North Carolina, 1830-1839*, p. 222.

a consul-general to Italy and a governor of Florida.[85] Out of the class developed prominent preachers, lawyers, and business men. The University could also boast of being the alma mater of Archibald D. Murphey and of John Motley Morehead, probably North Carolina's greatest *ante-bellum* builders. By an act of December 27, 1821, four charity students were admitted to the University free of tuition, room rent, and servant's charges, and the records thereafter show that adequate use was made of the provision.[86] The societies also educated two young men free of charge.

The work of the faculty and its contributions to the state are also significant. President Caldwell, in addition to being the author of a widely used textbook on geometry and a member of the commission which laid the boundary line between North Carolina and South Carolina in 1808, was a leader in the movement for internal improvements and public education and for trained teachers. Through his influence, it seems, *The Harbinger*, a literary paper of high merit, was begun at the University in 1824. The value of Caldwell to the state and the University is attested by the repeated statements found in the minutes of the board of trustees in praise of his work. Next to Caldwell, Mitchell probably stood out highest in his value and contributions to the state, in his influence on the young men with whom he came in contact, as well as in his scientific pursuits. Other members of the faculty, including Hooper, Olmsted and Hentz, were active in the writing of books. If the University was monastic during the period from 1804 to 1835, it was nevertheless the best exponent of light and learning, and the only institution of higher education in the state. That the University at least attempted to be progressive was attested by the frequent writing of letters and the making of inquiries of the condition of other institutions as a check on its own work. A letter received from Princeton in 1834 showed that the University of North Carolina was paying more for professors' salaries and devoting more at-

85. Battle, K. P. *op. cit.*, p. 258.
86. *Minutes of the Board of Trustees of the University of North Carolina, 1811-1822*, p. 233.

tention to science than was the New Jersey institution.[87] The organization of the North Carolina Institute of Education at the University on June 22, 1831, is further evidence of a progressive spirit and may be considered as an attempt on the part of the higher educational forces to lead the State Legislature to look with more favor upon the cause of general education. The University tended to unify the denominations and to bind the sections of the state more closely together. It was the agency by means of which most of the leaders of the state were educated during the period, and it furnished many ministers and most of the teachers of the academies. It was the guiding force for an expression of the best that was in the state. As Murphey said in his report of 1817: "It has contributed perhaps more than any other cause, to diffuse a taste for reading among the poor, and excite a spirit of liberal improvement; it has contributed to change our manners and elevate our character."[88] The University under Caldwell laid the foundations on which a greater institution was built under Swain.

David Lowry Swain was elected president of the University of North Carolina, November 21, 1835, on a motion made by Judge Cameron,[89] who said: "As Governor Swain has always swayed and managed men so perfectly, perhaps he is the very man to do as well with unruly boys."[90] Swain was born on a farm in Buncombe County on January 4, 1801, of English ancestry. His father, who was a New Englander of some education and learning, was desirous that his son should have a similar training. At the age of fifteen, David found himself at Newton Academy, a small local school near Asheville. In 1821, he entered the junior class of the University of North Carolina but, probably for want of means, was forced to withdraw after only four months of attendance. He spent the following year study-

87. *Reports from the Faculty to the Board of Trustees of the University of North Carolina, 1830-1839*, pp. 229-282.
88. Hoyt, W. H., *The Papers of Archibald D. Murphey*, Vol. II, p. 73.
89. *Minutes of the Board of Trustees of the University of North Carolina, 1823-1840*, p. 296.
90. Chamberlain, H. S., *Old Days in Chapel Hill*, p. 38.

ing law in the office of Chief Justice Taylor at Raleigh, received his license to practice, and returned to the mountains, soon to become a leader in his State. Serving first as a member of the state Legislature from 1824 to 1829, as Judge of Superior Court from 1830 to 1832, and as governor of the state from 1832 to 1835, he found his way for future political growth blocked at the time when the University, after the death of Caldwell, needed a president. He was very popular in the state and had little difficulty in securing the position.

He appeared to have few of the qualities and little of the formal equipment that would commonly be considered essential for a college president. He had less than a half year in conventional collegiate work. He was awkward in appearance and melancholy in countenance, and completely lacking in the quiet and dignified reserve of Caldwell. Henry Barnard, a New Englander and visitor to the state, in a letter from Chapel Hill to his brother on March 25, 1833, wrote: "I was introduced to Gov. Swain, decidedly the awkwardest man I ever saw in any public station. Nature has compensated him for his outward man by large mental endowments."[92] Later, a student while a little "fuddled with wine" made a remark that "Old Bunk (the students' nick-name for Swain) reminds me of chaos: he is without form and void."[93] A still better characterization was given by J. Johnston Pettigrew in a letter from Baltimore to his friend Bryan Grimes, Chapel Hill, on May 16, 1848: "Every thought of Chapel Hill suggests to memory the venerable old bladder, distended with wind and reviews. Has he decided yet whether the library shelves are to be perpendicular or horizontal? But although he is on most occasions rather amusing, he makes a most excellent President, and fulfills his duty in the world's economy as well as any person of his abilities; so that you must prepare to shed tears, when he gives you a final shake and

---

91. Vance, Z. B., *Life and Character of Hon. David L. Swain*, p. 6.

92. Bernard, Henry, "The South Atlantic States in 1833 as Seen by a New Englander" in *Maryland Historical Magazine*, September, 1918, p. 322.

93. Waddell, Alfred M., *The Ante-bellum University*, p. 9.

wishes you god-speed — sincere for once in his life."[94] Swain's
experience as a politician had taught him much about human
nature and had made him very practical. His kind humor and
good nature produced from other students the same fond reverence that it aroused in Pettigrew. Therefore, Swain's success
as president lay in his personal influence on the young men
with whom he came in contact.

But Caldwell's faculty did not accept Swain so kindly at first.
Dr. William Hooper, it seems, was responsible for the remark
that "the people of North Carolina had done every thing they
could for Swain in politics and now they were going to send
him to the University to be educated."[96] Swain did not take to
such remarks so kindly and Hooper found it necessary to resign
in 1837 after some sharp words with the president. Dr. Mitchell
was also in strong disagreement with Swain, but soon recanted
and wrote Swain asking for a settlement of their difficulties if
they were "to be associated for another session."[97] The relations
soon became harmonious and remained so. As an executive,
Swain proved very efficient and soon gathered around him
probably as strong a faculty as was to be found in the old South.
By an order of July 9, 1836, John De B. Hooper, a native of
North Carolina and graduate of the University, was made professor of modern languages. In 1838, further additions were
made to the faculty with the appointments of Manuel Fetter,
a Pennsylvanian of German descent as professor of Greek, and
the Rev. William M. Green, of Hillsboro, as professor of rhetoric and belles lettres.[98] The quality of the men selected by
the University was shown in a comment made by W. D. Williamson, Congressman from Maine, on Charles Fordyce
Deems, a native of Baltimore, who was appointed adjunct pro-

94. *Bryan Grimes Papers,* 1844-1863, Vol. I, p. 23.
95. For a good discussion of the activities of the *ante-bellum* college
president, see Schmidt, F. P., *The Old Time College President.*
96. Connor, R. D. W. *Ante-bellum Builders of North Carolina,* p. 85.
97. *Mitchell, Note Book,* (manuscript), p. 24.
98. *Minutes of the Executive Committee of the University of North
Carolina, 1835-1873,* p. 67.

fessor of logic and rhetoric in 1842; a man "blessed with fine intellectual powers, a brilliant imagination and a benign temperament, he is calculated to be both a popular preacher and professor."[99] In 1850, the university faculty included, in addition to Swain, Mitchell, and Phillips: William H. Battle, professor of law; Rev. Fordyce M. Hubbard, professor of the Latin language and literature; Manuel Fetter, professor of the Greek language and literature; the Rev. John T. Wheat, professor of rhetoric and logic; the Rev. Albert M. Shipp, professor of French language and history; and three tutors. Deems had resigned in 1847, Hooper in 1848, and Green in 1849. In the selection of his faculty, Swain had tried to avoid the criticism which Caldwell received in 1818, that the University was a Presbyterian institution. Swain, himself, although belonging to no denomination, favored the Presbyterians. Fetter, Hubbard, and Wheat were Episcopalians and Shipp was a Methodist. The department of law had been established under Battle in 1845, and that of French and history under Shipp in 1849. In 1854, the French part of Shipp's title was dropped. At this time Charles Phillips, who had already served as a tutor, was made professor of civil engineering; Benjamin S. Hedrick was added as professor of chemistry applied to agriculture and the arts; and Henri Herrisee was made instructor in French. In 1856, upon the death of Mitchell, William J. Martin, a graduate of the University of Virginia, was appointed to fill the professorship of chemistry. In 1859, the faculty included, in addition to the President, nine professors and seven tutors.

It was the policy of President Swain to make the chief function of the University that of training political leaders of the state, and as one who had been trained in the science of politics rather than the classics, he found this not so difficult to achieve. With his power as a leader already recognized, he found it somewhat easy to secure the support of the trustees in all cases. Gradually the entire domestic management of the University's affairs fell into the hands of Swain and his colleagues, and by 1845 no member was to be appointed to the

99. *Hillsborough Recorder,* February 1, 1844, p. 3.

faculty except by the President's consent. It became a policy of the University during this period to judge its success on the basis of numbers enrolled and graduated rather than the quality of the output. This is not saying, however, that the standards of the University were lowered. On the contrary, they were raised somewhat. In 1853, it was an accepted policy of the faculty that the minimum age for the proper admission of young men to the University was seventeen years. A committee of the faculty in 1858, in reporting on the entrance examinations, recommended "that they be made more severe, and that those who are not clearly fitted be vigorously excluded."[100] A further attempt at raising standards was shown in forcing students of the classical department to quit using interlinear translations.[101] As a contrast to the increase in student fees, it became a policy of the University, by order of the board of trustees in 1836, to admit any number of poor boys to the University free of tuition, room rent and servant's hire,[102] and as many as twenty-two such students were enrolled in one year. It was through a loan of $300 by President Swain that Zebulon B. Vance was able to enter the University. Students were also treated with more kindness, less aloofness, and it appears that they were trusted more than they were during Caldwell's administration. These charges were due largely to Swain's influence. Samuel T. Iredell, a student at the University in 1847, in a letter expressed his appreciation to Swain for not having him expelled from the University after such a resolution of expulsion had been passed by the faculty.[103] A young Mississippian of much talent, who had been expelled from the University, was later persuaded by Swain to return and graduate with honors.[104] Faculty members would

100. *Journal of the Faculty of the University of North Carolina, 1856-1885*, p. 131.
101. *Journal of the Faculty of the University of North Carolina, 1849-1855*, p. 149.
102. *Minutes of the Executive Committee of the University of North Carolina, 1835-1873*, p. 41; *Raleigh Register*, September 20, 1836, p. 3.
103. *Swain Papers*, no date, no place.
104. Spencer, C. P., *Pen and Ink Sketches of the University of North Carolina*, pp. 39-40.

often laugh and joke with the more rowdy students, and less attention seems to have been paid to the students' pranks. However, there was no laxity in the enforcement of the laws when it was deemed necessary. Immediately upon becoming president, Swain instituted the policy of holding regular weekly faculty meetings after which a little wine was served. Outrages against the University property in 1840 led to threats by the faculty of instituting criminal proceedings against the evil-doers. In 1845, students were forbidden to use servants other than those in the regular employ of the college. By a general agreement of the faculty in 1852 each class was to be admonished from time to time in order "to improve the standard of deportment at prayers, and particularly to avoid moving in their seats and to the aisle or towards the door during prayer."[105] In general, however, the policy followed was a progressive one, particularly in the matter of a more liberal curriculum. In December, 1844, President Swain, writing a letter from Chapel Hill to Charles Manly, in Raleigh, expressed his policy: "I am and always have been anxious to render our course of instruction practical to the greatest possible extent."[106] The discovery of mineral wealth in North Carolina in these years led to an attempt to make the instruction in geology and mineralogy more practical and useful. Students were urged to study civil engineering and scientific agriculture. In 1853, Professor Phillips was sent to make a study of the scientific school at Harvard. The gift of Dr. Emmons, state geologist, in 1859, was received as "a valuable collection of geological specimens which contribute interesting truths to science."[107] History as a subject for study was also urged as a part of this more liberal policy, and, in 1859, Francis S. Hawks was urged to become lecturer in the University on American history. And perhaps further evidence of a more liberal policy appeared in the privilege granted students

105. *Journal of the Faculty of the University of North Carolina, 1849-1855*, p. 177.
106. *Swain Papers*, (manuscript).
107. *Journal of the Faculty of the University of North Carolina, 1856-1885*, p. 243.

to see pageants of the type of "Bunyan's Tableau."

The difficulties faced by Swain's administration, although not so numerous and vexing as those that confronted Caldwell, were nevertheless trying. The opinion seemed to prevail among the faculty members that most of the students were not interested in their studies. A small number of students continued the disorders of Caldwell's administration and there was a corresponding attempt on the part of the faculty to check them. Serious outbreaks occurred in the years 1849 and 1859 and heavy drinking among the students appears not to have been uncommon In 1856, the college belfry was burned, an episode which greatly irritated the faculty. The faculty had about this time been accused by the executive committee of indulging the students. who stole rides on railroad cars, attended circuses and went to other forbidden places,[108] behavior over which the faculty had little control especially while the students were going to and from college. In 1858, the University was spoken of as "a theatre of evil and recklessness, of which the devil was the lessee, the students actors, the faculty, eye-shut and hand-tied witnesses — and the citizens, poor helpless unfortunate spectators."[109] The fear of denominational criticism was clearly revealed in 1856 when President Swain refused the seniors permission to invite Archbishop Hughes, a Catholic, to deliver the commencement address on the grounds that it would disturb the kind feeling which usually prevailed at commencement and would not be acting respectful to the great body of the community.[110] An attempt to allay bitter feeling between the denominations led to conducting Sunday services according to the ritualistic formalities of the Methodist, Baptists, Presbyterians, or Episcopalians; each church had a Sunday in the University chapel for its services and the students were required to conform to the customs of the presiding denomination.

108. *Minutes of the Executive Committee of the University of North Carolina, 1835-1873,* p. 192.
109. *North Carolina University Magazine,* April, 1858, p. 373.
110. *Journal of the Faculty of the University of North Carolina, 1856-1885,* pp. 6-7.

One of the most serious difficulties of the whole period arose over a political issue which involved the question of slavery Benjamin S. Hedrick, a professor at the University in 1856, declared himself a Freesoiler and for such was attacked by a university student in the *Raleigh Standard.* Hedrick replied in defense of his position by having an article printed in the same paper on October 4, 1856, stating his political position. It had long been a policy of the University to keep itself out of either political or religious quarrels; in fact, its laws forbade such participation by either faculty or students. The result was that a meeting was held by the faculty on October 6, and resolutions were passed condemning Hedrick for his action.[111] The situation waxed warm with the public press demanding Hedrick's resignation, and the students burning him in effigy and tolling the college bell. It was generally thought that Hedrick would resign; but since he failed to do so, the executive committee met and, after approving the action of the faculty of October 6, resolved on October 18, 1856, that "the said Benjamin S. Hedrick be and he is hereby dismissed as a professor in the University; and the professorship which he now fills is hereby declared vacant."[112] Professor Phillips said, in commenting on the action against Hedrick, that the University had to act or it would "have whistled for pupils here until doomsday."[113] The slavery issue also led to the agitation to keep Northern boys out of the University. Moreover, there was a constant attack on the faculty. The University was criticized for the salary which its president received,[114] for electing to the faculty professors who were not natives of the state,[115] for concealing the condition of its finances,[116] for offending the intelligence of the state, and for

---

111. *Ibid.,* p. 56.
112. *Minutes of the Executive Committee of the University of North Carolina, 1835-1873,* p. 198.
113. Spencer, C. P., "Old Times in Chapel Hill" in *North Carolina University Magazine,* 1890-1891, No. 1, p. 55.
114. *Hillsborough Recorder,* July 10, 1835, p. 3.
115. *The North Carolina Presbyterian,* October 8, 1959, p. 2.
116. *Washington Republican,* April 25, 1844, p. 3.

being a party institution.[117] In a series of seven circulars published in the *Raleigh Register* in June and July of 1837, the University was accused of wanting religious character, of excluding clergymen from its board of trustees, of being conceited, and of being badly located; and its laws were characterized as "calculated for the direction of a penitentiary, or of a company of slaves, than the sons of highminded freemen."[118]

In spite of these criticisms and difficulties, the *ante-bellum* University rose to a place of prominence during the administration of Swain, attracting attention both North and South. Andrew D. White, president of Cornell and a prominent liberal of his time, wrote to Professor Winston of the University in January, 1885: "I remember, in my young manhood, the University of North Carolina was always spoken of with the greatest respect among men who knew anything about an American collegiate education."[119] Aided by a more healthy endowment and with tuition fees passing the $10,000 mark the institution was able to secure that equipment which was essential: a progressive and able president, a strong faculty, an attractive campus, neat and well equipped dormitories, and a quite large student body. The enrollment at the University rose from eighty-nine in 1835 to 456 in 1858, and 178 of the students in the later year came from other states; while the total enrollment for the period was well in excess of 5000. The number of graduates showed a similar increase, from fifteen in 1835 to ninety-three in 1858, with a total graduation of more than 900 for the period. During the years 1858 and 1859, the states of New York, Iowa, Ohio, California, New Mexico, Missouri, and Kentucky were represented in the study-body in addition to large numbers of pupils from all the Southern States. Nor were all these students the sons of rich men. More than 200 of those enrolled from 1835 to 1859 were admitted free of tuition, room rent and servant's hire. Out of the students before 1860 came

117. *Fayetteville Observer*, February 21, 1859, p. 3.
118. *Raleigh Register*, June 26, 1837, p. 2.
119. "The Old University and Its Reputation" in *North Carolina University Magazine*, February, 1885, p. 216.

one President of the United States, ten cabinet officers, twelve foreign ministers, fourteen United States senators, thirty-five members of the Congress, fifteen governors of states, fifty-five judges, three presidents of colleges, and twelve prominent professors who served in posts outside the state.[120] This is not to mention the influence wielded by all the others of lesser prominence who attended the institution. As a variation from the usual classical curriculum, the University offered courses in Law, civil engineering, history, and science as applied to agriculture, in addition to the science courses offered before 1835. Beginning with 1847 definite interest was taken in beautifying the University campus, and in 1849 $1,000 was granted for this purpose. For the first time the trustees deplored the fact that the beautiful grounds had become the common pasturage of the cows and hogs of the village.[121] The University also favored better textbooks and as early as July 3, 1835, joined hands with other institutions of the country in an attempt to secure uniform adoptions for the higher institutions of learning. Two definite accomplishments for the period were the organization of the Alumni Association of the University on May 31, 1843, and the North Carolina His-torical Society in January, 1844. As first organized, the Alumni Association included thirty-three members. Its purpose was to renew and perpetuate the friendships formed in college days. and to promote the interests of the University and the cause of education generally.[122] The Association continued to prosper throughout the *ante-bellum* period and achieved, as one of its objects, the erection of a monument to President Caldwell. The North Carolina Historical Society had only a mythical existence. but through the belief that the Society was an entity, Swain was able to procure many valuable works relating to North Carolina history either by gift or permanent loan. The Univer-

120. Smith, C. L., *History of Education in North Carolina*, p. 96.
121. *Minutees of the Board of Trustees of the University of North Carolina, 1841-1868*, p. 273.
122. *A record of the Proceedings of the Alumni Association of the University of North Carolina*, p. 4.

sity under Swain, it seems, came nearer to the accomplishment of its purpose than it did under Caldwell.

By way of summary, it may be said that the University during the years from 1805 to 1860 passed from a period of meager economic resources to a period of relative economic security. Caldwell's administration was characterized particularly by a lack of funds. Sources of support were the escheated lands and arrearages granted by the state, a state gift of $10,000, private gifts of lands, subscriptions, lotteries, and tuition fees, and most of these were more or less uncertain. Internally, the University was controlled by a very strict code of laws which a rather able faculty made every effort to administer but without achieving any great degree of success. Prominent among the faculty members who made valuable contributions to the state and to the University were President Joseph Caldwell, President David L. Swain, and Elisha Mitchell. Although the administration of Caldwell was not so attractive because of the strong classical tendency and the poverty of the University, it was during his presidency that the foundations were laid on which a greater institution could be built. During Swain's administration, which was characterized by a strong political interest and an ideal of public service, the University earned a strong place in the life of North Carolina and was approaching a position of national significance at the outbreak of the war. Of the University during these years, Governor Vance wrote: "It emerged from swaddling clothes under President Caldwell; it passed into a splendid manhood under President Swain."[123]

---

123. Vance, Z. B., *Life and Character of Honorable David L. Swain*, p. 13.

IV

Denominationalism in Higher Education

The last quarter of the eighteenth century was a period of discouragement for the religious denominations. "The state of our Church in this commonwealth is truly deplorable," wrote Bishop Pettigrew from Tarborough, North Carolina, to the chairman of the Committee of Correspondence, Philadelphia, June 5, 1790, and added, "from the paucity of its clergy, and the multiplicity of opposing *sectaries*, who are using every possible exertion to seduce its members to their different communities."[1] Of the Presbyterians, who had been actively interested in higher education during the colonial period, it was said: "The pastors shed tears over departed worth," but "grieved most over the living who had renounced the religion of their fathers."[2] Probably the Baptists had the largest opportunity for influence, but their ideals of individualism were too strongly ingrained and they were divided over the question of an educated ministry.[3] The Quakers like the Lutherans and the German Reformed were segregated from the masses by a social cleavage, and the number of Catholics in the state was negligible. Only the Methodists, whose first circuit was organized in 1776, appear to have prospered during the Rev-

---

1. *Pettigrew Papers, 1772-1803*, Vol. I, p. 27.
2. Boyd, W. K., *History of North Carolina* (The Federal Period), Vol. II, p. 186.
3. Burkitt, Lemuel and Read, Jesse, *A Concise History of the Kehukee Baptist Association*. p. 70.

olutionary period. But as their appeals were evangelical and made primarily to the poorer classes, they had few strong convictions on the values derived from a college education even for the ministry. A Methodist minister at Wilmington in 1804 wrote of the results of one of his sermons. He said, "The cries of the distressed and the shouts of joy from those that were healed was (sic) truly awful and pleasing . . . The slain of the Lord were many. Every mouth was stopped and confessed that it was God."[4] A liberal estimate of the total church members in the State in 1800 would be 30,000 as against a population of 363,751.

At the turn of the century, religious interests felt the impulse of a new life. From 1800 to 1830 may be called an expansion period in which the foundations were laid on which the future denominational schools of higher education were built. The Methodists gave notice of the fight they were to make by holding an important conference in Baltimore in 1800. By 1802, interest in the denomination had spread from the western counties into the Cape Fear region and across the Albemarle section.[5] Other denominations followed with fervid religious revivals. Religious exercises were often marked by dancing, laughing, falling, shouting and much singing. The culmination of the Methodist revival came in 1811 with a meeting of the Virginia Conference at Raleigh accompanied by "sermons and songs and cries and shouts."[6] With the construction of a church building at this time, the growth of the Methodist denomination was assured. An increase in membership in the other denominations had also brought about more compact organizations. In 1813, the Presbyterians, who had been associated with the Synod of South Carolina, withdrew and set up the Synod of North Carolina and, in 1817, the Episcopalians organized a Diocese. The Baptists were also growing rapidly but there the movement for

4. Dow, Lorenzo, *Extracts from Original Letters to the Methodist Bishops*, p. 16.
5. Baldwin, J. A., "History of Methodism in North Carolina, 1800-1837" in *Raleigh Christian Advocate*, February 7, 1894, p. 1.
6. Burkhead, L. S., *Centennial of Methodism in North Carolina*, p. 87.

closer interassociational relations met serious opposition. Disagreements over the ideas concerning missionary work, an educated ministry, and the centralization of authority were evident. The Kehukee Association of Reformed Baptists meeting in 1827 protested against the new tendencies, agreeing to "discard all Missionary Societies, Bible Societies, and Theological Seminaries, and the practices heretofore resorted to for their support, in begging money from the public, and if any persons should be among us, as agents of such societies, we hereafter discountenance them in those practices, and if under a character of a minister of the gospel we will not invite them to our pulpits; believing these societies and institutions to be inventions of men, and not warranted from the word of God."[7] In other words this group of Baptists had taken a decided stand against the idea of an educated ministry.

Among the more influential members of all the denominations present in the state, however, there was a belief that ministers should be educated, but poverty among their parishioners and disorganization had prevented an early establishment of schools for this purpose. Class learning was valued highly, but only when it was consecrated to the services of religion; to them learning was connected with the church and if it appeared unsanctified it had no value. The *Western Carolinian,* for November 7, 1820, reported of the church: "Her eyes are upon the fountains of science, and she devoutly supplicates that they may be preserved pure." Among members of this group was much prejudice against the University because of its alleged skepticism, and the free thought expressed by its founders and early faculty. The apparent control of the University by the Presbyterians, particularly after Caldwell became president, tended to make it unpopular among many of the members of other denominations. Criticism of the morals of the students and the general rowdiness of their conduct was also apparent. But the selfish desire to promote the interests of a particular denomination seems to have been the strongest factor which led to the founding of the denominational col-

7. Boyd, W. K., *op. cit.,* p. 199.

leges. Out of a deep-seated religious consciousness came a demand for institutions in which particular religious doctrines could be taught. The Presbyterians had reported a deficiency of two hundred ministers in fifteen of the western counties. The demand for educated ministers was more than pressing among all the denominations at the beginning of the second quarter of the nineteenth century, and there was a need for schools in which the sons of religious people could be taught without compromising their faith.[8] Just as the Presbyterians had led the way for education in the Colonial era, they were now to lead the way in the establishment of the *ante-bellum* denominational schools.

1. *The Presbyterians*

On August 22, 1820, an article signed "Vox Populi" appeared in the Western Carolinian giving notice that the establishment of a "University" in the western part of the state was being contemplated. The writer, who exhibited a feeling of sectionalism, asserted that because Chapel Hill was too far away many youths were growing up in idleness who would otherwise be in school. Rivalry, it was said, would encourage the growth of the University at Chapel Hill rather than stifle it. The interests of religion and morality demanded another institution, for if all the youth of the state were collected at Chapel Hill it would "be difficult to preserve that order, that morality and virtue which are vitally important for the honor and interest of an institution."[9] The Presbyterians, who were the leaders in the movement, seem to have feared to come out for a strictly denominational school, and expected to get financial aid by

8. The idea assumed by Professor G. W. Paschal in his "History of Wake Forest College" (in *Wake Forest College Bulletin,* Vol. XIX, No. 4, p. 17) that the foundation of these colleges was in part due to the fact that the University, was unpopular because it did not represent "the democratic ideals of Jefferson," seems unfounded. The University, in fact, was founded on Jeffersonian principles, was at no time an institution of the classes, and admitted all, even the poorest.
9. *Western Carolinian,* November 7, 1820.

having the new institution chartered under the state, at the same time keeping it under their control. At a meeting held at Lincolnton on September 30, 1820, many letters were presented from citizens of South Carolina, the upper part of Georgia, and from the western counties of North Carolina, urging the establishment of the proposed institution. The *Western Carolinian*, commenting on the meeting, pledged itself to exert every effort "to achieve and obtain the equal rights of the western part of North Carolina."[10] A week later a writer to the same paper urged the establishment of the new school in order to get rid of the quack doctors who were "swarming about like Egyptian locusts, and whose nostrums are as destructive to the human race as those hateful insects are to the vegetation of the countries where they swarm."[11] The General Assembly, although somewhat reluctantly, granted the desired charter in the name of the "Western College of North Carolina."[12] Unfortunately, however, the charter provided no means of support except such subscriptions as the trustees might receive from private interested citizens. The result was the death of the movement in 1824. Probably the motives which directed the Presbyterians into activity were expressed by James McRee, the leader of the movement: "We hope to establish a Seminary of Learning, to prepare young men for public stations in life, and especially for the gospel ministry."[13] Failure of the movement has been attributed to too many discordant interests, poverty, disagreement about location, Presbyterian control, and opposition by the friends of the University.[14]

The idea of establishing a college in western North Carolina still prevailed in the minds of many Presbyterians. It was desired that such an institution should be located between the Catawba and the Yadkin rivers, that it should be under the con-

---

10. *Western Carolinian*, September 5, 1820.
11. *Western Carolinian*, September 12, 1820.
12. *Laws of North Carolina*, 1820, p. 19.
13. *Western Carolinian*, January 23, 1821.
14. The minutes kept by the trustees of this proposed institution are included in the *Minutes of the Faculty of Davidson College*, 1842-1861.

trol of the Presbyterians, that it should be thorough by electing scholarly men of the Presbyterian church, and cheap by the use of the manual labor system.[15]. But another decade passed before any action was taken. At a meeting of the Concord Presbytery in Rowan County in March, 1835, a memorial was approved which resolved:

> That this Presbytery deeply impressed with the importance of securing the means of education to young men, within our bounds, of hopeful piety and talents, preparatory to the Gospel ministry, undertake (in humble reliance upon the blessing of God) the establishment of a Manual Labor School.[16]

The purpose of the manual labor idea seems to have been twofold; to aid the financial support of the institution and to quell the evil tendencies of students. Plans were laid by the body for securing subscriptions to the proposed school and a committee was appointed to purchase a site as equidistant as possible from Salisbury, Statesville, Concord, and Charlotte. By May 13, 1825, a committee led by Robert Hall Morrison, a graduate of the University, had purchased 469 acres of land lying in the northern part of Mecklenburg County from William Lee Davidson, for the sum of $1,521. The finance committee reported in the meantime that the aid of the Presbyterys of Bethel, Fayetteville, and Morganton had been sought and gained and that subscriptions totaling $30,392 had been pledged. Two hundred thousand brick had been ordered by the building committee to be ready by November. The outlook for the school was promising.

Final preparations for the opening of the college were now laid. In an effort to rush forward the completion of the buildings, many of the nearby farmers contributed their labor instead of money, by clearing the grounds, making fences, and hauling brick. By the end of the summer, the steward's hall, the president's home, a professor's house, and four blocks of

15. Rumple, Jethro, "An Historical Sketch of Davidson College" in *First Semi-Centenary Celebration of Davidson College,* June 13, 1887, pp. 32-33.
16. Shaw, C. W., *Davidson College,* p. 12.

brick dormitories had been built. For a faculty, Robert Hall Morrison was selected as president and professor of moral and political philosophy; the Reverend Patrick J. Sparrow as professor of ancient languages; and Mortimer D. Johnston as tutor of mathematics. The Reverend Samuel Williamson, a devout and locally interested Presbyterian, was offered the professorship of science but he declined the post. The laws and constitution of the college were presented and approved on October 12, 1835. Among the articles of the constitution was the provision that the college should be established on the manual labor system whereby the student was required to spend a part of his time in physical labor, in the field at the plow, making brick, etc. The teachers were required by the regulations of the college to take the following oath:

> I do sincerely believe the Scriptures of the Old and New Testaments to be the Word of God — the only infallible rule of faith and practice. I do sincerely receive and adopt the confession of the Presbyterian Church in the U.S.A. as faithfully exhibiting the doctrines taught in the Holy Scriptures. I do sincerely approve and adopt the form of Government and discipline of the Presbyterian Church, in the United States and I do solemnly engage not to teach anything that is opposed to any doctrine in the Confession of Faith, nor to oppose any fundamental principle of the Presbyterian Church Government, while I continue as a Professor or Teacher in This Institution.[17]

A plan of education based on the classics and methods of punishment similar to those provided by the University were also outlined. At a meeting of the Concord Presbytery held on December 21, 1836, it was decided that the school should open on March 1, 1837. Tuition fees for the college at this same meeting were placed at $15 per session for languages and $10 per session for English grammar, geography, and whatever other subjects were taught. Sessions for the college year were to open on the first day of March and September; while August and February were to be months of vacation. The institution had

---

17. *Resolutions and By-Laws of the Board of Trustees of Davidson College,* 1836-1856, pp. 3-4.

also been given the name of Davidson College in honor of General William Lee Davidson, a patriot of the Revolution.

Davidson College opened on March 12, 1837, without chapel, society hall, library or scientific equipment, but with sixty-five students. Success at first did not seem so evident for the Presbyterians, but after a reluctant granting of a charter by the Legislature on December 28, 1838, Davidson College became a reality. The fact that this charter provided for the education of youths of all classes "without any regard to the distinction of religious denominations" seemed rather to please than to worry them, and little if any criticism was made over the clause which limited the life of the college to fifty years, its endowment to $200,000 and its tax exemption property to 500 acres. The regulations which provided for the control of the affairs of the students, and which were similar to those passed for the University, were heartly sanctioned by the trustees.[18]

From 1837 to 1860 the affairs of Davidson College were administered by three presidents, the Reverend Robert Hall Morrison, the Reverend Samuel Williamson, and the Reverend Drury Lacy, all very able men. Morrison had been graduated from the University in 1818, ranking third in a class of fourteen. Following his graduation, he had entered the ministry and had served as pastor of churches in Fayetteville, Charlotte, and the Sugar Creek Congregation of Mecklenburg County. Upon the failure of McRee to establish his western college, Morrison be-

18. *Laws of North Carolina*, 1838, pp. 102-106. As early as October 25, 1833, serious criticism appeared in the *Tarborough Free Press* on the chartering of the denominational schools. In an article, which was called "The North Carolina Whig's Memorial and Remonstrance" and said to have been signed by many citizens of the several counties of the state, it was asserted that the incorporation of theological schools was an abuse of power by the State Legislature and an attack on both civil and religious liberty. Such incorporation meant the first step toward a rich church and a proud and pompous ministry which had oppressed the peoples of all countries for fifteen hundred years. The history of France was referred to as the results which might be expected, and Spain was pointed out as a county in which such schools had been promoted. The writer favored the University and urged the establishment of a state medical school.

came interested in the manual labor school idea.[19] Being a man of influence and of strong personality, he was able to create the belief that a permanent Presbyherian school could be established. The result was the founding of Davidson College over which he was made President, somewhat against his will, but able men for such a position, at a salary of $1200, were hard to find. It has been said that he was a pleasant, impressive, and successful teacher, and a genuine pulpit orator with an easy, animated, and earnest style.[20] Because of the poor state of his health in 1840, he was forced to resign from his position, but after he had served with enthusiasm and vigor, begged funds, preached, taught, governed and supervised all the secular and religious interests of the college. In his Inaugural Address of August, 1838, he had asserted that religious education, based on the Bible, should be paramount to everything else.[21] His scientific turn of mind was shown in his interest in silk culture whose value he tried to realize by having many Morus Multicaulis trees planted on the Davidson campus.[22]

Reverend Samuel Williamson, who became president of the college on July 1, 1841, had already been serving as professor of mathematics since October 11, 1839. He was a native of South Carolina, of Scotch-Irish parentage, and was inured to hard work. His early education was gained by private teaching and attendance at Providence Academy, North Carolina. In 1821, he was graduated from the University of South Carolina where he was regarded as a young man of high rank and eminent abilities.[23] From 1822 until 1839, he served as a minister in the Presbyterian Church. He was a man of fine physique and of well trained mind and thus was able to handle the cares of the presidency satisfactorily. Difficulties arose, of course, but in desiring always to hear of the good that was in students

19. Ramsay, J. G. "The Administration of the Rev. Robert Hall Morrison" in *First Semi-Centenary of Davidson College,* June 13, 1887, p. 92.
20. Shaw, C. R., *op. cit.,* p. 28.
21. Morrison, R. H., *The Inaugural Address,* August 2, 1838, p. 11.
22. Rumple, Jethro, *op. cit.,* p. 47.
23. Shaw, C. R., *op. cit.,* p. 51.

rather than the bad, he made a deep impression on many of them.[24] He resigned in September, 1854, and was succeeded by Reverend Drury Lacy in March of the following year.[25]

Lacy, a finished gentleman and an accomplished scholar, was a graduate of Hampden Sidney College and of Union Theological Seminary. During the years from 1832 to 1855, he had served as pastor of churches in Raleigh and Newbern where he was spoken of as frank, generous, sincere, affectionate, and free from any sort of dissimulation or deception.[26] Coming at a time just following a serious break between the faculty and students (January, 1855), he added much to the confidence of the patrons and friends of the college. From 1855 to 1860 Davidson prospered, but difficulties arising among the members of the faculty over the maner of disciplining students led to much dissatisfaction on Lacy's part, and he resigned on October, 1860.[27]

The faculty of the college for the period seldom included more than two professors and one tutor, in addition to the president. Most prominent among the professors were the Rev. Patrick Jones Sparrow, who filled the chair of languages from 1837 to 1840, and Lieutenant-General Daniel Harvey Hill, professor of mathematics from 1853 to 1858. Sparrow was a firm believer in the value of the classics and strongly asserted their value to the educated man.[28] Hill was a West Point graduate of 1842, and immediately upon his entrance into Davidson tried to institute rules of discipline similar to those of his alma mater, and was successful to a degree. Through his influence, the demerit system was instituted into the college along with an exacting grading system. Other members of the faculty included the Rev-

24. *Ibid.*, p. 52.
25. White, A., "The Administration of Reverend Samuel Williamson", in *First Semi-Centenary Celebration of Davidson College*, June 13, 1887, pp. 109-119.
26. Shaw, C. R., *op. cit.*, p. 81.
27. Johnston, R. Z., "The Administration of Reverend Drury Lacy," in *First Semi-Centenary Celebration of Davidson College*, June 13, 1887, pp. 121-139.
28. Sparrow, P. J., *Inaugural Address*, August, 1838, p. 8.

erend Samuel Blain Owen Wilson, professor of languages, 1841 to 1853; Mortimer Davidson Johnston, A.M., professor of mathematics and natural philosophy, 1841 to 1853, the Reverend Elijah Frank Rockwell, A.M., D.D., professor of chemistry, natural philosophy and geology, 1850 to 1854, and of Latin and modern history from 1854 to 1868; the Reverend James Ruet Gilland, A.M. professor of languages from 1852 to 1854; Celement Daniel Fishburne, A.M. professor of Greek and ancient history, 1858 to 1860; John Adams Leland, professor of natural philosophy and astronomy, 1854 to 1860; Washington Caruther Kerr, professor of chemistry, mineralogy, and geology, 1855 to 1865; and Alexander McIver A.M., professor of mathematics, 1859 to 1869.[29]

Aside from the education of ministers and the promotion of the welfare of the Presbyterian Church, which were the major interests of the founders and patrons, it was stated that the policy of the college would be to afford "sober and conscientious citizens an institution to which they may send their sons, and feel that their moral and religious principles are safe."[30] Students were to be trained under the restraints of Christianity and to recognize the Bible as the infallible rule of life. In order to afford "an opportunity of thorough education, at a moderate expense and free from temptations to immorality," the manual labor school idea, as suggested in the first plans for the college was adopted.[31] A farm was provided near the college campus on which there were blacksmith shops, cabinet shops, harness shops, carpenter shops and a brick-yard. In addition to raising ordinary farm crops, an interest was also encouraged in hemp growing, rope making and the culture of silk.[32] Tools, materials, seeds, etc., were furnished by the col-

---

29. *The Semi-Centennial Catalogue of Davidson College,* 1837-1887, pp. 13-17.
30. *Western Carolinian,* November 14, 1835, p. 3.
31. *Catalogue of the Trustees, Faculty, and Students of Davidson College,* 1842-1861, p. 2.
32. *Minutes of the Board of Trustees of Davidson College, 1836-1861,* p. 31.

lege. Students were divided according to their size and age, a full grown boy receiving $15 per session for his work, the second size $12, and the smallest boys $9. The average manual work per student was three hours a day. The supervision of the farm and the work of the students were placed in the hands of the "Steward and Farmer," while faculty members made weekly visits to the shops and farm, to examine the work. The manual labor system, however, did not prove successful, either as an agency for financially aiding the college and poor students or keeping students out of mischief, and it was abolished in 1841. In 1851, a new financial policy was instituted in the attempt to sell 1000 one hundred dollar scholarships, covering twenty years of instruction. Two hundred of these scholarships were sold, to the high satisfaction of the board of trustees.[33] Such further financial policies, however, were made unnecessary by the gift of $250,000 by Maxwell Chambers in November, 1854, but because of the limitations of the charter the institution received only $200,000.

Many difficulties were faced both by the trustees and the faculty in keeping the college open. The manual labor school had proved a financial failure; the students destroyed the implements of work whenever opportunity offered. Rest, it was found, could be gained by breaking a hoe handle or a plow point, or throwing away shovels and axes in the night hours. And working under an overseer was too much like Negro work, not to speak of the fatiguing effects which often made the students unfit for intellectual pursuits. A small number of the students were inclined to break the laws of the college. In 1838, six students were suspended for immorality and another for assault on a fellow student.[34] Expulsion for intoxication was the fine imposed upon two students in 1845 and to thirteen in 1849. Corporeal punishment was also resorted to as a method of pun-

33. Shaw, C. R., *op. cit.*, p. 64.

Following the close of the Civil War, these scholarships proved a great burden to the institution whose endowment of $130,000 had been made worthless.

34. *Ibid.*, p. 32.

129

ishment, but often led to many withdrawals from the institution. A serious break between the faculty and students occurred in 1855 with the majority of the students threatening to withdraw unless their suspended member was restored to good standing. Aside from their riotous tendencies, many students had little interest or ability in the classics which they were required to study, to the great annoyance and worry of their teachers. The fact that the preparation of the students in general was bad increased the worry. If the minutes of the board of trustees of the institution may be believed, the cares of college routine proved to be very trying on the health of men who had been used to the comparative quietude of ministerial life. Disagreements rising among the members of the faculty over the disciplining of students became so tense in 1859 that a committee of the board of trustees, who investigated the situation, reported that it would be impossible for confidence to "be restored so as to make it practicable for members of the faculty as at present constituted . . . ever to act pleasantly and usefully in administering discipline in the institution."[35] The result was the resignation of Colonel Leland and, in the following year, of the president. The filling of the presidency and of the professorships before 1860 proved to be difficult tasks for the trustees who were forced to accept many refusals before securing an executive or teacher. Davidson College seems to hve suffered most of the evils and difficulties possible for a small *ante-bellum* denominational college.

The accomplishments of the college while not conspicuously large were nevertheless real. The manual labor system, although abandoned in 1841, probably made the beginning of the institution possible in securing the support of those of small means. An optimistic spirit over the experiment had been shown in 1838 when the trustees reported that the manual labor performed by the students contributed much to their good health and lessened considerably the expenses of their education.[36] Had the system been on a permissive rather than a compul-

35. *Ibid.*, p. 97.
36. *Western Carolinian*, February 23, 1838, p. 3.

sory basis its chances for success would probably have been larger. With the Chambers' gift in 1854, the trustees were able to erect the best college building in the state, at a cost of $81,000, a distinctive building of southern architecture, containing a large chapel eighty feet square, seventy-two sleeping rooms, five class rooms, and three laboratories.[37] Laboratory and library equipment were purchased with a part of the fund so that by 1860 the physical plant of the institution was creditable for a small college. In its curriculum, the institution showed a liberalizing tendency by 1860 with some science, history, and French being taught. The curriculum continued to be largely classical, however, since such a type of education was necessary for those who expected to enter "the Gospel Ministry."[38] In 1837, the Reverend Mr. Morrison boasted of the fact that the school had enrolled "twelve or fifteen students who have the ministry in view.[39] During the period from 1837 to 1860, 1912 students were enrolled and 222 were graduated. The largest enrollment for any year was 109 in 1838-1839 and the smallest was fifty-two in 1842-1843. Out of the graduates of 1840 and 1841, numbering twenty-three, came eleven ministers, four physicians, three farmers, two lawyers, and two teachers.[40] Others of the graduates became merchants, bankers, scientists, druggists, manufactuers, editors, etc.[41] In general, the purpose for which the institution was established was met, in large part, at least, although the college never showed the prosperity which its founders had hoped. It promoted the interests of the Presbyterian faith and was a source of refuge to many local poor boys who would have found it difficult to attend college elsewhere. Standards, although not high, were not reproachfully low for the time.

---

37. Shaw, C. R., *op. cit.*, p. 90.
38. Sparrow, P. J., *The Inaugural Address, Davidson College,* August 2, 1838, pp. 15-16.
39. Shaw, C. R., *op. cit.*, p. 31.
40. Ramsay, J. G., *op. cit.*, p. 105.
41. *The Semi-Centennial Catalogue of Davidson College,* 1837-1887, p. 168.

2. *The Baptists*

The Baptists were not slow in following the Presbyterians. With the organization of the Baptist State Convention in 1830, composed of many missionary societies which existed in the various sections of the state, the centralization of power, necessary for the establishment of a denominational college was achieved. Opposition to such an objective had been eliminated by the withdrawal of the anti-missionary Baptists in 1826. At a meeting held by the Convention at Roger's Cross Roads Church in Wake County, 1831, a delegation of fifty-one members determined that the primary object of their meeting was to be "the education of young men called of God to the ministry and approved of by the churches to which they respectively belong."[42] As there was no Baptist school then in existence, it was arranged that private instruction should be given to such young men by Elder John Armstrong, and that the Reverend Samuel Wait should canvass the state for funds and impress upon the people the importance of educating men for the ministry. This situation did not prove satisfactory and at a second meeting of the convention at Rives Chapel in 1832 it was decided that a Baptist Literary institution should be established on the manual labor principle.[43] This type of school had already appeared in some of the northern states, and, as the funds at the convention were low, it seemed to offer a partial financial remedy. A board of managers was appointed, however, to work out further details of the plan. The plan, as worked out by the board, called for the establishment of "The Wake Forest Institution" whose purpose was "to enable young ministers to obtain an education on moderate terms, and to train up youth in general to a knowledge of

---

42. Purefoy, James S., "Wake Forest College — Its Birth" in *The Wake Forest Student,* 1886, Vol. V, No. 5, p. 181.
43. This idea seems to have originated with Fellenberg who established a manual labor and literary institution at Hofwyl, Switzerland, in 1806. See Knight, Edgar W., *Public Education in the South,* Chapter IV.

science and practical agriculture."[44] The latter purpose, it seems, "was deemed advisable for the sake of economy and bodily health" of the young ministers.[45] It would also keep down the baser passions of youth such as envy, selfishness, ambition, and tendencies to dissipation. Students were at work at manual labor three hours a day, subject to the control of the principal teacher, who was to be a minister. Expenditures were not to be over $60 a year, and due credit was to be given to each student for his work. Students above twelve years of age were to be admitted who brought with them an axe, hoe, a pair of sheets and a pair of towels. Students were required to board in the institution so that the introduction of "news, customs, temptations and other undesirable commodities would be avoided."[46] There was to be only one vacation in the year, from the middle of December to the first of February. In approving the plan, the convention on September 28, 1832, stated that it seemed "expedient and highly important to afford our young ministers facilities for obtaining such an education as will qualify them to be able ministers of the New Testament."[47] Another probable reason was expressed by a writer in the *Raleigh Register,* July 24, 1837, when he said: "There is not one of all the denominations, that feel satisfied with the University as a place where to educate their young men for the ministry." The statement was supported by the fact that only about twenty of the several hundred ministers in the State had been educated at the University. The farm of Dr. Calvin Jones, of Wake County, consisting of 615 acres, had already been recommended and purchased for the sum of $2000. Reverend Samuel Wait was elected to take charge of the school and it was hoped that students could be admitted on February of the following year.

With the plan of education outlined, a farm purchased, and a teacher hired, the convention in 1833 turned to the state for a charter. Opposition was expected particularly from the anti-

44. *Raleigh Register,* November 23, 1882.
45. *Baptist Interpreter,* January, 1833.
46. *Baptist Interpreter,* August 2, 1834, p. 190.
47. *Minutes of the Baptist State Convention,* 1832, p. 5.

missionary Baptists. In a little pamphlet published about that time, called "The American Telescope" and signed by "A Clod hopper," the proposed plan for qualifying men to preach was said to be of the devil and to come from high-minded men who wanted to maintain their cause by human strength and an arm of flesh. Schools, it was said, disfigured preachers "by cropping their long ears of humility in dress and manners," by teaching them "to run straight for the purse; and where the most money and high salaries are to be got," and "to speak in high flown words and pompous expression, so that the poor and unlearned are not able to understand them; . . . . . ."[48] The idea of the unification of the state and church was flaunted, and the horrors of the Spanish Inquisition and French Revolution were referred to as resulting from such schools. Some opposition probably came from some of the friends of the University and also from other denominations.[49] The result was a bitter struggle in the Legislature with W. D. Mosely, speaker in the senate, and a graduate of the University, breaking a tie vote in favor of the charter.[50] The provisions of the charter itself showed with what reluctance it was granted. The property of the institution was to be subject to taxation "as other real estate" and was never to exceed $50,000. No right was given to the trustees to confer degrees and the provisions of the act were to remain in force twenty years "and no longer."[51]

The years from 1834 to 1838 proved to be a period of experiment and preparation. In February, 1834, the school opened with an enrollment of sixteen students, but by the end of the year as many as seventy-two had registered. The average maintained for the period 1834 to 1838 was probably more than seventy pupils. Students on entrance found seven log cabins built for slaves as sleeping quarters, a former carriage house, eight

---

48. Howard, George, *Miscellaneous Publications Printed at the Office of the Press at Tarboro, North Carolina*, 1833-1837, pp. 21-22.
49. Huffman, J. D., "How We Got the Charter" in *The Wake Forest Student*, 1898, Vol. XVII, No. 6, p. 435.
50. *Raleigh Register*, December 24, 1833, p. 3.
51. *Laws of North Carolina*, 1833, p. 58.

een by twenty-four feet, for a chapel and lecture room, and a large cloth tent, covering seventy feet of space, for a dining hall. Wait, who was the only teacher for the first few months, was said to have complained of having some students who wished to be fitted for college and others who could hardly read in a common spelling book.[52] No division of the students was made at first, but by 1836 there were sixteen students enrolled who were ranked as freshmen and sophomores. In the preparatory department of fifty-seven students, there was a division into first and second year classes. A separate class of forty-five students primarily interested in English had also been arranged by a faculty which at that time consisted of three professors and two tutors.[53] The system of government that was followed was paternal, with the professors eating at the same table as the students. Prospects for the future were made to look somewhat better with the beginning of work on a $14,200 brick building in 1834, a building of four stories containing a chapel, recitation rooms, and literary halls. On the other hand, the school was rapidly going into debt, and closed the year 1838 with an indebtedness of about $865. Payments on promises, totaling $38,000 by May, 1838, had practically stopped as a result of the panic which swept the country in 1837; and the profits from the manual labor system were never of any material value, the average made by the student for a year's work being only four dollars and four cents.[54] Little more could have been expected, however, as the salaries paid students were three cents an hour for those over sixteen years of age and two cents an hour for those under sixteen and over twelve.[55] Only ordinary farm crops such as oats, corn, and potatoes were raised and there was little if any scientific experi-

52. Brewer, J. B., "Early Days at Wake Forest" in *Wake Forest Student,* 1896, Vol. XV, No. 5., p. 203.
53. *Catalogue of the Trustees, Faculty, and Students of the Wake Forest Institute,* 1836.
54. Mills, L. R., "Our College" in *The Wake Forest Student,* February, 1884, p. 227.
55. *A Record of the Proceedings of the Board of Trustees of Wake Forest College,* 1834-1888, p. 3.

mentation. As the work was dull and tiring to the student, he often played sick or found some means of getting rid of his working tools. The result was that the manual labor system was given up in 1838. The fact that the president and the professors were northern men was also taken advantage of by the opponents of the institution.[56] Such was the condition of the school when the state granted a new charter in 1838, giving the institution the full rights of a college, exempting its property up to 600 acres from taxation, permitting an endowment of $200,000 and an existence of fifty years.[57]

From 1834 to 1860, Wake Forest Institute and College was administered by four presidents, the Reverend Samuel Wait, (1834-1846), the Reverend William Hooper, D.D., LL.D. (1846-1848), the Reverend John B. White (1849-1852), and the Reverend W. M. Wingate, D.D. (1854-1879).[58] During the years from 1852-1854, Professor W. H. Owen acted as president *pro tem.* Wait was a native of New York, born in 1789, and received his ministerial training at Columbia College, Washington, D.C. Before coming to North Carolina in 1827, he had served as pastor of the Baptist Church at Sharon, Massachusetts, and as tutor in his alma mater. From 1827 to 1832, he served as pastor of the Baptist Church at Newbern. To him more than any one else is due the credit for the founding of Wake Forest College. Not only did he create the sentiment which led to the interest in founding the institution, but he also spent much of his time from 1832 to 1838 in visiting all parts of the state, begging funds for the welfare of the struggling institution. Hooper was a native of North Carolina and a graduate and a former professor of the University. Following his resignation from the University in 1837, he had served as professor of theology at Furman University from 1838 to 1840, and a professor of Roman literature in the University of South Carolina from

56. Paschal, G. W., "A History of Wake Forest College" in *Bulletin of Wake Forest College*, Vol. XXII, July, 1827, p. 18.
57. *Laws of North Carolina*, 1838, pp. 106-107.
58. Taylor, C. E., *General Catalogue of Wake Forest College*, 1834-1892, pp. 3-4.

1840 to 1846. His work at Wake Forest, although covering only a short period, was able. White was a native of New Hampshire, born in 1810, and was graduated from Brown University in 1832. Teaching first at New Hampton Institute, New Hampshire, and serving as professor of mathematics at Wake Forest from 1837 to 1849, he was well prepared to fill the president's chair. His New England ways and ideas, however, made him neither so popular nor his task easy, and he resigned in 1852. Wingate, probably the most influential of the early presidents, was born at Darlington, South Carolina, in 1828. Following his graduation from Wake Forest in 1849, he studied theology at Furman University, South Carolina, and from 1852 to 1854 served as an agent for Wake Forest. In addition to his able work as president, he was able to raise the endowment fund from $25,000 to $46,000 by 1861, most of which, however, was lost as a result of the war.

The turnover of the faculty was also quite heavy, thirteen professors and thirteen tutors serving for an average of only three years each. In addition to the president, the faculty usually included two professors and one tutor. The number of New Englanders on the faculty, although quite large, was probably due to the fact that Baptist teachers were hardly to be found elsewhere.[59] Most able among the professors were John Armstrong, professor of ancient languages (1835-1837); Stephen Morse, professor of Latin and Greek (1839-1843); William Hays Owen, professor of ancient languages (1843-1858); William Thomas Walters, professor of mathematics (1842-1868); and William Gaston Simmons, professor of chemistry and natural history (1855-1888). Prominent among the tutors was Henry Lea Graves, a graduate of the University in 1835, and who, after leaving Wake Forest, became the first president of Baylor University, Texas, in 1846.[60]

In administering the affairs of the college, a policy was followed similar to that followed at Davidson. Expenses were made reasonably low for the time, particularly as an aid to

59. Paschal, G. W., op. cit., November, 1926, Vol. XXI, p. 20.
60. Taylor, C. E., op. cit., pp. 18-19.

poor boys who anticipated entering the ministry. In some cases students were admitted free.[61] Tuition was placed at $22.50 each session and board and washing at $8 a month. The expenditures for a year were estimated at $131. Degrees offered were the A.B. and M.A., four years of languages being a strict requirement for the A.B. Students were admitted on the basis of good moral character and an ability to do the work of one of the two departments of the college, academic or collegiate. As in the case of the University, the law of the state forbade the sale of liquors within one mile of the college, the use of a billiard table, and theatrical tricks without the written consent of the faculty. An extremely monastic policy was followed in order that students might be taught to be pious, humble, and reverent, and no student was allowed to go to Raleigh more than twice during a session of five months.[62] During the study hours, the faculty regularly occupied rooms in the college building and no student was allowed to leave his room without the consent of the president. Students were punished by private reproof, public admonition, probation, suspension, dismissal or expulsion, according to the number of demerits received. All forms of gambling, drinking, swearing, fighting, and association with persons of bad character were forbidden, as well as any kind of noise or splitting of wood in the buildings. Students were to rise and retire according to the hours prescribed by the president. Attendance at prayers, Sunday services, and revivals was required of all students and any student denying the existence of God was subject to expulsion. Each faculty member was required to keep a close and careful record of each student's activities, and to report such at each faculty meeting as a basis for estimating the student's scholarship. Public examinations were held at the end

---

61. A *Record of the Proceedings of the Board of Trustees of Wake Forest College*, 1834-1888, p. 13.
62. *Record Book of Faculty Meetings of Wake Forest College*, 1856-1897, p. 4.

of each session, particularly for the trustees' approval of the work done.[63]

The difficulties faced by those administering the college were many. In addition to the opposition of the "Primitive Baptists," who were continually assailing the school and those working for it,[64] there was much severe criticism from many of the churches and individuals represented in the Baptist Convention. According to Wait, "the institution was grievously slandered, and that, too, not infrequently, by its pretended friends. The most ridiculous tales are often set on foot."[65] No interest was manifested in the institution by the western part of the state, while in the eastern part there were many who were always ready to tell the trustees how to improve its management. Many said that the institution should confine itself to teaching only ministerial students and that only theological subjects should be taught. One old Baptist preacher of Wake County stopped taking the *Raleigh Standard* because of a series of articles which it printed on Wake Forest.[66] Complaints were made about paying professors salaries of $800 a year, and tutors $300, while others refused to pay their subscriptions to the college in 1838 because the manual labor school was abolished.[67] In fact the difficulty of financing the institution was more than discouraging until after 1856. In 1838, the college had an indebtedness of approximately $20,000 due for building, faculty salaries, and the steward's accounts. This was reduced somewhat by the sale of public lots around the college (amounting to about $6,000 by 1845), and the quarrying of granite by the students. The pressure of the debt became so heavy by 1841 that an appeal was made to the Legislature for a loan of $10,000, which was granted on January 11, by a vote of nineteen to twenty-three in

---

63. *The Charter and Laws of the Wake Forest College*, 1839.
64. *The Primitive Baptist*, February 12, 1842, pp. 33-37.
65. Paschal, G. W., *op. cit.*, Vol. XXII, July, 1927, p. 13.
66. *Ibid.*, p. 13.
67. Wait, Reverend Samuel, "The Origin and Early History of Wake Forest College" in *The Wake Forest Student*, October, 1882, p. 58.

the Senate.[68] The note was renewed in 1845 and was not finally paid until 1858. Every effort to have the interest on the note cancelled failed, as well as the attempt to get the state to make appropriations to the institution. Sentiment against the loan was evident throughout the state. A writer to the *Raleigh Standard* in 1846 suggested that the institution hoped to secure the loan as a grant and entered a solemn protest "against all such religious incorporations. . . . as they are mere entering wedges to the alarming amount of property held by similar institutions in France, at the time of the Revolution, as well as other nations."[69] Difficulties also prevailed among the members of the faculty at times, and the students were probably as mischievously inclined as they were at Davidson, Trinity, or the University.[70]

Considering the difficulties which the college faced, its achievements were considerable. During the period from 1834 to 1860, 1020 students enrolled at the institution, and of these ninety-eight received A.B. degrees and twenty-nine received M.A. degrees.[71] The enrollment for 1849, which was a fairly representative year, included two resident graduates, five seniors, twelve juniors, thirteen sophomores, twenty-four freshmen, and fifty-two academic students. Of this grouup, probably more than thirty per cent entered the ministry, while the majority of the remainder became teachers, farmers, merchants, doctors, and lawyers. Although the quality of work done by the college would not take very high rating when measured by modern standards it was, nevertheless, fairly creditable for the period.

68. *Laws of North Carolina,* Session of 1840-41, p. 109.
69. *Raleigh Standard,* November 25, 1846.
70. The failure of the faculty to keep a complete record of its meetings makes it impossible to investigate the activities of sudents. Only a few brief reports of several meetings in 1856 were kept. There is no reason to believe, however, that the students were any more decorous in conduct than they were at the University, Davidson, or Trinity. The few records that exist show that students were expelled from the institution for various reasons. — *Record Book of Faculty Meetings of Wake Forest College,* 1856-1897, p. 4.
71. *General Catalogue of Wake Forest College,* 1834-1892.

In spite of the dispirited teachers and the dry classical texts, many students learned and profited much by their attendance; and in spite of poverty and many rowdy students, able teachers came to the institution. As an agency of the Baptist Church, Wake Forest promoted well the interests for which it was founded, as well as aiding in bettering the general social, economic, and intellectual conditions of the state. By 1860, the institution was firmly established, free from debt, and with an endowment of $46,000 and, as in the case of the University and Davidson, was showing a more liberalizing tendency in favor of the science courses.

3. The Methodists

The Methodists tardily took an interest in the establishment of an institution for the education of ministers in North Carolina. This may be accounted for by the fact that prior to 1830 higher education was not considered a prerequisite for a "minister of the Gospel" by the majority of the members of the denomination and when the need for such training came to be felt. Randolph-Macon College, which was established in 1830, was being regularly patronized. An interest, however, was manifested in the more elementary types of education which often took the form of private schools. It was in such a school that the Quakers and Methodists first came together in Randolph County, a school first taught by a mother in her home, but in 1832 by Allen Frazier in a log house which had been build for that purpose.[72] As Braxton Craven expressed it: "The founders of the institution did not think of a college; their most sanguine dream did not include the curriculum and the diploma; their utmost intent embraced only such instruction as is usually given to a good academy."[73] The school which came to be called Union Institute, signifying a unity of feeling between the peoples of

72. Peacock, Dred, "Some Things Not Generally Known About Trinity College" in *Greensboro Daily News*, October 23, 1929, p. 3.
73. Craven, Braxton, "Historical Sketch of Trinity College" in *Centennial of Methodism in North Carolina*, p. 179.

the Methodist and Quaker denominations, was supervised by a board of trustees appointed by the patrons of the community. In 1839, this board, deeming Frazier's school too distantly located from the community, built a two-story frame building nearer by and hired the Rev. Brantley York, a Methodist, as teacher at a salary of $200 a year. A charter for the school was granted by the state in 1841.[74] When it became necessary to hire an assistant in 1842, the Quakers demanded one of their faith, and Braxton Craven, who had been in atendance at New Garden Boarding School for two years, was hired. In 1843, with the departure of York, Craven was made head of the school and Miss Irene Leach, a former pupil of York, was made his assistant. Such was the humble origin of Trinity College. The story of the attempts to make this school a college is best told in the life and work of Craven.

Braxton Craven was nineteen years of age when he took up his work as a teacher. Born in Randolph county of humble parentage, he became an orphan at the age of seven and spent the rest of his childhood in the home of a Quaker by the name of Nathan Cox.[75] Hard labor and the monotonous routine of daily chores did not deprive him of the opportunity of study, first in a spelling book given by the proprietor of a way-side store, and later at a subscription school in the community. At the age of sixteen, he set up a subscription school of his own, and with the proceeds derived was able to attend the New Garden Boarding School, a Quaker institution, for two years. After his entrance into Union Institute as a teacher and principal he continued his studies, and by taking the examinations at Randolph Macon College in 1850, was granted the A.B. degree. The following year, the degree of master of arts was conferred upon him by the University.

During the years from 1842 to 1850 Union Institute prospered being patronized by families in nearly all parts of the state, by Virginia, and by South Carolina. The average annual income for the period was probably about $1,200 and the enrollment

74. *Laws of North Carolina,* 1841-1842, p. 116.
75. Dowd, Jerome, *Life of Braxton Craven,* D.D., LL.D., p. 17.

105. During these years the sum of more than $1,570 was granted as an aid to worthy, needy young men.[76] But Craven had larger ambitions for his school. The beginning of the public school system in the state in 1839 made more acute than before the need for trained teachers, and this need Craven felt very keenly. In 1849, he outlined a rather comprehensive plan for the training of teachers which he published the following year under the title of "Theory of Common Schools."[77] In order to carry out this plan, it was Craven's hope to change his institute into a state normal college, and he gave notice of his intention by placing a bill in the hands of Senator Lane, of Randolph, to be presented at the meeting of the General Assembly. The Legislature passed a bill (January, 1851) rechartering Union Institute as Normal College, but refused to give the college any support. Calvin H. Wiley was among those who opposed the provisions of this bill, although Craven had written to him soliciting his aid.[78] The bill as passed provided that graduates from the school should be given certificates as sufficient evidence of ability to teach in any of the public schools of the state. It was also stated that those entering the college must sign a pledge declaring to devote themselves "to the business of teaching common schools" in North Carolina.[79] In 1853, the charter was amended, giving the institution the right to confer all degrees characteristic of a high grade literary institution, and directing the Literary Board of the state to make a loan of $10,000 to the college.[80]

---

76. Craven, Braxton, *op. cit.*, p. 180.
77. *The Southern Index*, July, 1850, Vol. I, No. 3, pp. 42-44.
78. *Calvin H. Wiley Papers*, 1835-1852, Vol. I, p. 33.
79. *Laws of North Carolina*, 1850-1851, pp. 56-58.
80. Craven said in regard to teacher training: "Funds must be increased and taxes levied. We must have normal schools and teacher institutes. The people cannot be taught with untrained teachers. Instructing and training the immortal mind should be done as significantly as practicing law and medicine or preaching the gospel. Shall the immortal part be given up to unlearned and unskilful instruction." — Spencer, H. E., "The Development of Duke University" in *The Alumni Register of Duke University*, January, 1926, p. 14.

The failure of Craven, however, to secure for his school the support of the state caused him to turn to the Methodists for aid. At this time, the North Carolina Conference was patronizing Randolph-Macon College, even to the extent of providing beneficiaries and scholarships to worthy and needy students who were planning to enter the ministry.[81] In 1851, the trustees of Normal College agreed to educate young men preparing for the Methodist ministry free of charge if the Conference would endorse the college and agree to appoint a visiting committee. To this the Conference agreed, although it was given neither ownership nor control of the institution. Only an agreement of mutual cooperation was established. The fact that the Rev. A.B. Andrews, at the request of the Conference, was appointed to the chair of English literature (English Bible and ancient and modern history) in 1851, however, showed a close connection between the college and the Conference.[82] There was also a growing feeling among the Methodists against the continued patronizing of Randolph-Macon. This opposition was led by Dr. Charles F. Deems, a leader in the Conference and president of the Greensboro College for Women, who had had a heated controversy with President Smith of the Virginia institution while Deems was a professor there in 1848.[83] The differences between the two men grew and Craven was not slow in making use of his opportunity. In 1854, he was able to perusade the Conference that, although his college was not under Methodist control, it was to "all practical purposes Methodistical."[84] Following the attempt of the Virginia Conference to prefer charges against Deems in 1856, the North Carolina Conference completely broke with the Virginia body. The trustees of Normal College now authorized Craven to propose to the Methodist Episcopal

81. *Minutes of the North Carolina Methodist Conference*, 1840-1848, p. 79.
82. *Ibid.*, p. 107.
83. Brooks, E. C., "The First State Normal Becomes Trinity College" in *Trinity Alumni Register*, July, 1815, p. 102.
84. *Ibid.*, p. 268.

Church, South, that Normal College be placed under Methodist control. The proposals also called for the raising of $25,-000 by the denomination. Craven's proposals led to a spirited debate, for there were many who still favored the Virginia institution, but at a meeting of the Conference in Greensboro in 1857, the college was accepted and trustees were appointed from the Methodist body.[85] In the following year, an appeal was made to the Legislature for a new charter which was granted on February 19, 1859. By this charter old Normal College was abolished in favor of Trinity College, and all authority for the control of the institution was vested in the hands of the Methodists. Provisions similar to those acts passed for the regulation of the University, Davidson, and Wake Forest were included in the bill. The sale of liquors, the erection of a billiard table, and the presentation of theatrical pieces within two miles of the college were forbidden. The state had little interest in teacher training at this time and the Methodists desired to have an institution for the education of their ministers. It was but natural, therefore, that the transfer of the control of the institution should be made.

Craven's ideal for his college was stated by himself: "The College shall be theoretically and practically religious in creed and in heart; religious doctrinally and by conversions . . . The whole tone of the college must be one of piety, and revivals and conversions a part of the ordinary life."[86] In reality, the policy of the college changed during the years 1850 to 1860 from that of a teacher training institution to that of an institution for the education of ministers and the promotion of the interests of the Methodist Church. This seems to have been largely due to financial difficulties which hampered the growth of the school in a way similar to that of Wake Forest and Davidson. Strong opposition was also manifested by some of the best men in the state who designated Craven's teacher training project as "trash" and "humbug." The contempt of the old line academies and colleges was also evident. In May, 1843, Craven wrote to

85. *Ibid.*, p. 268.
86. Brooks, E. C., *op. cit.*, p. 94.

President Swain of the University: "The University, *as a whole,* treats us ungenteely, and with but little of that courtesy due an honorable inferior."[87] The fact that the teachers of the state favored the county institute, that Wiley did not strongly recommend Normal College, and that many of those granted certificates by the institution did not measure up to expected standards, all added to Craven's difficulties.

The institution prospered, nevertheless, and the standards of scholarship were probably as creditable as those maintained by the other denominational colleges. With the loan of $10,000, granted by the state in 1853, the first brick building was constructed on the campus, and by a vote of the trustees and the board of visitors in 1857 to raise $50,000 the financial success of the college was assured. An annual average collection of $5,000 from the students also aided in the payment of faculty salaries. An able faculty which had been collected by 1859 included, in addition to President Craven, Lemuel Johnson, professor of mathematics; W. T. Gannaway, professor of Latin and Greek; I. L. Wright, professor of natural science; and two tutors.[88] During the years from 1853 to 1859, the average number of matriculants was 187, with a majority of them in the preparatory school. The report for 1859 showed an enrollment of nine seniors, twenty juniors, thirty-three sophomores, twenty-five freshmen, and 107 preparatory students, or a total enrollment of 194. Fifty-one students were graduated during this period, the lowest for any one year being two in 1852, and the highest being twelve in 1858. Of these graduates, twenty-five became teachers, nine became ministers, and the others entered law, medicine, journalism, and farming.

4. *Other Denominational Efforts*

The other denominations which attempted to establish institutions of higher education, but which were below the college level, were the Quakers, German Reformed, Episcopalians, and

87. *Ibid.,* pp. 95-95.
88. *Catalogue of Trinity College,* 1859-1860, p. 5.

Lutherans. Of these, the Quakers were probably the most successful. They had entered North Carolina as early as 1660, and in 1789 were estimated to have made up more than half of the population of the colony. Even before 1757, the Quakers were holding regular yearly meetings, one of the purposes of which was to look after the "education and order of Friends' children."[89] In 1830, much concern was shown at the North Carolina Yearly Meeting over the question of Quaker children attending the schools of other denominations, and a plan was presented whereby a boarding school under the control and direction of the Quakers could be established. The result was the founding of New Garden Boarding School on a site six miles northwest of Greensboro. Through the efforts of George C. Mendenhall, a charter was secured from the state in 1833,[90] and by August 1, 1837, the day for the opening of the school, the main building was completed. Twenty-five Quaker boys and twenty-five Quaker girls were enrolled the first day under the supervision of Mr. and Mrs. Douglas Clark, with J. L. Slocum, of Rhode Island, serving as principal of the boys and Catharine Cornell as principal of the girls. The restriction limiting the school to Quaker children was soon necessarily removed, and by 1850 the enrollment, which was ninety, included forty students who were not Quakers. Only girls over ten and boys over twelve were admitted. Pupils were advised constantly to engage in prayer and to guard against everything that would provoke them to wrath.[91] In spite of the spirit of optimism which pervaded the Yearly Meeting of 1851,[92] serious financial difficulties came upon the institution ($25,245.52 by 1860) and there were threats of selling

---

89. Klain, Zora, *Quaker Contributions to Education in North Carolina*, p. 49.

90. *Laws of North Carolina*, 1833, p. 50.

It was generally believed that had the Legislature known that the charter was for a Quaker Institution, the petition would have failed to pass. Mendenhall was a Methodist.

91. Smith, C. L., *History of Education in North Carolina*, p. 145.

92. *Minutes of the North Carolina Yearly Meeting of Friends*, 1851, p. 14.

the school plant for the debt, but the Friends, North and South, rallied to the support of the school and paid off the indebtedness. In 1889, the Legislature rechartered the school as Guilford College.

As early as 1834, the German Reformed people, meeting at the Grace Reformed Church in Catawba County, founded an education society for the purpose of aiding "indigent and pious young men within the bounds of this Classic for the Gospel Ministry."[93] In 1841, this interest was continued by the founding of the Loretz ($5,000) and Boger ($1,500) beneficiaryships, made up of gifts coming through the central and western churches of the state.[94] With these funds, it was hoped that many prospective young ministers could be educated in desirable northern institutions. However, the difficulties of travel, expense, and probably the establishment of schools by the Presbyterians and Baptists, led to an interest in establishing a German Reformed school in North Carolina. At a meeting of the managers of the beneficiaries in 1849 a favorable decision was made. In 1851, Catawba College opened in the "Old Academy Building" in Newton, North Carolina, and the following year a charter was secured without opposition from the state.[95] The leader of the movement was M. L. McCorkle, a prominent lawyer of Newton, who had made the proposal for the school in 1849, and who now led in the attempts to secure funds for the institution. But financial difficulties proved too great, and the years from 1830 to 1860 proved to be years of futile effort, the institution probably never reaching more than a high school level.

The work of the Episcopalians and the Lutherans hardly materialized before 1860. At a meeting of the State Episcopal Convention at Warrenton, June 1, 1833, the Rev. Levi Silliman Ives urged the importance of establishing a "Diocesan Episcopal School" on the grounds that children should be educated in "the

---

93. Leonard, J. C., *History of Catawba College*, p. 21.
94. Walker, G. W., *Reformed Church in North Carolina*, p. 86.
95. *Laws of North Carolina*, 1852, p. 657.

principles of the Church and hence by pious Churchmen."[96] In accordance with these expressed wishes, a school was opened near Raleigh in 1834 with sixty-seven pupils enrolled under the supervision of Rector Joseph G. Cogswell and with a curriculum embracing religious instruction, ancient and modern languages, mathematics, and history.[97] Disciplinary and financial difficulties proved too large for the founders, however, and the school closed its doors in 1838.

The Lutherans, who began their work late, opened up an Academy in 1855 at Mt. Pleasant which, in January, 1859, was rechartered as North Carolina College.[98] By 1861, two buildings had been erected, the college had an endowment of $20,000 and 100 students had been enrolled under a faculty of four.[99] The Rev. D. H. Biddle was President. But the institution had only a short life for it closed its doors shortly after North Carolina entered the Civil War.

In sum, the Revolutionary period brought about a general decrease in denominational interest and in denominational schools. This period of indifference, however, was short-lived. With the coming of the new century, revivals among the Methodists, Baptists, and Presbyterians became quite frequent and by 1810 most of the denominations were more securely established. The growth of theological interests and the increase in denominational pride and competition between the denominations led to an increased demand for well-trained ministers and the education of boys according to sectarian beliefs. First in the field were the Presbyterians who, as early as 1820, attempted to establish the "Western College of North Carolina." Failing in this attempt, they finally succeeded in establishing David-

96. Ives, Levi Silliman, *The Importance of Christian Education*, 1833, p. 11.
97. *Report of the State of the Episcopal School of North Carolina*, November, 1834, p. 5.
98. *Laws of North Carolina*, 1858-1859, p. 79.
99. Bernheim, G. D. and Cox, G. H., *The History of the Evangelical Lutheran Synod and Ministerium of North Carolina*, p. 64; Raper, C. L., *Church and Private Schools in North Carolina*, p. 230.

son College in 1837. In 1834, the Baptists, who were somewhat more successful in their first attempts, opened Wake Forest Institute which in 1838 became Wake Forest College. The Methodists, who had patronized Randolph-Macon College in Virginia after 1830, finally became interested in a college of their own and rechartered Normal College as Trinity College in 1859. Other attempts were made by the Quakers, German Reformed, Episcopalians, and Lutherans. In all of this work it appears that the denominational schools grew out of the conviction among the church people that higher education was a function of the church — which was an old view — not only its legitimate prerogative but its imperative obligation.

V

The Curriculum

It was suggested in Chapter II that a change in ideas as to the purpose of education had come about during the revolutionary period, and that in keeping with this change a curriculum had been set up at the new State institution which would satisfy the social, economic, and political needs of the masses rather than the classes. Such a curriculum, however, for the *ante-bellum* period, proved to be only an ideal in the field of higher education and was soon lost amid other rising interests. The curriculum which developed at the University of North Carolina after 1804 and later at the various denominational institutions is now to be considered. Special attention will be given to the most important textbooks used in those institutions during the *ante-bellum* period.

Throughout that period the requirements of the curriculum called for practically all of the student's time every day of the week. Daily classes were held from Monday to Friday. On Saturday, an English composition was presented to the professor, the subject of the student's own choosing, which was corrected and returned to the pupil. On Saturday morning, speeches and readings were required, while in the afternoon the students were free. W. D. Williamson, Congressman from Maine, and a visitor to the University in the eighteen forties, noticed that two or more students declaimed every evening after prayers, that "the three lower classes" were "required to declaim in private before the professor of Rhetoric, and afterwards periodically in presence of the faculty," and that members of the "senior class" were required "to deliver orations of their composition, on the public stage, twice at least in each term."[1] Morning and evening prayers were held daily. Regular attendance at church in the morning, and a Bible class in the afternoon composed a part of the schedule for Sunday. Regular meal hours, regular study hours, and regular sleeping hours were also prescribed.

At sunrise the students arose and attended prayers. Then followed a study period. From 8:00 A.M. until 9:00 A.M. was the breakfast hour, and the period from nine o'clock until twelve o'clock was set apart for study and recreation. Then came the dinner hour and recitation period which lasted until 2:00 P.M. The hours from 2:00 P.M. until 5:00 P.M. were devoted to study and recitation work, and the period from 5:00 P.M. until 8:00 P.M. was given up for supper, prayers, and recreation. At 8 o'clock, students were required to "retire to their prospective lodgings and not leave them without the consent of their teacher until prayers the next morning."[2] In the supervision of this schedule, the professors or tutors often visited the students' rooms in the night hours. Similar practices also prevailed at the denominational schools of Davidson, Wake Forest, and Trinity.[3]

Except for the extremely religious interests, which were dominant in the denominational schools and the scientific interests which marked the State University, at least in part, the curricula of the various higher educational institutions of North Carolina were not altogether unlike during the period considered here. The University after 1804, largely through Caldwell's influence, returned to the classical fold, the elective system was abandoned and Greek and Latin became the core of the curriculum. Similar conditions existed in the denominational schools in respect to the classics.

1. Williamson, H. D., "The University of North Carolina" in *Hillsborough Recorder*, February 1, 1844.
2. *Minutes of the Board of Trustees of the University of North Carolina, 1790-1797*, p. 167.
3. A discussion of the curriculum for the higher education of women will be found in Chapter VIII.

Entrance requirements at the various institutions were also quite similar and showed a progressive degree of difficulty throughout the *ante-bellum* period, especially at the University. A letter written by Joseph Caldwell, Chapel Hill, to A. D. Murphey, Alamance County, on July 6, 1800, shows the nature of the entrance requirements to the University at that time. In regard to the son of a Mr. Haralson, it was

concluded to join him to the freshman class. His Latin course had been passed through, but I dare say he will find several in the freshman class who will be equal to him. In the Greek he has not had anything but grammar, whereas the sophomores had studied actually the whole of John and fourteen dialogues of Lucian. He appears not sufficiently versed in Mair's introduction and in prosody. In all he will be more regularly and completely brought forward by entering the Freshman class.[4]

The entrance requirements at the University in 1810, in addition to reading, writing and spelling, included a knowledge of Aesop's *Fables*. By 1850, the University was requiring for entrance a knowledge of algebra through equations of the first degree, arithmetic, ancient and modern geography, and an approved examination in the languages of Greek, Latin and English.

The final examinations of all the colleges were also oral and were held at the end of each term, there being two terms to the collegiate year. According to the regulations adopted at Davidson in 1836, an examination was held at the end of each term in the presence of the board of trustees or a committee appointed by the board who determined whether the examination should be sustained or not. A student, commenting on his examination in 1837, said, "We had a considerable examination. We had a great many spectators and sustained our examinations tolerably well. It lasted for two days."[5] J. L. Connor writing from Chapel Hill to his brother, George Connor, Pasquotank County, North Carolina, on November 10,

4. *Murphey Papers*, 1797-1817, Vol. I, p. 47.
5. Shaw, C. R., *Davidson College*, p. 30.

1805, said, referring to the strenuousness of examinations at the University: "To give you an idea of their close application it is only necessary to mention, that some of the members of our class for three weeks past, have studied until two o'clock in the morning; and for a week past, there has been an instance of one, who studied until day break. Their principal dread is Geography, which they nearly all get by rote."[6]

The class work at the University was somewhat difficult, according to a letter written by James K. Nisbet, a student at the University, to his sister on January 25, 1826. After commenting on the dullness of the place and his discouragement he said, "The studies are so hard and so confining that it is enough to kill any person. You can't imagine how hard times are here. We have three lessons to say everyday, two or three compositions every week, and not infrequently speeches to learn. We have so many things to do that it is impossible to do any of them well as the old saying is, too many irons in the fire to keep them all warm.[7] But if the minutes of the Faculty of the University of North Carolina are to be believed, life was neither so hard nor so dull to the student as Nisbet would picture it.

In general, a four-year collegiate course was followed at all the colleges during the *ante-bellum* period with the A.B. degree as a reward to the student after his earnest endeavors. But the degree in itself counted for little, for the measure of a student's success in his college work was determined largely by the number of honors he received at the time of his graduation.[8] During his freshman and sophomore years the students' time was largely taken up by the study of the classics, reviewing the grammars of both Greek and Latin, and reading after such writers as Xenophon, Horace, Isocrates, Livy, Plato, Cicero, Virgil, Thucydides, and Herodotus. The Bible was also read and studied in the Greek. Other subjects that were studied included arithmetic, algebra, geometry, ancient and modern geography, history, rhetoric, trigonometry, surveying and nav-

6. Weeks, S. B., "The University of North Carolina in 1805" in *University Magazine*, April, 1894, p. 338.
7. *Chapel Hill Weekly*, March 15, 1929, p. 2.

8. The following is a chart of the standing of the senior class at the University in 1832:

	Philosophy	Chemistry and Rhetoric	Math	Languages	Total	Averages
Thomas L. Clingman	1	1	1	1	4	1
John M. Parker	2	2	2	2	8	2
Thomas Ashe	3	2	3	3	11	3
James C. Dobbin	3	2	3	3	11	3
John L. Hargraves	3	3	3	3	12	3
James A. Stedman	4	4	4	3	15	4
John H. Houghton	5	2	4	5	16	5
Thomas F. Jones	5	3	4	5	17	6
Samuel B. Stephens	4	3	4	6	17	6
Thomas L. Armstrong	5	4	4	5	18	7
Samuel L. Biddle	4	4	5	6	19	8
Mitchell W. Holt	6	3	5	5	19	8

Reports from the Faculty to the Board of Trustees of the University of North Carolina, 1830-1839, p. 112.

igation. The junior and senior years offered some relief from the classics, particularly at the University, with more attention being given to scientific subjects, political economy, mental and moral philosophy, national and constitutional law, history and French. Written and oral lectures were also rendered by the President, the professors of chemistry, mathematics, and natural philosophy. The following chart served as a basis for the work at the University in 1841:

Course	Weeks	No. of Recitations	Fresh.	Soph.	Junior	Senior
Latin Freshmen	37	4	10 4/9			
Latin Sophomores	37	4		10 4/7		
Latin Juniors	18	3			3 6/7	
Latin Seniors	16	2				2 2/7
Greek Freshmen	37	5	13 3/4			
Greek Sophomores	37	4		10 4/7		
Greek Juniors	19	3			4 1/4	
Greek Seniors	18	2				2 4/7
French Seniors	16	1				
French Juniors	19	3				
Rhetoric	37	½				
Logic	18	1½				
Moral and Mental Philosophy	14	3				4 1/3
Internal and Const. Law	15	3				4 1/2
History	18	1½			2	2
Political Economy	11	3				3 1/10
Algebra	18	5	6 3/7			
Geometry	19	5	6 11/14			
Logarithms	1	3		3/4		
Plane Trigonometry	9	2		2		
Surveying	7	2		1		
Mensuration	7	2		1		
Navigation	5	2			5/7	
Conic Sections			None			
Spherics	5	3			1 1/4	

Course	Weeks	No. of Recitations	Fresh.	Soph.	Junior	Senior
Astronomy	18	2				3 3/5
Analytical Geometry	23	3	5			
Differential Calculus	8	5		3	3	
Integral Calculus	7	5			2 1/2	
Mechanics	11	3				
Application of Algebra and Geography	3	3		9/14		
Hydrostatics	2	5		2 5/4	5/7	
Pneumatics and Acoustics	4	5			1/ 3/7	
Optics	2	5			5/7	
Magnetism	3	5			5/7	
Chemistry	34	2				6 4/5
Use of the Globes	1 1/5	5		3/7		
Botany	2					2/5
Mineralogy	14					2/5
Geology	9	1				
Other Branches of Natural History	2	2				
Electricity	3	5			1 1/4	[9]

The second column represents the number of weeks the student was required to pursue the course; the third column represents the number of recitations per week; while the last four

9. *Minutes of the Faculty of the University of North Carolina, 1821-1841,* pp. 518-519.

columns give the approximate values of the courses taken leading to the A.B. degree.[10]

Not only obedience to law, but a knowledge of the purpose of law was considered necessary to good government. Thus, it was quite natural that a study of law should have occupied a place in the University curriculum. One of the first books to be studied in this field was Burlamqui's *The Principles of Natural Law*, published in 1791. Such subjects as the nature of man, his rights, the principles of will and liberty, of reason and virtue, the rule of conduct, the morality of human actions, the law of nature, and the formation of civil societies were discussed. Vattel's *The Law of Nations* was also studied. First printed in 1793, the little book set forth the many duties of a nation, and of its right to protect and to better itself. The object of government, the just cause of war, the rights to security, and the freedom of the seas were all studied. The study of the constitutions of the United States and of North Carolina occupied an important place in the curriculum of the University, and after Swain became President in 1836, the political phase of the college study was even more emphasized. In 1846, a law school was estab-

---

10. An exception to the general college curriculum in North Carolina during the ante-bellum period was found at Normal College, which later became known as Trinity College, and which continued in session from 1853 to 1859. According to the plan drawn up by Braxton Craven, president of the Institution, a student could elect either a classical or an English Course, only three years of study being required for the latter. During his first year, in the English course, a student studied the subjects of orthoepy, orthography, reading, writing, arithmetic, geography, English grammar, natural philosophy, bookkeeping, the history of the United States, and lectures on the mode of conducting and teaching school, while practice teaching for the prospective teacher was to be provided every week in a model school. Generally the opinion seemed to prevail that there existed a definite system of rules for forming habits and the communication of ideas, and along with the memorizing of such rules the teacher was "to obtain such a knowledge of the philosophy of the mind" as to "enable him to understand the reason of these rules and apply them with judgment and discretion." Brooks, E. C., "The First State Normal School Becomes Trinity College" in *Trinity Alumni Register,* July, 1915, p. 100.

lished at the University, and although the professor received no salary from the institution, his students were given the degree of Bachelor of Laws after two years of study and the passing of an approved examination. Blackstone's "Commentaries,' the "Commentaries" of Judge Story, lectures, state legislation and the judicial decisions of North Carolina made up the larger part of the law curriculum.

A study by Abel Parker Upshur, called *A Brief Inquiry Into the Nature and Character of Our Federal Government* (1840) and a review of Judge Story's "Commentaries" indicated the growing interest of the South to count her slaves as property and at the same time for representation. The discussion of the book closed with the statement that "The truth is, the slaveholding states have always contributed more than their just proportion of the wealth and strength of the country, and not less than their just proportion to its intelligence and virtue."[11] Throughout the whole period the ideas of Hume, the great apostle of empiricism, continued to be popular, while Montesquieu's *The Spirit of Laws*, a critical interpretation of customs and laws was thought to contain an inexhaustible mine of information and suggestions quite useful to the practical legislator.

In the study of political economy, most of the colleges offered courses which were thought to have practical value; the best of the texts was Carey's *Principle of Political Economy* (1832). Treatments of the value of goods, production, wages capital, profits, and revenue, then bore a close similarity to present college courses in economics. The text closed with a study of the causes which retard the improvement of the political condition of man, discussed chiefly under the subjects of population and wealth. Wayland's *The Elements of Political Economy*, a series of lectures first delivered at Brown University and published in 1837, seems to have been studied. The author of this book reflected the strength of localism in school administration. He favored the district system of school support on the grounds that a more lively interest would by this means be

11. Upshur, A. P., *A Brief Inquiry Into the Nature and Character of Our Federal Government*, p. 115.

maintained in behalf of education, the appropriation of public money would be more zealously guarded, and the appointment of teachers would be made because of their skill and ability.

Intense interest was continually manifested in oratory probably because oratory was useful in both politics and religion when the means of communication now so common were very meager. Public speaking was a very necessary activity in both fields of endeavor. There was much illiteracy in the state, and the masses were often led then as now more by emotion than intellect. The success of the student speakers of the University in 1805 led to this comment: "These examples of elegant speaking afford the highest satisfaction as they afford an happy presage of the future usefulness and respectability of the speakers."[12] So important was public speaking in the education of the college man that it continued to be the most important part of the annual college commencement. The morning exercises of the University commencement in 1820 consisted of a prayer, a salutatory in Latin, four debates, and four orations The orations of Cicero, both in Latin and in the English translation, were studied and analyzed. The most popular of the general collections of orations was *The American Speaker* (1826) which included speeches of the ancient orators, particularly Cicero, speeches of American orators, including Patrick Henry, Hancock, Clay, Washington, and Webster, and speeches of English and Irish orators such as Burke, Grattan, Plunket, and Sheridan. An even more simple collection was Enfield's *The Speaker of Miscellaneous Pieces*, published in 1798. The titles of some of the speeches were "The Dead Ass," "Modesty," "Happiness," "Liberty and Slavery," and "Satan's Soliloquy." A collection which especially showed the moral purpose of teaching was Noah Webster's *An American Selection of Lessons in Reading and Speaking* (1803). After giving a very elaborate discussion of the rules of reading and speaking, the author presented short sketches on such phases of character as piety, devotion, obedience, innocence and happiness. A variety

12. *Journal of the Faculty of the University of North Carolina*, 1800-1809, p. 126.

of axioms, such as "To err is human, to forgive is divine," or "a good word is an easy obligation" were sprinkled here and there in the book.

It was during the *ante-bellum* period that the lecture method of teaching, which had come down from practices in mediaeval universities, became so popular in the colleges, particularly for the junior and senior classes. Political interests, moral philosophy, and the development of an interest in the historical subjects offered the best opportunity for a display of the pedagogue's wit, although the sciences were by no means left out. This was especially true in the teaching of such subjects as moral and political philosophy, and chemistry in the senior class, where the lecture method of teaching was largely used. Occasionally an outsider dropped in to lecture. The report went out from the University in 1837 that "The montony of our situation here, has been agreeably relieved for several days, by the presence of Mr. Perdicanis, a Greek gentleman, who is now engaged in delivering a short course of condensed lectures on the History of Modern Greeks."[13]

Series of lectures were often presented in book form for class use. One of the most popular of these texts was John Witherspoon's[14] *Lectures on Moral Philosophy and Eloquence,* published at Philadelphia in 1810. The student was required to memorize in detail the laws of duty and nature as laid down in the text, and to familiarize himself with the principles most tantamount in the fields of ethics and politics. Ethics dealt with man's duty to God, to society, and to himself, whereas politics considered man's position in domestic and civil society, the laws of nature and of nations, jurisprudence, and eloquence. A series of lectures which dealt with all sorts of questions was Joseph Priestley's[15] *Lectures on History and General Policy* (1793),

---

13. *Raleigh Register,* April 18 1837, p. 3.
14. Scotchman by birth — elected president of Nassau Hall (Princeton University) in 1768 and was the only clergyman to sign the Declaration of Independence.
15. English chemist and radical clergyman, supposed to have been the first producer of oxygen (1784).

especially emphasizing the sciences and the economic activities of man. Volney's[16] *Lectures on History,* first delivered at the Normal School of Paris and translated and published at Philadelphia in 1801, also found a popular place.

History, although studied at the University from the day of its opening in one form or another, and although a professorship was established in the subject in 1849, was never held in very high repute as a course for study. Dr. Elisha Mitchell in speaking of the studies of history and rhetoric in 1831 said "These branches of learning are not such as require great ability to enable a person to prosecute them with a good degree of success . . ."[17] Romulus M. Saunders in making an address at Wake Forest in 1852 noticed that history was "too much neglected, or if studied at all, but superficially."[18] Indeed, most of the histories that were written were partisan.

One of the best examples of American patriotism, as it was then viewed, was Butler's *Complete History of the United States,* a study in three volumes, published in 1821. The author assumed that "by the laws of nature occupancy, and possession, is the only law of title; the law of force gives no just right of property, because it is a maxim of nature 'that might often overcomes right.' "[19] The author concluded after an elaborate discussion of the Revolutionary War, that the Colonies were undoubtedly right in all their activities against the mother country. A similar study, but less biased, was David Ramsay's *History of the United States,* also in three volumes, published in

---

16. Compte de Volney, an eminent French savant and liberal of the French Revolutionary period — one time professor of History at Ecole Normal. In 1795, he made a visit to the United States where he was accused of being a French spy.

17. Coon, Charles, *North Carolina Schools and Academies, 1790-1840* (A Documentary History), p. 499.

18. Saunders, R. M., *Address Delivered Before the Two Literary Societies of Wake Forest College,* June 9, 1852.

19. Butler, Frederick, *A Complete History of the United States,* Vol. I p. 3.

1816. Other histories which were read and studied were Rollin's *Roman History from the Foundation of Rome to the Battle of Actium,* (1950); Hume's *History of England,* (1792); Smollet's *History of England,* (1793); Lyttleton's *History of the Life of King Henry the Second,* (1769); Strahan's *Political Essays Concerning the Present State of the British Empire,* (1772); Raynal's *Philosophical and Political History* (1782); Manor's *Historical Account of the Most Celebrated Voyages, Travels and Discoveries,* (1803); Voltaire's *Essay on Universal History,* (1759); and Adam's *Summary History of New England,* (1799). Due to the scarcity of books the student was often required to read whatever he could find, especially during the first quarter of the nineteenth century.

In the original plans for the state university, as we have already said, English was made the dominant course for study, being considered as absolutely useful to all pupils for social happiness and economic prosperity. Gradually, however, as the classics assumed their former major role, the English course came to be considered an aid to oratory and declamation and seems to have been so taught. The subject was intended as an aid to clear thinking, logical expression, and distinctive enunciation, to be used primarily by those who could speak to the public in the capacity of lawyers, statesmen, or ministers of the gospel.

The first of the texts used for a study of English was Robert Lowth's *Short Introduction to English Grammar,* published at Philadelphia in 1775. Beginning with a simple introduction in which the author commented on Swift's remonstrance of the neglect of the English language, and stating that "our language has so little inflection, that its construction neither requires nor admits many rules,"[21] the author continued by saying he would "teach us what is right, by showing what is wrong."[22] In gen-

---

20. English divine and orientalist. In 1741, he was appointed professor of poetry at Oxford.
21. Lowth, Robert, *A Short Introduction to English Grammar,* pp. 5-6.
22. *Ibid.,* p. 9.

eral, the study was quite brief as the author merely set forth a group of rules to be followed, the various parts of speech with examples for each, and the proper use of punctuation marks. A more elaborate study was Noah Webster's[23] *Dissertation on the English Language,* published in 1789, and dedicated to Benjamin Franklin, from whom he seems to have gained many of his ideas, especially that of a reformed mode of spelling. Murray's *English Grammar,* published in 1795, and regarded as a standard text for many years in England as well as in America, has been criticized "for its obscurity, blunders, and deficient presentation of etymology."[24] In addition to emphasis on the written and spoken language, the text also contained a strong moral emphasis.

Closely connected with the study of English grammar was the study of rhetoric, for which a professorship was established at the University in 1819. Richard Whatley in his textbook, *Elements of Rhetoric,* (1858) used by the colleges in the last decade of the *ante-bellum* period, said that the study of rhetoric stood only a few degrees above logic in popular estimation, that it was commonly employed in referring to public speaking, and that it suggested to some people "an associated idea of empty declamation or of dishonest artifice; or at best, of a mere dissertation on Tropes and Figures of Speech."[25] But the subject at least attempted to set forth the sophistical tricks of the art of writing and speaking, discussing such important techniques of writing as method of address, propositions to be maintained, style, and elocution. One of the earliest of the texts used in this general subject was Blair's[26] *Lectures on Rhetoric and Belles Lettres,* published at London in 1787. Much attention was devoted to the rules of grammar and to taste, genius, the sublime,

---

23. American lexicographer and journalist. In 1806, he brought out *A Compendious Dictionary of the English Language.*
24. Knight, E. W., *Education in the United States,* p. 432.
25. Whatley, Richard, *Elements of Rhetoric,* p. 3.
26. A Scotch Presbyterian divine, professor of rhetoric and belles lettres at Edinburgh 1762.

and beauty in writing. Rollin's *Method of Teaching and Studying the Belles Lettres,* first used at the University of Paris in the latter decades of the eighteenth century, and designed particularly for use in higher education, gave elaborate instructions with regard to the eloquence of the pulpit, the bar, and the stage. A most interesting feature of the book was the author's discussion of the government of classes and colleges, in which he said that the first step for the successful education of youth was "to lay down the end we should propose, to inquire by what means it is to be obtained, and to choose out an able and experienced guide, who is able to conduct us safely."[27] Another text was Campbell's *Philosophy of Rhetoric,* which was almost entirely a study of the phases of eloquence.

The eighteenth century witnessed much progress in scientific interest. Following Franklin's experiments with electricity and study in many other practical fields, came Priestley's electro-chemical experiments with ammonia gas in 1775, while the work of Sir Humphry Davy, Berzelius, Lavoisier, and others was attracting notice. Yet, outside of the University of Pennsylvania (due largely to the influence of Franklin) and the College of William and Mary (due largely to the influence of Jefferson) little interest was taken by the American colleges in the study of scientific pursuits until later. In 1768, the Medical School of the University of Pennsylvania was established, and in 1779, Jefferson, as governor of Virginia, abolished the chair of divinity and oriental languages at the College of William and Mary and established chairs of law and politics, of medicine, and of modern languages.

In Chapter II it was shown that the University of North Carolina first gained outside recognition because of the scientific interest manifested in the institution. A report of the committee on education in 1792 had provided for the purchase of scientific equipment, the proposed plan in general being sim-

---

27. Rollin, *The Method of Teaching and Studying the Belles Lettres,* pp. 248-249.

ilar to that later passed by Congress in the Morrill Act.[28] Science was supposed to ennoble the mind, to promote happiness, to serve as a remover of superstitious fears, and to promote a love of beauty, "especially in the natural objects as they are seen in their constitution and external appearance."[29] The mottoes of the two university societies reflected their scientific interest. The motto of the Dialectic was "Love of virtue and of Science" and that of the Philanthropic was "Virtue, Liberty, and Science." Although scientific interest appears to have waned somewhat in the University during the first decade after 1804 due to extreme classical interests, yet the spark of the early interest continued to grow and possibly was the contributing factor which "led to the establishment of the first astronomical observatory in the United States, to the first geological survey by public authority in America, and to the first equipment for the teaching of electricity."[30]

In December 1817, with the appointment of W. E. Mitchell as professor of mathematics, and of W. D. Olmsted as professor of chemistry, the faculty and administrative officials of the University again recognized the value of the sciences. These appointments marked the beginning of a departure from the old curriculum, and a continued scientific interest was evident at the University from this time on. It was then stated that "the endowment of a professorship of chemistry would not only enhance the fame and add to the growing reputation of this infant establishment, but would also operate in a way highly

---

28. This act, passed by Congress in 1862, provided among other things for the sale of 10,000,000 acres of public lands, the proceeds for which were to be distributed among the states for the support of higher institutions of learning, in which technical and agricultural subjects were taught. Proceeds from this fund led to the founding of such universities as California, Maine, Montana, Nebraska, Nevada, West Virginia, Wyoming, and Cornell.
29. "The Beauty of the Study of Science" in *The University Magazine*, November 1, 1844, p. 429.
30. Cobb, Collier, *Some Beginnings in Science*, p. 764.

beneficial to the community at large, and particularly to the agriculturist of our country."[31]

Olmsted's[32] *Outlines of the Lectures on Chemistry, Mineralogy and Geology*, published at Raleigh in 1819, was the first text to be used in presenting the new course for study. After introducing the course with the conventional definition of chemistry, its history, its application to medicine and the arts, and the motives for studying the subject, the author proceeded to outline lectures on such phases of chemistry as light, water, atmospheric air, alkalines, earths, metals, animal chemistry, vegetable chemistry, and agricultural chemistry. Although the work today would be considered elementary, it was nevertheless a forward step.

Even Caldwell, the great advocate of the classics in the first years of his administration as president of the University, became engrossed in scientific pursuits. His interest in mathematics led him to do a text on the subject of geometry; in 1827, he erected at the University the first collegiate astronomical observatory in America, instruments for which were brought by him from London.[33] In order that he and his seniors could study the constellations with more accuracy, Caldwell had a platform built on the roof of his residence, while a true meridian was achieved by building two pillars of brick in his garden and grounding them in the same plane. A third pillar was also built near these two pillars, on the top of which was placed a sun dial for marking the hours of the day. In 1829, Caldwell purchased from London the necessary equipment for an electrical laboratory at a total cost of 153 pounds, four shillings, and six pence. The first item on the bill was for a three-foot plate elec-

---

31. *Minutes of the Board of Trustees of the University of North Carolina, 1811-1822*, p. 146.

32. Professor of chemistry at the University of North Carolina from 1818-1824 and later at Yale.

33. On this same trip, Caldwell became a very strong proponent for the building of railroads in North Carolina, the ideas for which he later set forth in a series of articles called "The Numbers of Carlton."

trical machine with a large branch conductor.[34]

Most influential of all the *ante-bellum* leaders for the cause of science was Elisha Mitchell. Coming to the University in 1818, he remained as one of its leading professors until 1856, when he died while engaged in an effort to measure the height of Mt. Mitchell. Mitchell began his scientific work with the publication of the second of the state geological reports in 1826. In 1836, he urged the faculty and board of trustees to purchase the "Griscom Cabinet of Minerals"[35] which contained some 3000 common specimens as well as many rare ones, stating that although the contributions had been liberal, there was a need for more equipment in the field of chemistry.[36] A unique feature of the commencement of 1842 was a group of experiments carried out by Dr. Mitchell with a recently purchased electro-magnetic apparatus. Although powerful and rapid motion was produced by magnetism, Mitchell was convinced that such would never enter into competition with steam because of the cost of the materials.[37] Among the articles of Mitchell which were published in the American Journal of Science were "The Geology of the Gold Regions of North Carolina" (1839), "On the Causes of Winds and Storms" (1831), and "Observations on the Black Mountains of North Carolina" (1839). Some of the other publications were *A Geography of the Holy Land, Notes on Natural History,* and a *Manual of Chemistry.*

N. M. Hentz, professor of modern languages at the State University from 1826 to 1831, ranked as one of the leading pioneers in the field of American entomology, being a recognized authority on American spiders. Among his best writings were *Some Observations on the Anatomy and Physiology of the Alligator*

---

34. Cobb, Collier, *op. cit.,* p. 770.
35. This was a very valuable collection of minerals held at Frierd's Boarding School, Providence, R. I. Mitchell made a special visit to Providence, R. I. to observe the cabinet, as well as observing similar equipment at Yale, Brown University and Amherst.
36. *Reports from the Faculty to the Board of Trustees of the University of North Carolina,* 1880-1839, p. 306.
37. *Tarboro Press,* June 18, 1842, p. 3.

of North Carolina (1825), *Description of Some Species of North American Insects* (1825), and the *Description of Eleven New Species of North American Insects* (1830). David H. Hill, professor of mathematics at Davidson from 1854 to 1859, was author of a treatise on algebra which exhibited very strong sectional feeling in the stating of its problems. The book was praised very highly by General Jackson. Other University professors at the denominational institutions of the State were engaged in the writing of books, especially for the use of their classes.

In January of 1852, President Swain proposed the instituting of "a department of civil engineering" in the University, and requested "the Faculty to prepare and to report a plan for organizing the same."[38] As a result, a professorship of civil engineering and analytical chemistry was established at the University in the same year. At a meeting of the faculty on October 29, 1852, some conversation was given over to the plan of organizing a new department, in which the application of science to the arts should be taught."[39] Seniors at the University in 1853 were given an opportunity to elect courses in the scientific school, while in this same year Professor Hedrick was giving instruction in the analytical laboratory. Finally, in the plan of the School for the Application of Science to the Arts, as worked out in January of 1854, preparation was to be provided for the professions of engineers, artisans, farmers, miners, and physicians. Daily work in the laboratory came as a result; but the professor usually performed the experiments. If a student pursued his studies in the science department for two and one-half years, he was awarded the Bachelor of Science degree. A similar plan was instituted at Davidson in 1858.

As a part of the science studies, there was also a study of geography, geology, and the various fields of mathematics. A book which stood high in the estimation of college pupils and teachers in the first decade of the nineteenth century was

38. *Journal of the Faculty of the University of North Carolina, 1849-1855,* p. 137.
39. *Ibid.,* p. 174.

Morse's *American Universal Geography*, published in 1784, and criticized by a contemporary critic as "a mere aggregation and index of rich materials, a lexicon rather than a true text book."[40] The best that Morse could say of North Carolina for the period was that many of her women were grandmothers at twenty-seven, and that "temperance and industry" were "not to be reckoned among the virtues of the North Carolinians." The time which they "wasted in drinking, idling and gambling," left "them very little opportunity to improve their minds."[41] The book was one of the principal studies of the sophomore class in 1807, while Robert Heron's *New and Complete System of University Geography*, a very ponderous, musty-looking text, was used at a later date. In the latter text, the author attempted to present his geography along with the history of the discovery, settlement, and growth of the United States, while his comment on North Carolina women was that "they possess a great deal of kindness, and except that they suffer their infant babes to suck the breasts of their black nurses, are good mothers, and obedient wives."[42]

Geology texts were written with much care in order that there should be no conflict between science and the prevailing interpretations of the Bible. One of the texts used, and a book which was almost a classic, was Joshua Trimmer's *Practical Geology and Mineralogy*, (1842). After dealing with the practical applications of geology, the author stated in the third chapter of his text that "The discoveries of geology are not opposed to revealed religion."[43] In another chapter he gave an elaborate discussion of the Noachian deluge, and then concluded his argument by saying that when the geological discoveries "shall have had the sanction of another century, or even less, they will not be deemed more dangerous to religion than the discoveries of Newton."[44] Other texts used were Charles Lyell's *Elements of*

40. Knight, E. W., *op. cit.*, p. 439.
41. Morse, Jedidiah, *The American Universal Geography*, p. 581.
42. Heron, Robert, *A New and Complete System of Geography*, p. 473.
43. Trimmer, Joshua, *Practical Geology and Mineralogy*, p. 55.
44. *Ibid.*, p. 65.

Geology, published in 1839, and Gustav Bischof's *Elements of Chemical and Physical Geology*, published in 1854.

President Joseph Caldwell seems to have used his own text while teaching geometry at the University. The text was completed in manuscript form in 1806 and was published at Philadelphia in 1822 under the title of *Compendium System of Geometry*. The book was somewhat similar to the modern texts on geometry, but it had a strong moral tone. In summarizing the discussion on the definitions and principles of geometry, Caldwell suggested that "They also have a singular power to sway the understanding in its deductions concerning human conduct."[45] Mathematics was studied as a means for mental training, beauty of structure, mathematical truth, and moral and demonstrative reasoning.

A companion text to Caldwell's text was Hutton's *Treatise on Mensuration*, published in London in 1802, which, in addition to the subjects of plane and solid geometry and trigonometry, contained a number of problems on surveying. Gunmer's *Treatise on Surveying* (1825) was also used for study as well as Garland's *Elementary Treatise on Plane Trigonometry* (1842). In the field of astronomy, James Ferguson's[46] *Astronomy Explained Upon Sir Isaac Newton's Principles* (1799) proved to be the most popular text. But it was very detailed and contained elaborate discussions on the values of astronomy.

Gough's *Practical Arithmetick*, published at Dublin in 1800, and used extensively by Charles Phillips, Professor of Mathematics at the University, discussed such simple arithmetical problems as fractions, the extraction of roots, and mercantile arithmetic, especially banking. As for algebra, only the simpler forms were taught at the University before 1820, Simpson's *Treatise of Algebra* (1809) being an example of the type of textbook which was used. Young's *Elementary Treatise on Algebra*, published in 1832, and used by most of the colleges, marked

---

45. Caldwell, Joseph, *A New System of Geometry*, manuscript, p. 15.
46. Ferguson, A Scottish astronomer of humble origin, elected fellow of the Royal Society in 1763.

an advance over the Simpson text, at least in difficulty, and discussed such problems of mathematical interest as cubic equations, indeterminate equations, and diophantine questions. One other text used at odd times was Mackay's *Complete Navigator* (1810), a text based upon the theories and problems of navigation.

Scientific interest probably reached its height in the *antebellum* curriculum in the course popularly known as mental science, the field in which the word "reason" came to be most popularly used. Stewart,[47] in his *Elements of the Philosophy of the Human Mind*, (1818), — the text most often quoted in this field, — presented the subject best when he said "among the various characteristics of humanity, the powers of devising means to accomplish ends, together with the power of distinguishing truth from falsehood, and right from wrong, are obviously the most conspicuous and important; and accordingly it is to these that the word reason, even in its most comprehensive acceptation, is now exclusively used."[48] The author outlined his process of indoctrination by providing a detailed study of the logic of Aristotle, Locke, Bacon, and Newton, and what many writers had said about the art of reasoning, at the same time taking care that all the material should correlate with the idea of good morals and the Biblical teachings. Thomas Reid's[49] *Essays on the Intellectual and Active Powers of Man*, a text published in 1785, had a quotation from Micah on the fly leaf — "He hath shewed thee O man, what is good." Abercrombie's text, called *Inquiries Concerning the Intellectual Powers and the Investigation of Truth*, published in 1859, maintained that miracles were not a violation of the established order of nature, and that the aim of the study of mental science was to exercise and strengthen the reasoning faculties, "to think clearly and

---

47. Scottish philosopher, professor of moral philosophy at the University of Edinburgh from 1785 to 1820.
48. Stewart, Dugald, *Elements of the Philosophy of the Human Mind*, p. 4.
49. Son of a Scotch minister and founder of the "Scottish School" of philosophy, Professor of Philosophy at King's College, Aberdeen, 1752.

reason clearly."[50] A student's comment, found in one of these texts, defined the value of the intellectual powers as "the capacity to gratify desire."

Wayland's[51] *The Elements of Moral Science,* published in 1858, proved so popular that more than 35,000 copies of the text were sold. Perhaps the method which he suggested for the study of his book enhanced its value. "Let the portion previously assigned for the exercise, be so mastered by the pupil, both in plan and illustration that he will be able to recite it in order and explain the connection of the different parts with each other, without the necessity of assistance from his instructor."[52] The lesson was to be reviewed on the following day, and reviewed again when the section was completed. For subject matter, the author discussed moral action and moral law, natural and revealed religion, piety and the duties of man, physical, intellectual, and religious liberty, justice, chastity, and marriage, and generally concluded that the improvement of moral character was "The surest method of promoting" the "physical, intellectual and social happiness" of man.[53] Brown's[54] *Lectures on the Philosophy of the Human Mind* (1824) contained lectures on habits, duties, fears, emotions, associations, morals, and happiness. Other similar texts were Enfield's *History of Philosophy* (1792), Hedge's *Elements of Logic* (1824) with the characteristic brown back and dull print, Whatley's *Elements of Logic* (1843), and Cavallo's *Elements of Natural or Experimental Philosophy* (1813). In general, these texts attempted to make a science out of the question of right living, and in doing so included in their study various branches of such modern courses as physics, physiology, philosophy, psychology, and literature. The last-named

50. Abercrombie, John, *Inquiries Concerning the Intellectual Powers and the Investigation of Truth,* p. 11.
51. American educationist and Baptist theologian, President of Brown University 1827-1855.
52. Wayland, Francis, *The Elements of Moral Science,* p. 8.
53. Wayland, Francis, *op. cit.,* p. 386.
54. A Scottish metaphysician and one time professor of moral philosophy at the University of Edinburgh.

text even included a study of the art of flying in which the author concluded: "Though the expense, the time, and the trouble, which attend the construction, and use of aerostatic machines, will perhaps ever prevent their being used as vehicles of travel . . . .; nevertheless the use of balloons may prove advantageous."[55]

A student's opinion on the teaching of mental science is shown in a letter written by Harrelson, a student at the University, to A. D. Murphey, Alamance County, in 1811: "When we read authors we examine the propriety of their reasons, sift and weigh their arguments and the accuracy of their deductions — the eccentricity and often times alacrity marks our discussion, yet we feel tolerably confident of the benefits arising from it.[56] Archibald Baker, delivering an address before the two literary societies of Davidson on July 31, 1845, summed up the purpose of the study of mental science when he said: "In the study of the mind, it is not to be expected that we shall be able to pry into its essence; and the end is gained for all practical purposes when we trace out the faculties and laws, by which it is governed; nor do we expect so much to obtain practical knowledge, as to acquire an ability to wield that which we have already secured."[57]

Scientific interests had also aroused the attention of the collegiate commencement speakers. James H. Dickinson, delivering an address before the alumni association of the University in June, 1853, concluded in his speech on "Science", "Thus has it come to pass that fact has outstripped fancy, and the scientific wonders of Watt and Arkwright, of Fulton, Morse, and Ericsson have transcended the boldest imagining of romance."[58] The idea of the conflict of science and theology was also receiving notice. B. M. Palmer, delivering a commencement address at Da-

---

55. Cavallo, Tiberius, *The Elements of Natural or Experimental Philosophy*, p. 531.

56. *Murphey Papers*, Vol. I, 1797-1817, p. 79.

57. Baker, Archibald, *The Science of the Mind*, p. 7.

58. Dickinson, J. H., *An Address Delivered Before the Alumni Association of the University of North Carolina*, June, 1853, p. 12.

vidson in 1852, said "The alarmists, too peal the tocsin throughout the church, as though vanquished Christianity was about to surrender to her armed assailant."[59] He continued: "The dapper infidelity of our day sits, with a spruce and jaunty air, in the halls of science and in the chairs of philosophy. Too bland and nice ever to distort its features with a sneer, a smile of vanity ever lurking upon its lips, it simply handles and ignores the Bible."[60]

If the words of a student are to be accepted, the professors were not so successful in their teaching of the sciences, especially the Copernican theory. A University student's comment showed that he concluded rather boldly: "I am resolved to believe what I see, after all they have to say about such things. Is it not as plain as a pike staff that the earth stands stock still? — If the earth turns upside down as they say it does what is the reason that the dinner pot never falls out of the chimney — and that if we are whirling around at such a rapid rate, we do not all fly off like so many slingstones."[61]

The popularity which the French language gained in the first University curriculum did not last very long. With the decrease in popularity of the French Government with the American peoples during President John Adams's administration went a decrease in the emphasis for teaching French in the colleges. The connection of the French language with the infidelity of Paine and Voltaire; rising denominational interests; the failure of the French teachers to understand American students or vice versa; the dominant revival of an interest in the classics, all must have contributed to the waning interest in the French language. However, interest in the language did not completely die, for a French teacher or tutor seems to have been available at the University off and on during the whole period. A professorship of modern languages set up at the University in 1824 was soon abolished, but Caldwell again suggested to the Board of Trus-

---

59. Palmer, B. M., *Baconianism and the Bible*, p. 5.
60. *Ibid.*, p. 28.
61. *Letters, University of North Carolina*, Manuscripts, 1796-1855, p. 160.

tees in 1834, "The employment of a Tutor of French if the funds will allow, the same to be not a foreigner, but an educated American. This opinion is made up after mature consideration and consultation with gentlemen who have had opportunities of experience on this subject."[62] The question as to whether the study of French could be elected instead of Latin or Greek was submitted by Swain to the faculty of the University in 1856, only to be decided in the negative; however, the professorship of modern languages was restored in the following year. At Davidson, French was not added to the curriculum until 1858, while at Wake Forest the modern languages were given only meager recognition until after the Civil War. Spanish seems to have been taught at the University at one time or another for an examination was given on the same in 1828. The German language seems to have attracted but little attention at any of the institutions during this period.

It is probably fair to say that the teaching of the classics dominated the curriculum of all the ante-bellum colleges. Although professorships in Greek and Latin were not provided at the University until 1828, the classic interest had been quite strong for more than a quarter of a century, Latin having become a required subject in 1800 and Greek in 1804. On July 11, 1804, it was resolved by the University faculty "that after the present junior and senior classes of the establishment shall have taken their degrees of Bachelor of Arts, no student shall thereafter receive the Honors of this institution without having first attained a competent knowledge of the Greek language."[63] Generally, no freedom was offered the student from the classics until the second half of the senior year, and as late as 1854 fully one-half of the student's time at the University was devoted to the classics, while English was taught only three hours a week for one collegiate year. It was required that the student should have a minute acquaintance with the classical grammars and

---

62. *Reports from the Faculty of the University of North Carolina to the Board of Trustees,* 1830-1839, p. 177.
63. *Minutes of the Faculty of the University of North Carolina to* 1810, p. 56.

dictionaries and that, at commencement, such students as selected should deliver salutatory orations in Greek or in Latin.
Wake Forest went so far as to establish a professorship of Hebrew in 1839.

A good education in the classics was considered as "the foundation of correct taste in literature, and of eminence in the
mathematical and physical sciences."[64] The study of Latin and
Greek was supposed to accustom the mind to a process of
thought by which the analysis of complex ideas could be carried on. Such studies were to give the mind habits of activity
and discrimination, and to prepare the mind for "the difficult
and abstruse investigations of science,"[65] as well as providing
the most delicate shade of moral excellence. Greek provided
excellent models in poetry and eloquence, with beauty and sym-
metry of construction, for the refinement of the taste and the
imagination of the individual, while Latin provided the greatest examples of oratory, with strong ideals for obedience to law
and government. It was claimed also that a knowledge of the
classics gave the student a foundation for the English language
and enabled him to read the Bible in the original.

In his inaugural address at Davidson College on August 2,
1838, Professor P. J. Sparrow laid down what he considered as
essential to a classical education. Among the requirements he
suggested were a thorough knowledge of the grammars of the
languages concerned, a familiar acquaintance with the idioms
of such languages, a history of the authors read, a knowledge
of the thoughts of the author whose works were read, a course
in classical literature, a knowledge of the geography of the countries mentioned by Greek and Roman authors, including such
things as manners, arts, and customs of the peoples, and being
able to read and write in the Greek and in the Latin. Generally
speaking, such ideals formed the basis of the classical curriculum in the colleges. At the University, the freshman and sophomore classes were required to study the gospels of St. John

---

64. *Reports from the Faculty of the University of North Carolina to
the Board of Trustees*, 1809-1829, p. 183.
65. *Ibid.*, p. 183.

and Luke in the Greek and to review the grammars of the two languages which were supposed to have been mastered in preparatory courses; while at Davidson and Wake Forest regular study of the Greek Testament was required. Most popular among the Greek writers were Homer, Xenophon, Thucydides, and Herodotus. Collections of writings, Graeca Minora, which contained many of Aesop's Fables, and Graeca Majora, which contained some of the writings of Herodotus, Thucydides, Xenophon, Isocrates, Demosthenes, Aristotle, Plato, Homer, Sophocles, Theocritus, and others, were used. Cicero's "Orations," Horace's "Odes," Virgil's "Eclogues" and the "Aeneid," Ovid's "Metamorphosis," and Caesar's "Commentaries" were most extensively studied in the Latin courses.

For grammar and sentence study in the Greek, Fisk's *Greek Grammar* and *Greek Exercises* (1831) absorbed much of the attention of the student. The latter text, presented in interlinear form, emphasized the important uses of the verb, adverb, adjective, and other parts of speech. The exercises were selected for useful information, beauty of sentiment, or the inculcation of some moral maxim. Neilson's *Greek Exercises* (1810) was quite similar to that of Fisk, except that the quotations were longer, while Kuhner's *Grammar of the Greek Language*, published in 1840, had many similarities to the modern text in the subject.

In the field of Latin, Mair's *Introduction to Latin Syntax* (1820) was the most popular text. The learner was to be improved in the elegance and beauty of the Latin tongue, as well as finding in the study of Latin "a fitter system for initiating youth in the youthful study of history."[66] William Hooper's[67] *Short System of Latin Prosody*, first published in 1819, and of pocket size, was used extensively for the purpose of scanning hexameter verse and Horace's "Lyrics." As a grammar, Ruddiman's *Rudiments of the Latin Tongue*, published in Raleigh in 1809, seemed best for all purposes.

66. Mari, John, *Introduction to Latin Syntax*, p. x.
67. One time professor of foreign languages at the University and later president of Wake Forest College.

Partly due to custom and tradition, and partly due to the attacks made by the Deistic followers on the theology of the eighteenth century, the teaching of revealed religion became an important part of the college curriculum; and although the major emphasis of religious teachings was at the denominational colleges, the Bible and certain theological writings were regularly taught at the University throughout the whole *ante-bellum* period. On Sunday afternoon at four o'clock students were required to "read compositions on some text or paragraph of scripture previously given out."[68] In 1841 at the University, all classes were reported as reciting the historical portions of the old and new Testaments, with the seniors being heard by the president, juniors by the professor of chemistry, sophomores by the professor of Latin, and freshmen by the professor of rhetoric.[69] One of the usual themes at the Wake Forest chapel service, which was held twice a day in addition to required attendance at Sunday services, was the thirty seventh verse of the thirty seventh Psalm, "Mark the perfect man, and behold the upright; for the end of that man is peace." Attempts, however, to establish a theological department at Wake Forest in 1838 failed possibly due to the problem of finance. Regular Bible courses were given at all the denominational schools with an average of three recitations per week in the freshman year, while the "Evidences of the Christian Religion" were taught in the higher classes, usually along with the course of moral philosophy. As early as 1830, the Concord Presbytery earnestly recommended to the trustees of Davidson College the introduction of the daily study of the Holy Scriptures into the curriculum."[70]

A very narrow and confining text which was used for the purpose of religious indoctrination was Gilbert West's *Defense of the Christian Revelation*, published in 1748. The text pre-

68. *Journal of the Faculty of the University of North Carolina*, 1800-1809, p. 24.
69. *Minutes of the Faculty of the University of North Carolina*, 1821-1841, p. 518.
70. Shaw, C. R., *Davidson College*, p. 209.

179

sented from the argumentative point of view suggested a "submissive confidence to Divine Wisdom," and the casting down of all "imagination, and every high thing that exalteth itself against the knowledge of God."[71] Thomas Wood, author of *Germs of Thought* (1821) was convinced that a "religious obligation" was "above everything else, indispensably necessary in the earlier as well as the latter years of life."[72] Another of the texts which came out to support the doctrine of revelation as against that of reason and nature was Sykes's *Principle and Connection of Natural and Revealed Religion,* published at London in 1840. James Beattie's[73] *Evidences of the Christian Religion* (1788) was extensively used in the colleges as a text. The author suggested that a student should accept the ideas of the pious fathers and use his reason only in cases "whereof he" was "a competent judge."[74] Students were urged to follow the humility and meekness of Christ and to recognize his poverty and his wisdom. Other works of a similar type were William Paley's[75] *View of the Evidences of Christianity* (1787) and Joseph Priestley's *Discourses Relating to the Evidences of Revealed Religion* (1797). In general, these writers asserted that Voltaire, Hume, Paine, Gibbon and Bolinbroke had made many unbelievers, but that the rapid rise of infidelity, by Biblical proof, was destined to destruction.

A more different type of text was Horne's[76] *Introduction to the Critical Study and Knowledge of the Holy Scriptures* (1825). The work consisted of two volumes, and the student must have given a deep sigh of relief when it came time to close its lids, — that is, if he ever opened them. The material of the text dealt with the history of the Bible, the origin of its language,

71. West, Gilbert, A *Defense of the Christian Revelation,* pp. 245-246.
72. Wood, Thomas, *Germs of Thought,* p. 111.
73. Scotch poet and writer on moral philosophy, one time professor of moral philosophy at Marischal College, Aberdeen.
74. Beattie, James, *Evidences of the Christian Religion,* Vol. II, pp. 33-34.
75. English divine and philosopher. His books were used extensively at the University of Cambridge.
76. English theologian and bibliographer.

its many editions, versions, etc., provided a proper method for the interpretation of the Scriptures, and asserted the necessity of divine revelation and miracles. Along with the teaching of the Bible went also a teaching of the geography of the Holy Land, Rosenmuller's *Biblical Geography of Asia Minor, Phoenicia and Arabia* (1841) being most often used as a text. Prideaux's *Old and New Testaments Connected* (1815) was widely used. Quite an odd text was Melmoth's *Sublime and Beautiful of Scriptures* (1795) which after discussing such subjects as "The Formation of the Earth," "The Origin of Dress," "Institutes of Moses," and "Scriptural Beauty and Sublimity," was concluded with the idea that Adam and Eve before the fall brought to view the times when "Error and affectation had no dominion and when the fantastic passion for external finery had no sway, even in the breast of woman."[77]

Outside of the writing of compositions and the preparing of declamations and orations, the library played only a small part in the functioning of the *ante-bellum* curriculum. As a general rule, there were no regular librarians. The library was kept by a member of the faculty and remained open only for one hour during one day of the week. After 1838, the librarian at the University was a senior tutor who was paid a salary of $100 a year for his library services. In addition to the college libraries at the various institutions, there were the libraries of the societies, usually two in number, which were looked after by students appointed by the organizations. In spite of the interest taken in securing books both by the faculty and by the societies, little care was taken for their preservation. Rats and mice proved destructive. The University library journeyed from a student's room, to a room in the President's house, to a basement, to an attic, and finally found a resting place in Smith Hall in 1850. At Davidson, the library found its first resting place in Professor Sparrow's class room. Neglect was evident at the other schools of college rank.

Outside of the money contributed by the societies for the

77. Melmoth, C., *The Sublime and Beautiful of Scriptures*, p. 20.

purchase of books, most of the library books came as gifts from interested friends and alumni. At the University, Joseph Gautier made the earliest of the large contributions, giving one hundred volumes, mostly in French. A plea sent out by the University in 1804 for gifts to the library found the people more or less indifferent, and similar efforts put forth at Davidson and Wake Forest brought in only a few books, mostly of a theological nature. Too much material written by so-called infidels was not desired at the denominational schools, as was shown by the purification of the library at Davidson on May 9, 1857, when all the works of Paine, Voltaire, and Rousseau were burned.[78] Possibly the largest donation for library books during the period came in 1824 when President Caldwell of the University spent $3,234.74 of the $6,000.00 entrusted to him by the Board of Trustees, for the purchase of library and scientific equipment for 979 books. The levy of a student library fee of fifty cents per term, begun at the University in 1813, was soon abolished. The promise of $250.00 per annum by the Board in 1827 was unfulfilled, as were the promises on the part of the boards of trustees of the other institutions for similar purposes. The sizes of the libraries in 1860 varied from about 14,000 volumes at the University, including the libraries of the literary societies, to possibly 2,000 at Davidson.

The distribution of the volumes of the Dialectic Literary Society, from an inventory taken in 1835, showed a predominance of novels and romances with periodicals, history, and poetry coming next in order. Biography, theological material, and drama also ranked high.[79] Books purchased by the Philanthropic Society at the University in 1800 included such works as Godwin's *Reflections*, Volney's *Travels*, Rousseau's *Political and Social Contract*, and a life of Benjamin Franklin.[80] Among the books purchased by Caldwell on his European trip were Ward's *Oratory* ($4.00), a classical journal of sixteen volumes ($28.00),

78. Shaw, C. R., *Op. cit.*, p. 217.
79. Pugh, J. F., "The History of the University of North Carolina Library" in *North Carolina University Magazine*, March, 1914, p. 209.
80. *Minutes of the Philanthropic Literary Society*, 1799-1803.

and Buckman's four volume *History of Inventions* ($15.50).

If the distribution of the volumes of the Dialectic Literary Society be accepted as an indication of the student's interest, the reading of novels and romances must have absorbed much of the student's time. Circulation in the college libraries proper was always very low, with probably less than a fourth of the students making use of the libraries. Only juniors and seniors were permitted to use the encyclopedias, which could be taken out, one volume at a time, if desired. James K. Polk's reading from the University library for the collegiate year beginning in August, 1817 consisted of Gibbon's *Rome*, Volume I, Ramsey's *History of the United States*, Volume III, and one volume of an encylcopedia.[81] Other books which were widely read by students were Robertson's *Charles Fifth*, Clarke's *Travels*, and Rollin's *History of Rome*.

In general, *ante-bellum* teaching was characterized by a close study of words and a careful statement of facts. To recite Morse's *Geography* "like a speech, page by page, was the test and the glory of a good scholar."[82] An interesting story was told of the action of Zebulon B. Vance while in a law class one day with Richard H. Lewis. The students had been asked to memorize a large number of cases, and Lewis, whose memory was short, had written them down on his left boot. Vance, who saw Lewis reading the cases, asked for the lending of his leg, but without waiting for his consent, he jerked Lewis's leg up in his lap and rapidly read off the cases. Shortly afterwards, Lewis was called up to the front of his class to recite the cases, but was only partially successful, while Vance, who was asked to take his place, walked leisurely to the front and gave the cases with remarkable accuracy. On returning to his seat, he was reported to have said, "Lewis, why don't you study your lesson, you lazy fellow."[83]

Each member of the class had to "attend exclusively to the subject of the recitation or the lecture as it proceeded," and

81. Demerit Roll, *University of North Carolina*, Manuscript.
82. Hooper, William, *Fifty Years Since*, p. 12.
83. Dowd, Clement, *Life of Zebulon B. Vance*, p. 19.

"for this reason their text books" were not to "be brought into the recitation room."[84] Fast reading was abhorred, while the slower a student read, the better student he was supposed to be. A speaker was neither to carry his manuscript upon the stage, nor to be prompted in any way, and if departing from his speech, was subject to a dismissal from the institution.[85] No recitation was to take place except from a clean page, and no interlinear book was allowed in the class room. There was much drilling, especially in Latin. Professor Sparrow, speaking of the classics in his inaugural address at Davidson said, "We do not believe in any railroad system on this subject, by which the results may be obtained without the labor. Like most other things, a classical education decreases in value, in proportion to the small amount of labor which it costs."[86]

In spite of the attacks made upon the classical education, its advocates continued to uphold it. In 1838, William Hooper, in a valedictory address delivered to the students of the University of North Carolina, contended that "such persons should reflect that the system of studies usually pursued in colleges, has been the results of the combined wisdom of the world."[87] Against such opposition, the liberal, social, and scientific interests, present at the founding of the University, gained headway in the decades from 1830 to 1860, but a new South had to dawn before the task could be completed. The strong influence of the ancients was dying but only slowly. At Davidson, the break came in 1858 when a science course was set up with a required three years of study for a B.S. degree. The University had already been active in making changes, and rumblings of discontent were heard at the other institutions. President Swain, of the University, a politician with a brilliant record, particularly influenced members of the senior class to whom he taught consti-

84. *Minutes of the Faculty of the University of North Carolina, 1821-1841,* p. 267.
85. *Ibid.,* p. 541.
86. Sparrow, P. J., *Inaugural Address,* 1838, p. 12.
87. Hooper, William, *A Valedictory Address Delivered to the Students of the University of North Carolina,* January 21, 1838, p. 14.

tutional law. In the face of the tiresome classics, the rewards of a professional life were secure and enticing; thus, public speaking, as a necessary part of the training of politicians and preachers, continued to grow in recognition.

In sum, the higher education curriculum in North Carolina before 1860 was centered around the study of the classics, although tendencies toward a more liberal education were evident. The policy followed was one of intensive rather than extensive training, of memorizing rather than reasoning and of much exacting drill. Along with a high moral interest went an attempt to indoctrinate the student with the ideals of revealed religion. Training for the speaking professions was the rule of the day, although an attempt was made by President Swain of the University to connect that institution more closely with the larger interests of the state.

VI
Collegiate Interests

The *ante-bellum* college campus was a secluded place and to many students it appeared dull. Occasionally an unfounded scare of a slave insurrection or a political campaign, such as that of the "Log Cabin and Hard Cider" of 1840, would bring a ripple of excitement. Or perhaps a matter such as the Hedrick case, which occurred at the University in 1856, would stir the students into a frenzy. The discovery of gold in North Carolina in the eighteen thirties caused some excitement with debates in the University societies as to its value to the state. But these were transitory interests, and soon the life of the college resumed its monotony.

The letters of the students reveal the dullness of academic life. John G. Mason, a student at the University of North Carolina in 1810, wrote to his friend John H. Bryan, of Newbern, on May 2 of that year: "Since our examinations which occurred about two weeks ago, time has hung so heavily on my hands that I have wished myself at Old Nick twenty times . . . . Tired of Chapel Hill and its dependencies, hissed to an excess which I never expected to experience."[1] "My noctural labors have not yet been attended with success," wrote T. D. Donoho, from Chapel Hill, to his friend Martin Armstrong, in Stokes County, March 14, 1819. And he added: "Delay and disappointment torment me as yet. But hope still leads me on."[2] W. I. Bingham,

1. *John H. Bryan Papers*, 1773-1825, Vol. I, p. 37.
2. *Reports from the Faculty to the Board of Trustees of the University of North Carolina*, 1809-1829, p. 305.

a student at the University in 1825, seems to have been discouraged about his work. He wrote to A. D. Murphey, of Alamance County, April 2:

My senior year has been spent rather unprofitably, so far as the studies of college life are concerned. I lost so much ground last session in consequence of sickness, that I despaired of recovering it, and gave myself up to much promiscuous reading, to the neglect of my studies except such as amused me. I look back with regret to my loss of standing. But after all, college distinctions are of not great advantage in after life. Perhaps you will say the grapes are sour? Very true. But a poor fellow is in a wretched predicament when he can find nothing to console him.[3]

James K. Nisbet, writing of his troubles to his sister Mary C. Nisbet, from Chapel Hill on January 25, 1826, said: "How often have I heard people say what an easy time that student has, nothing to do but lie in the shade and talk. On the other hand how often does the student exclaim: 'How glad I would be if I were out home on the farm.' "[4] In 1815, Zebulon B. Vance expressed himself as feeling very miserably over the disagreement which he had had with his girl:

Cousin Kate I will make a part of a confession to you under the seal of my honor and tell you that in my reflecting hours, and they are more frequent than of old, alas yes I am the most miserable man alive I suppose. My confounded, excuse for saying *accursed,* rash, headlong and inconsiderate folly has led me into more awkward difficulties and unhappy situations, than you could well imagine. . . The why and the wherefore of this Kate I shall take the liberty of withholding from you, hoping to rid myself of it before long in some way or other. But remember me to Miss Sallie when she comes up in the kindest manner, and don't say anything about this confession of mine to her or anybody else, mind that.[5]

Writing about his "Lady Fair" seems to have consumed quite

3. *Murphey Papers,* 1825-1830, Vol. III, p. 24.
4. *Chapel Hill Weekly,* Friday, March 15, 1929, p. 3.
5. *Vance Papers,* 1827-1863, Vol. I, p. 21.

a bit of the student's time, and sometimes the student enclosed in his letter to her a poem, for which he had paid fifty or seventy-five cents to the old college servant.[6] Writing from the City of Oaks, Tyrrell County, on May 25, 1847, J. Johnston Pettigrew wrote to his friend J. Bryan Grimes, a student at Chapel Hill:

> My Dear Bowlegs: —
> Don't mention your Chapel Hill visits to me again; five minutes conversation with Livy Daniel is worth all that ever was said at the hill of Science, except at commencement two years ago, when she was there. It is perfectly ridiculous that I should attempt to describe such a person: imagine to yourself ten thousand such as Miss Jeannie Iredell all concentrated into one, add six bushels of beauty, two barrels of excellent intellect, 3 hundred weight of rhetoric and even then you will not have the faintest idea of Livy Daniel.[7]

Evidently Pettigrew had been guilty of writing doggerel parodies on the ladies for he says in reference to a doggerel called "More's Funderal to Miss Helen": "It was written under a promise of secrecy and I received a most awful raking down for it, Miss Helen not seeming over fond of paying compliments."[8] Later when Pettigrew had journeyed to Baltimore, and had entered the work of the national government, J. Bryan Grimes wrote to him from Chapel Hill on March 20, 1848: "Stud Whitaker is in Raleigh on a courting expedition but fortune showers not her choicest gifts on the poor fellow as

---

6. George Horton, a self-taught negro slave, wrote poems for the University boys for which he charged fifty and seventy-five cents depending on the length. Here is a verse from a poem which he wrote on *Love*,

> "Whilst tracing thy visage I sink in emotion,
> For no other damsel so wond'rous I see;
> Thy looks are so pleasing, thy charms so amazing,
> I think of no other my true love but thee."

Horton, George Moses, *The Hope of Liberty or Poems by a Slave*, Philadelphia, 1837, p. 8.

7. *Bryan Grimes Papers*, 1844-1863, Vol. I, p. 6.

8. *Ibid.*, p. 6.

Reports had it that he either is or will be discarded."[9] Pettigrew had by now it seems lost all love for "Livy Daniel" for he wrote on March 27, 1848 in reply: "For my part I should be woefully troubled at present, to commence life with 150 pounds of beauty around my neck, a very fine thing to look at, and love, kiss, etc., but a most costly article of furniture."[10]

Of the activities about the campus, J. Bryan Grimes wrote from Chapel Hill on April 13, 1848, to J. Johnston Pettigrew at Baltimore: "Wiley the novelist is engaged in writing another tale wherein a scene is laid at Chapel Hill. This item was communicated by his poterized (sic) brother .... Thomas and Saunders have departed from the Hill of Science to try their fortunes at Yale .... They say that Reed of New Hanover County is the democratic candidate for governor ... In a fortnight from this time I rise before a gaping audience and glide down the stream of life — Sit cross legged for me."[11]

Sometimes the call from the student to family or friend was for money. A student by the name of Harrellson wrote from Chapel Hill to A. D. Murphey, Alamance County, on September 13, 1811, that he needed "a pair of shoes and some money" and that he would not make this unreasonable demand if he had not purchased a ticket in the W. M. Lottery. Then to show he had some intellectual interests, he wrote that he was fond of reading Hume, or as much of him as he understood. He had also been reading some of the writings of Rousseau and had found that "this wood hand philosopher" had led him into a spirit of arguing. He further stated that he had just received the American Whig Review and that it contained a "great account of useful and entertaining matter both literary and political."[12] In 1815, Martin Armstrong while writing from Chapel Hill to his father Thomas A. Armstrong, Raleigh, suggested, among other things, that he must have a few dollars to discharge his expenses. "If I remain here I must have 10 Dollars. If not 5 will

9. Ibid., p. 18.
10. Ibid., p. 19.
11. Bryan Grimes Papers, 1844-1863, Vol. P. 20.
12. Murphey Papers, 1797-1817, Vol. I, p. 79.

do to get me home." He added that, although his examination had been "particularly strict," he thought it was such as would be approved.[13]

Students tried to drive away dull care by engaging in activities within the college buildings. If it were thought that no professor was about, a stag dance would be staged in one of the halls of the dormitories. Professor Phillips, of the University, came upon such a party on Friday night, May 3, 1850 — "engaged in a boisterous dance in the passage of the old South Building, and told them that such an assemblage and such an amusement in study hours was unlawful, and directed them to go to their rooms. These two students (the two that were called before the Faculty) defended the proceedings in a disrespectful manner, the candle was blown out, a great yell ensued, and a pitcher of water was thrown upon the professor from the upper story. Mr. Ruffin upon being told to go to his room declared that he would not do it."[14] Occasionally, a tutor would report to the faculty that a great uproar had been going on in the dormitories about supper time, "occasioned by fiddling, dancing, stamping on the floor and shouting in a very tumultuous manner."[15] Often wood was thrown at night from the third floor of the South Building (at the University) to the first with such force that the floor was broken through in places. Sometimes when a student was caught and was examined too closely by a member of the faculty, the professor or tutor would be threatened with ejection through the window, as was Joseph Caldwell in 1797 by Johnston Blakely.[16] In an effort to keep faculty members out of their rooms, students quite often placed "a large pan or bucket of water mixed with lamp black or some other substance above the door so as to fall and empty the con-

13. *Reports from the Faculty to the Board of Trustees of the University of North Carolina,* 1809-1829, p. 279.

14. *Journal of the Faculty of the University of North Carolina,* 1848-1855, pp. 39-40.

15. *Minutes of the Faculty of the University of North Carolina,* 1821-1841, p. 81.

16. Johnson, William, "Biographical Sketch of Capt. Johnston Blakely" in *North Carolina University Magazine,* February, 1854, p. 3.

tents on the first one who should enter,"[16] and the arrangements were such that a faculty member would be the first to enter. One of the chief inconveniences experienced by faculty members was "a drenching with water clean or foul" as they passed the steps or walked the passages.[18]

Similar activities were engaged in outside the college buildings and in the night hours. Sometimes the yells coming up from the nearby woods were those of a poor freshman who was being hazed by the sophomores. W. A. Smith, a student at Davidson in 1859, wrote that "one form of hazing was to invite a Freshman to join a party to rob a hen roost. The Freshman had to climb the tree, then some one of the party would slip to one side and shoot. The party would run leaving the freshman to shift for himself."[19] Sometimes a freshman was taken out "snipe hunting." Hazing by blacking often befell the freshmen. On the night of July 22, 1853, at the University a number of students bent on blacking up a group of freshmen accomplished their task, but not until one member of the party had been shot through the arm and a freshman had had his scalp laid open with a club. The appearance of Tutor Brown broke up the fracas.[20] Quite often the freshman was invited to tell a joke, which he was never allowed to tell to the satisfaction of his tormentors. Occasionally, the freshman was made quite drunk with "ardent spirits" and sent before the faculty with a petition for admittance to the "Ugly Club" which was active at the University in 1853. Weather permitting, a number of students would band together for a parade of the campus in the nights hours, first, however, seeing that the tutors were locked up in their rooms. Ringing of bells, "hallowing" and screams of terror would break forth as the riotous mob wandered from one

17. *Minutes of the Faculty of the University of North Carolina,* 1821-41, p. 403.
18. *Reports from the Faculty to the Board of Trustees of the University of North Carolina,* 1809-1829, p. 509.
19. Shaw, C. R., *op. cit.,* p. 102.
20. *Journal of the Faculty of the University of North Carolina,* 1849-55, p. 206.

building to another. In the Minutes of the Faculty of the University for September, 1840, it was recorded that

the disorders of Saturday night the 29th which commenced with a freshman treat and which continued with occasional intermission through the greater part of the night during which the tutor's windows were shattered by stones and other missles, several members of the faculty endangered by being thrown at, the college bell rung violently and long, the doors of the laboratory, junior and sophomore recitation rooms broken open and nearly destroyed, the stables of several members of the faculty entered, their horses taken out and ridden.[21]

Again on Octoter 9, 1840 a meeting of the faculty was held for the

purpose of inquiring into the disorders of the last night, which commenced about eleven o'clock and continued until a very late hour, during which time, a large company assembled at the door of the South Building, made, many loud, unusual and disorderly noises, as calling loudly for several members of the faculty by names known among the students, singing indecent songs, imitating certain exercises usual at camp meetings, such as singing hymns, shouting and crying out as mourners at camp meetings. This party, or the greater portion of them, was seen by one of the tutors to approach the belfry, and shortly after it was broken open and the bell rung at that time and twice afterwards. The horse of a member of the faculty was also painted, and his mane and tail cut and then fastened up in Person Hall.[22]

Students at the University, finding that they were being checked up on in their practice of parading the campus at night, found it necessary to "black up" or to tie cloths around their heads and bodies so that they would not be recognized if and when seen by a member of the faculty. It was in such a disguise that Tutor Graves saw a student making for the belfry one night. On seeing Graves, the student fled through the

---

21. *Minutes of the Faculty of the University of North Carolina,* 1821-41, p. 476.
22. *Ibid.,* p. 496.

passage of the South Building only to be caught at the other end; however, there followed a struggle in which the student was able to secure his freedom, but left his gown and sheet behind.[23]

Similar conditions prevailed at Davidson. The faculty in 1849 recorded that the students had been engaged in such disorderly acts as "destroying the college bell, disturbing of the neighbors and in two instances by firing at them with a pistol, and actually wounding one of them, the taking of the Bible from its place in the college Chapel, the tearing away of the lining from the pulpit, and the scattering of shot and pebbles during prayers."[24] In 1859, a student at Davidson climbed on top of Chambers Hall and tied a wire to the bell. "The wire could not be seen and the bell rang all night."[25]

Students often became hungry under the exactions of such mischief at such late hours at night, and in absence of a lunch counter in the village supplied one in their rooms. The meat was usually chicken, obtained from some near-by neighbor's roost, or opossum, partridge, or rabbit caught on a hunt during the night or the previous day. In season, the students had watermelons, potatoes, corn on the cob, and sometimes honey, also procured by trespass. Biscuits and coffee came in some way from the steward of the commons. Even the killing of a hog which belonged to a neighbor, but which ranged over the campus, was not uncommon. And now and then the student invaded a professor's kitchen. Late one Sunday evening in 1856, a member of the University faculty caught students Hamer, Thompson, and Washington, all of whom admitted their guilt when placed on trial, but protested that it was their first offense.[26]

The students at Wake Forest seem to have bought their chicken in the form of pies from a Negro named Peter. One night Peter was attacked by the boys for selling them "puppy

23. *Ibid.*, p. 345.
24. Shaw, C. R., *op. cit.*, pp. 57-58.
25. *Ibid.*, p. 102.
26. *Journal of the Faculty of the University of North Carolina,* 1856-85, p. 82.

pies," to which his reply was "dar ain't no dog in 'em a 'tall. When old hen ain't handy, old har'll do jus' as well."[27] At still another time, Peter sold the students pumpkins for watermelons, and when later questioned about, it, he admitted having picked them in the dark.

Interests in the neighboring towns and villages were sometimes strong enough to draw the student away from the college campus in spite of a protesting faculty and the violation of the rules of the institution. A student at the university who was admonished for going to Pittsboro without permission replied that "he felt bound to return with some ladies who came on a visit from that place under his escort."[28] Court sessions were also attractive to the student, and, above all, when a murder trial was going on. Many students went to Hillsboro on April 30, 1859, to attend a murder trial without permission from the faculty, "and several in spite of a refusal."[29] Students at the University also attended cock fights and horse races, and, in order not to be distinguished from the masses, "they disguised themselves in the garb of negroes."[30] Other attractions were the circus, theatrical performances and the concerts which usually dodged the college towns because of forbidding statutes.

Students also enjoyed annoying their professors. They were

---

27. Paschal, G. W., "A History of Wake Forest College" in *Bulletin of Wake Forest College*, November, 1926, p. 33.
28. *Journal of the Faculty of the University of North Carolina*, 1849-55, p. 197.
29. *History of the University of North Carolina*, manuscript.
30. Those engaged in manipulating the races or cock fights contributed "all the facilities and inducements in their power to such students as" could "be tempted to attend. It may display the nature of such races as these to mention that money does not constitute the principal prize, for the necessity of providing this would possibly prove a competent interdict, except such small sums as negroes may be able to collect before the appointed day. To make out a stake of high interest, fifty barrels of corn are brought together by the six or seven persons who enter their horses, and this is borne off at last by the owner of an animal, which would have to be improved upon for fifty years to bring it to any tolerable standard." — *Reports from the Faculty to the Board of Trustees of the University of North Carolina*, 1809-1829, pp. 246-247.

called before the faculty for talking at prayers, talking at recitation, slumping in the reading room, laughing in time of recitation, cutting the bench during prayers, sleeping in the recitation room, clucking in the recitation room, scrapping in the recitation room, scuffling in the reading room, throwing a chalked rag, pushing a fellow classmate from the bench, eating walnuts in the recitation room, exploding torpedoes in the prayer hall, tarring the chapel seats, swinging in the study hours, expressing political opinions while on the stage, reading at morning prayers while the worship was going on, laughing and indecorum at prayers, slighting the duty of declamation, playing marbles at study hours, firing pistols, rolling stones through the passageways, carrying off parts of the bell, uttering threats of violence against the faculty, fighting in chapel, exploding gun powder in the night, making "great and tumultous" noises in the passage ways, pinching a fellow classmate in chapel, blowing trumpets at night, leading a procession behind a member of the faculty to chapel, disturbing a recitation "by groaning in concert and rolling marbles along the bench,"[31] answering improperly at prayers,[32] exercising on the campus in time of study hours, throwing peaches about the class room, kicking the door on the outside, sitting on the back of the fences at prayers, throwing copper coins at the professor's head,[33] scattering asafetida in the classroom, riding horses through the halls of the buildings, throwing missiles from the outside into the

---

31. *Journal of the Faculty of the University of North Carolina*, 1849-1855, p. 238.

32. Richard H. Lewis of the class of 1852 reported that in answering the word "Here" to the calling of his name he pronounced the first portion "with the note of a key bugle and the latter a deep bass. It always brought down the house, raising a smile from the placid face of Dr. Mitchell, but ridging a frown on the face of Professor Brown the roll caller, who thought it was a put up job." — Lewis, R. H., "Athletics in the University, Muscular and Vocal, Forty Years Ago," in *North Carolina University Magazine*, November, 1894, p. 100.

33. This happened often in Professor Fetter's room at the University — *Journal of the Faculty of the University of North Carolina*, 1849-1855, p. 69.

classroom, lying down or other improper postures at prayers, especially at the morning service, stopping up the key hole of the recitation room doors, playing with fire balls, refusing to recite, impertinence to the faculty, buffoonery at recitation, throwing acorns on recitation, habitual tardiness, shooting chinquapins during recitation, exploding squills under the recitation room doors, and unscrewing the locks of the recitation room doors and throwing the screws away. Yet in spite of the punishment which the student was to receive, if caught, the practice of irritating the faculty continued to be considered manly and spirited by the students.

Such behavior often led the student to many excesses. John Allen, a student at the University in 1809, stated to President Caldwell that his purpose in throwing a rock at the window before which Caldwell was standing, was not to injure "but rather to irritate and perplex him."[34] A young sophomore by the name of DeRossett was in 1851 "reprimanded for laughing and talking in church."[35] In 1856, Freshman Huggins was admonished for "coaxing a dog after him into the South Building."[36] Junior Morrison was admonished the same time for having "a basket of champagne at Durham's depot" and was "required to place the same in the hands of the President."[37] Badger and Boylan, two students at the University in 1857, who were often guilty of entering the classroom late, each gave as excuse: "I stopped to change my shirt," and if the professor saw fit to argue, each replied, "I am not tardy, my watch is as good as yours."[38] On Friday, September 21, 1860, Hunt, a senior, was caught "in the chapel during the session of the Faculty, in the act of eavesdropping."[39] Two juniors, Taylor and Shorter, were

---

34. *Records of the Faculty of the University of North Carolina,* 1795-1815, p. 197.
35. *Journal of the Faculty of the University of North Carolina,* 1849-55, p. 97.
36. *Journal of the Faculty of the University of North Carolina,* 1856-85, pp. 11-12.
37. *Ibid.,* pp. 11-12.
38. *Ibid.,* p. 117.
39. *Ibid.,* p. 234.

admonished in 1851 for "sporting a dog" in Professor Hubbard's room.[40] Whitaker in this same year "went and stood in the door of Professor Fetter's room, when another class than his own was in attendance." The Professor directed him to retire, and his reply was, "I will go when I get ready."[41] "Highly improper conduct" was the description given to the actions of a group of students who had led a "retreat of the class" from Professor Fetter's room in 1851.[42] Students Ashe and Hughes could not resist the temptation in 1856 to unhitch some farmers' horses which were standing in the street and ride them in a hard gallop out of town and back, as well as answering their names at the morning prayers "through the windows on the outside of the chapel."[43]

In the earlier days of the University, students poked fun at the Frenchman, who taught French, to such an extent that the trustees found it necessary to secure an American to teach the subject. At Davidson, students were active in tying geese to the chairs of the professors and placing rams on the college stage. Stamping in the classroom was a sign to the professor that the lecture was dry or that he was disliked by the students. In 1852, the practive became so bad at the University that an act was passed by the faculty which subjected any student caught in such an act to suspension.[44] Promiscuous applauding in the recitation room or in chapel was also engaged in, to which the Strudwick boys of Hillsboro contributed their part. J. B. Williams, a student at the University in 1851, was noted for his activity in leading "a procession of the Freshman class in the rear of Tutor Brown on his way from the recitation room to evening prayers in the chapel."[45] It was no uncommon thing

40. *Journal of the Faculty of the University of North Carolina,* 1849-55, p. 120.
41. *Ibid.,* p. 121.
42. *Ibid.,* p. 105.
43. *Journal of the Faculty of the University of North Carolina,* 1858-85, p. 70.
44. *Journal of the Faculty of the University of North Carolina,* 1849-55, p. 147.
45. *Ibid.,* p. 125.

for a faculty member to find himself caricatured with black paint on his recitation room door, often with "ridiculous and scandalous imputations."[46] Sometimes a professor took pleasure in chasing a student, as did President Caldwell, who caught Faulkner in the act of building a fence across the street. Three times around the Old East Building they went. Finally, when it appeared that Faulkner would get away, he tripped over a root, and on top of his sprawling body went the President.[47]

War with England in 1812 offered an exceptional opportunity for an outburst of students' feeling at the University. William B. Shepard, a student from Newbern, took the opportunity while delivering a senior speech in Person Hall, to denounce President Chapman, a former Englishman, who was thought to have expressed his feelings too freely. Attempts were made by the faculty to call the young man down, but the students urged him to go on, and he did to a grand climax.

> - - - - and - - - - are men of note,
>   But as for - - - - he's a damned old goat.[48]

This attitude towards President Chapman was still more vividly expressed in a letter addressed to him by a group of students.

Chapel Hill

President Robert Chapman,
Dear Sir,

Having been informed that you are anxious to know why your gate post was decorated with tar and feathers, this is to inform you that it was intended by the patriotic students to deride Toryism and as a monument to the memory of the inspired politician and designing traitor.

In a balmage, Sir of humble tar you will be as secure as pharoah, and in a hieroglyphic of feathers rival in finery all the mummies of Egypt.[49]

---

46. *Ibid.*, p. 88.
47. Hooper, William, *Fifty Years Since, An Address Delivered Before the Alumni Association of the University of North Carolina*, June 1, 1859, p. 28.
48. Creecy, R. B., "University Days Seventy Years Ago" in *North Carolina University Magazine*, December, 1902, p. 95.
49. *Records of the Faculty of the University of North Carolina*, 1795-1815.

198

Too much faculty control and too little student freedom resulted in Manly's being "admonished for playing the fiddle in the front door of the East Building, Sunday afternoon at four o'clock" in 1857 at the University.[50] A graduate of the class of 1858 at Davidson wrote that "in spite of Dr. Lacy's fondness for us, he could not control those industrious associates of his in the Faculty who practiced their schemes upon us, and vied with each other in their extravagant demands upon us, until the greater part, and perhaps the more spirited fellows of us, were so possessed and rushed and hurried and pushed that they left the college in disgust, leaving not a baker's dozen to graduate, and we so exhausted and belittled that we could not reasonably fill the high expectations."[51]

In the field of sports, students found some freedom from the cares of college life. Many students kept dogs in spite of the oppositions of the faculty, and with them and their guns and horses spent much of their leisure time hunting in the woods, chasing rabbits, squirrels, opossums and partridges. Walking was also popular. At the University, the most popular walk led to the "Meeting of the Waters," and here on a large beech tree, which stood at the fork of two small streams, students carved their names. Buggy rides and horse races were participated in by many of the students. There was no serious objection to the teaching of boxing, fencing, single stick, and dancing.[52] Students participated in swimming contests and in such gymnastic contests as "chinning" and drawing up over the bar. The game of marbles was allowed only to seniors at the University.[53] A college band seems to have existed at the University for the records show that those participating in the "College Band" in

50. *Journal of the Faculty of the University of North Carolina*, 1795-1815.

51. Johnston, R. Z., "The Administration of Reverend Drury Lacy, D.D." in *First Semi-Centenary of Davidson College*, June 13, 1887, p. 23.

52. Dancing was not regularly taught at the University until 1850, after which time a Mr. Frensley made annual visits to the Hill.

53. Lewis, McDaniel, "Early Athletics" in *North Carolina University Magazine*, May, 1914, p. 358.

1860 were "released from attendance on morning prayers and recitations during senior speaking week."[54] However, the college boy's attitude toward vocal music was such that the editor of the *North Carolina University Magazine* in 1853 suggested: "Show us a youth that is a good singer at eighteen, and we will show you a foo-foo at forty-five."[55]

Students had an interest in the game of bandy which was pronounced by a graduate of the University in 1894 as being "more ferocious than football."[56] Played in the same manner as it was in the highlands of Scotland, the game was found to be so rough that University officials passed an act in 1803 requiring that no ball should be used by the students "composed of harder materials than wound yarn covered with leather."[57] The game continued to grow in interest, however, and to be played with a wooden ball rather than a ball of yarn. In 1830, President Caldwell of the University reported to the Trustees that as a result of the game of bandy, "Frequent instances have recently occurred, of students knocked apparently lifeless for a time and disabled for many days."[58] Broken arms, broken legs, and broken jawbones were not unknown. James Reid Cole, who attended Trinity College from 1857 to 1861, gave a good description of the game as it was played:

> Imagine 30 or 40 athletes, from 16 to 25 years of age, half on one side and half on the other, with big clubs bent around at the lower end, stretched out facing each other, on the campus — watchful, ready to spring as the leader says, "High Buck or Low Doe", and as the big hard ball is thrown up or down, see them rush upon it withuplifted clubs, and strike right and left crying "Shin on your side", and see them jump in the air to dodge a savage blow, and

---

54. *Journal of the Faculty of the University of North Carolina*, 1856-1885, p. 221.

55. *North Carolina University Magazine*, May, 1853, p. 208.

56. Lewis, R. H., *op. cit.*, p. 99.

57. *Minutes of the Board of Trustees of the University of North Carolina*, 1801-1810, p. 109.

58. *Reports from the Faculty to the Board of Trustees of the University of North Carolina*, 1830-1839, p. 44.

the ball is knocked whirling, and all rush for it, and sticks fly, and hands are hurt, and limbs are bruised, and heads are struck, and still the exciting panting players rush after the ball to gain the victory. It was exciting, it was fun, it was battle, and the weak timid boy was not in it.[59]

Another sport of much interest, but partcipated in much less than that of bandy, was ice skating. On extremely cold winter days when classes were abandoned because of insufficient heat students skated upon the near-by mill ponds. "We have had two holidays to skate," wrote James K. Nisbet to his sister from Chapel Hill on January 25, 1826. He continued by saying that he had attempted to learn skating, that it was "very easy to learn," and that there was no amusement that he ever liked so well.[60] During the first session of the year 1852 at the University on a day which was pronounced too cold to have classes ladies of the neighborhood turned out *en masse* with the students for a skate on the pond. Members of the faculty also were present. A student wrote that the ladies were "provided with a chair and an accommodating gallant to push them about, and wrapped up in furs to protect their delicate forms from the driving blasts . . . ."[61]

The most dominant of all the collegiate interests were the literary societies. To the students the societies offered a democratic form of government in which there was majority control Students had a chance to imitate the state and national legislative bodies, and to set through individual initiative rather than compulsion. The societies also served to develop student loyalty, student cooperation and student competition.

In time, there grew up at each of the institutions for higher education in the state two societies. Society work at the University began on June 3, 1795, when "The Debating Society" was organized by a group of students with the help of the faculty. Soon it was found that competition was desirable for the promotion of interest in society work; the result was the or-

59. Cole, R. J., *Miscellany*, p. 253.
60. *Chapel Hill Weekly*, March 15, 1929.
61. Lewis, McDaniel, *op. cit.*, p. 359.

ganization of the "Concord Society" on August 1, 1795. By the end of the following year, the two societies had taken on new names, the mother society becoming known as the Dialectic and the Concord as the Philanthropic, names which are still retained. At Wake Forest, the Euzelian and the Philomathesian societies were organized in February, 1835. The Ecumenican and Philanthropic societies of Davidson were organized in June, 1837; while at Trinity there were the Columbia and the Hesperian societies, organized in June, 1846, and June, 1851, respectively.

These societies soon grew to power and prominence in the institutions in which they existed, as their role of alumni and members increased. So small was "The Debating Society" at the time of its organization at the University that two objections were sufficient to reject an applicant for membership. The membership fee was only twenty-five cents, and the library, which consisted of only a few musty volumes, was contributed by those who had already joined the society.[62] But by 1834, the University societies had become so strong that Charles Manly concluded in an address delivered before the senior class and the alumni of the institution:

> Your societies, young gentlemen, are identified with this University. They have become great arteries in the system, indispensable to its vitality. Without your active cooperation, the laws of the college are impotent, and nugatory. The dread of your displeasure carries more terror than all the majesty of the laws and the authority of the Faculty and the Trustees combined; you are emphatically an "imperium in imperio," a power behind the throne greater than the throne itself." There is not an individual in this assembly, acquainted with this place, who does not know that what I say is true.[63]

At the denominational schools, such a power on the part of the societies was much less evident for the membership was small-

---

62. "Sketches of the History of the Dialectic Literary Society" in *Catalogue of Members of the Dialectic Society, p. 5.*
63. Manly, Charles, *An Address Delivered Before the Alumni and the Senior Class of the University of North Carolina,* June, 1838, p. 15.

er; there was more faculty control, and membership was determined by choosing from the student body by lot. The usual run of officers included a President, Vice-President, Secretary, Treasurer, Censor, Librarian, Supervisor, Reader, Senior and Junior Critic or Correctors, and various committees. Terms of office were for a period of six weeks.

The activities of the societies were many and varied. Their chief activity was public speaking. In 1878, it was said in the presentation of the Heck-Williams Building at Wake Forest where the two societies were located: "Here young men are taught to write with accuracy and speak with power, and in after life to wield the pen and use the rostrum for the progress of truth and advancement of the kingdom of Heaven."[64] At the University, the chief end was training for political life. In general, the weekly program of all the societies consisted of debates, declamations, essays and dissertations, and was usually carried out in the evening. In some cases meetings were semiweekly, in which case one of the meetings was on Saturday morning. Students often spoke with boldness and fervor, and sometimes with skill and wit. It was said of Zebulon B. Vance: "His wit and humor always lengthened the list of fines whenever he spoke — and the treasury grew fat; for who could resist laughing."[65]

The subjects discussed by the members of the societies were very varied. Here students were at their best and in some cases showed clear thinking on the problems of the day, sometimes tinged with sectionalism. In a speech on "Youth," delivered before the Dialectic Literary Society in 1806, A. M. Rogers asserted: "To set for oneself is the inherent principle of every man. It is confirmed by experience; whilst in the affairs of life, has been made indispensable. Nothing contributes more to enliven in youth, brilliant expectations of happiness, than the idea of becoming the complete master of his own actions."[66] John

64. Williams, C. B., A History of the Baptists in North Carolina, p. 95.
65. Lewis, R. H., "A Brief History of the Dialectic Society, 1848-1852" in Catalogue of Members of the Dialectic Society, p. 14.
66. Addresses of the Dialectic Society, Vol. IV, P to Y, p. 113.

Williams, speaking before the same society in the same year on "The Nature of Man," felt that "To unfurl and discover to mankind the great number of indolent thoughtless actions attending the youth of the present age could not fail to make them blush and revolt from the present neglect of improving and cultivating their minds."[67] In an excellent speech on "The Benefits of Reading" in November, 1830, Thomas P. Pitchford, of the Dialectic Society, declared: "Letters cherish and invigorate the mind in its greener years and amuze at a more advanced period of life. The acquisition of a new idea will give a greater ornament to the head than any dress we can bestow upon it."[68]

Almost every imaginable question was discussed pro and con in the society debates. In 1800, the Philanthropic Society of the University decided that marriage was very advantageous to a community and that the flood was not universal but was confined to a single country.[69] In 1812, the Dialectic Society decided that a public education was more desirable than a private education, that late marriage was the better, that it was more laudable to advocate justice than mercy, and that a woman who had lost her chastity should at times be admitted into respectable society. In 1813, the same society decided that capital punishment should not be inflicted for stealing a horse. In 1814, it was decided that North Carolina should establish a penitentiary, that the slaves should be emancipated, and that wealth was a greater enemy to virtue than poverty. In 1815, the minds of females were decided to be as susceptible to learning as those of males. H. C. Jones wrote from Chapel Hill on August 14, 1816, to Major Abraham Staples that his society had just discussed the question "Do we experience more pleasure from contemplating the works of nature or of art?" He had taken the side of nature and among other things had said in his speech that "no painter nor sculpturer can produce in the mind of man that exquisite sensation which is produced in the mind

67. *Ibid.*, p. 455.
68. *Ibid.*, pp. 3-4.
69. *Minutes of the Philanthropic Literary Society*, 1799-1803.

of the lover from contemplating the fascinating charms of his dulcinea."[70] He won the debate.

In 1817, the Dialectic Society decided that it would be consistent with the policy of the United States to encourage agriculture and to discourage domestic manufactures, and that it would not be wise to establish a colony of free blacks in the Northwest Territory. Opposition was raised to a standing army in 1818 on the grounds that it was not conducive to the most good in a republican form of government. Students of both the University societies during the year 1818 decided that North Carolina should erect schools for the public education of the poor. In 1848, the Philanthropic society of the University discussed the question: "Does Congress have the power to exclude slavery from the territories?" and decided in favor of the negative.[71] During this same year at Wake Forest, the students of the Euzelian Society were discussing the question: "Will the Roman Catholic Religion ever prevail in this country?"[72] The Hesperian Society of Normal College in 1851 discussed the question whether virtue had more of an effect on man than a classical education and voted strongly in the affirmative. At the Davidson societies, about the same time, the question "Is love voluntary?" was being discussed. Other subjects discussed dealt with "perserverance," "law," "natural rights," "denominationalism as conducive to Christianity," "the worthlessness of a miser or a spendthrift," "Should a man be allowed to whip his wife?" "Is slavery a blessing or a curse?" This last question was not debated after 1845.

Outside of the regular program, the societies attempted to keep the campus clean, beautify it, repair the walks, plant shrubbery, elect and pay for commencement speakers, provide a band at commencement, sponsor the commencement dances,

70. *Reports from the Faculty to the Board of Trustees of the University of North Carolina,* 1809-1829, p. 291.

71. *Records of the Philanthropic Society of the University of North Carolina,* 1847-1853, p. 124.

72. *The First Records of the Euzelian Society of Wake Forest,* 1835-1852, p. 301.

and aid in the financing of the college buildings. And in 1852, the Philanthropic Society of the University contributed $25 for the purchase of a hearse for the use of the college and the village. But the societies were especially active in building up libraries.

Library interest was largely promoted by the keen rivalry which existed between the two societies of each institution, and often led to the duplication of many books. If money were not available from membership fees and fines, members went out and begged for books wherever they could find them. On one occasion, the libraries of the literary societies of Wake Forest secured books valued at $800.[73] A member of each society was hired as a librarian who kept the library open one hour twice a week. At the University the society libraries far surpassed the University library throughout the whole *ante-bellum* period. Such magazines and papers as the *American Review, Democratic Review, Merchant's Magazine,* and the *Southern Literary Messenger* were regularly subscribed to by the society libraries. Books with beautiful bindings were preferred. In 1814, the Dialectic Society voted to sell all the old Greek and Latin books in its library and to purchase other books.[74] Henry Barnard, a New England Yankee, who made a tour of the South Atlantic States in 1833, wrote to his brother from Chapel Hill on March 25: "Was invited by several to visit the libraries — did so — the dialectic is one of the finest I have ever seen. I noticed mostly all very fine standards works — English works — English Editions and in English binding — several portraits of members who have become distinguished — visited the Philanthropic library — about the same no. of volumes — but less splendidly bound and many new books."[75]

As disciplinary agencies, the societies of the University came to exert a more powerful influence on the students than the

73. Paschal, G. W., "A History of Wake Forest College" in *Bulletin of Wake Forest College,* November, 1926, p. 51.
74. *Minutes of the Dialectic Literary Society 1812-1818,* p. 112.
75. Barnard, Henry, *The South Atlantic States in 1833,* p. 327. A more detailed discussion of the libraries will be found in Chapter V.

faculty. J. Bryan Grimes wrote from Chapel Hill in August, 1847, to J. Johnston Pettigrew, Washington, D.C., that boys on being called before the societies for trial "often burst into tears."[76] In all the college societies, a general check was kept on each member's deportment in the classroom and on the campus. The police work was usually done by secret monitors or committees, and cases were handled by expulsion, reprimand, suspension, and fines. At Davidson, members who were "found guilty of intoxicaion or lying to the faculty were fined heavily for the first offense and expelled if the action was repeated."[77] When the chapel bell was destroyed at Davidson in 1849, the Philanthropic Society put all its members under oath to tell what they knew.

The records of the societies are replete with the fines and punishments imposed upon members. John L. Graves, tried before the Dialectic Society of the University in 1812, was found guilty of breaking the society laws and was suspended for a term of three months. In 1815, Durant A. Hall was expelled for robbing the treasury of the same society. James Sampson was tried in the same year for card playing and was declared guilty. The fines for James Patrick in 1817, totaling seventy cents, were for "spitting amber on the floor." Robert C. Clopton at the same time was fined twenty-five cents for not wearing stockings in the society hall, while Charles G. Rose was fined in the same amount for speaking a speech too often in the society. In 1818, the Dialectic Society concluded in a resolution "That a wilful violation of the decorum of college (sic) such as throwing stones through the passages, scrapping feet or such like conduct, subjects any member to admonition from the president, and if persisted in to suspension."[78] Fines became so numerous that it was found necessary to keep them in a special account book, and it was not unusual for them to total more than $50 a head annually. During the year 1858-1859, the fines of Thomas P.

---

76. *Bryan Grimes Papers*, 1844-1863, Vol. I, p. 12.
77. Shaw, C. R., *op. cit.*, p. 254.
78. *Minutes of the Dialectic Society*, 1812-1818, p. 289.

Bonner totaled $70.25.[79] Fines in the Dialectic Society for March, 1859, totaled more than $110.[80] Five dollars was the fine for not paying all the society dues at the end of each session at the University. To be caught reading a book in church, which was not connected with the services, there was a fine of $2.00, while to leave the church unnecessarily, there was a fine of only $1.00. Twenty-five cents was the fine for failure to wear a sock or cravat at the society meetings. Casting personal reflections on a member, or disrespect to the hall, subjected the guilty one to a fine of $1.00. For urinating out of one of the college buildings there was a fine of fifty cents, while only twenty-five cents was the fine for urinating against a tree within ten feet of the college. The smallest fine at the University was ten cents and was levied on that member who was guilty of leaning his chair against the "mantle (sic) piece." In 1835, at Wake Forest, it was "Resolved that the fine for sleep during the session of the society be reduced from twenty-five cents to five cents."[81]

Sometimes members were prone to create frivolity and amusement in the society halls, and then to deny the charge of misconduct, but usually the societies were administered with much dignity and grace. The president, who was always a first honor senior, sat in a large velvet-covered chair on a raised platform, regaled in a large beaver hat, and carried a gold-headed cane as an emblem of authority. During the year the freshman "felt crushed to the earth when in attendance, and he hardly dared call his soul his own. The lordly senior had everything his own way, and brooked no opposition from any of a lower class."[82] There was an elaborate ritual and heavy fines were imposed upon those who revealed any secrets of the society. At the end of each meeting of the Columbian Literary Society at Trinity

79. *Record of the Fines imposed by the Philanthropic Society*, 1856-1858, p. 237.
80. *Minutes of the Dialectic Society, 1856-1867*, p. 161.
81. *The First Records of the Euzelian Society*, Wake Forest, 1835-1852, p. 27.
82. Lewis, R. H., *op. cit.*, p. 14.

all members had to rise and fold their arms across their breasts as a sign of perfect harmony. If any members were offended, they should hold their arms at their sides.[83] The Philanthropic Society of the University was horrified when it learned on July 31, 1848, that a woman of disreputable character had been wearing one of its badges. The committee in reporting the affair said in words: "Can you behold with untinged cheek our motto upon such prostitute wretches, 'Virtue, Liberty and Science.' Virtue upon one whose whole life has been spent in entrapping virtue, Liberty upon one who has ever been a slave to passion, Science upon one whose only science is the art of alluring unhappy admirers."[84] Nor did the societies hesitate to reprimand the faculty when they deemed it necessary. In 1816, a committee was appointed by the Dialectic Society to investigate and inquire into "some disrespectful observations" made by Mr. Chapman, President of the University "concerning some proceedings of the Dialectic Society."[85] In 1839, the Philanthropic Society sanctioned a letter sent by some senior members of their group to the faculty protesting against the refusal of the faculty to grant Mr. Maultsby first distinction in the coming commencement. Members of the society further asserted that they would take no part in the coming commencement unless justice was granted to their fellow member.[86]

Membership fees varied from $1.00 at the Hesperian Society at Trinity to $10.00 in the societies of the University (1857). A literary fee of $2.00 each quarter was also levied in the University societies. A comparison between the funds collected by the University societies and those of Wake Forest is shown in the treasurers' reports. In 1848, the treasurer of the Philanthropic Society of the University reported a balance of $1491.37 as

---

83. Barnard, W., "The Columbian Literary Society" in *Trinity Alumni Register*, October, 1915, p. 169.
84. *Records of the Philanthropic Society of the University of North Carolina*, 1847-1853, p. 72.
85. *Minutes of the Dialectic Society*, 1812-1818, p. 183.
86. *Minutes of the Faculty of the University of North Carolina*, 1821-1841, pp. 372-374.

compared with a report of $33.75 at the Euzelian Society of Wake Forest in 1850. Expenditures were for books, diplomas, candles, candlesticks and snuffers, paper, and tombstones. In 1816, the Dialectic Society advanced $50 to Simon P. Jordan to help pay his board bill in the community. Interest was also taken in fixing up the society halls. In the earlier days of the University, the societies met in the little old chapel, Person Hall, with no fire in the winter and the "north wind pouring through many a broken pane,"[87] but by 1861 new halls, adorned in silk and tassel, had been provided in the New West and New East buildings. A similar development was also noticeable at the denominational schools. The society halls at Wake Forest were pronounced in 1878 as the most attractive in the South.[88] Expenditures for portraits of members who had become distinguished totaled more than $5000, that of James K. Polk alone costing $341.50. Portraits of other great *ante-bellum* North Carolina leaders, such as William R. Davie, W. R. King, Willie P. Mangum, George K. Badger, James C. Dobbin, David L. Swain, Joseph Caldwell, and Elisha Mitchell still adorn the society halls. In 1852, the Philanthropic Society of Davidson had painted the portrait of President Williams of that institution. Diplomas and seals, awarded for membership and for honors and worn at commencement with much gusto, also called for a large expenditure in the budget.

Students took much pride in, and were jealous of, their societies. Those members who had become famous in the world were often written to and heard from. James K. Polk, writing to the Dialectic Society from Washington on March 15, 1847, said: "I remember with pleasure my association with our common and hallowed fraternity — the Dialectic Society, and though nearly twenty-nine years have elapsed, since I closed my connection with it, I am deeply sensible of the great value of the instruction which I derived from its exercises."[89] Members of one society witnessed with great pleasure the intoxication of a

---

87. Hooper, William, *op. cit.,* p. 7.
88. Williams, C. B., *A History of the Baptists in North Carolina,* p. 95.
89. *Autographs, Manuscripts,* University of North Carolina Library.

member of the other, and an honor to any member was also considered an honor to the society to which he belonged. Sometimes false reports would be circulated by a member of the society against the other society or a member thereof. A resolution passed by the Dialectic Society February 18, 1816, said in part that the report which had "circulated respecting the D.S.'s promising and failing to concur with them (Philanthropic Society) in some improper conduct during last session was without any foundation in truth."[90] Competition between the two societies in each institution became so strong at times that jealousy and antipathy arose between the members of each. The *Biblical Recorder* reported on September 7, 1835, referring to the two societies at Wake Forest: "Jealousies arose and then antipathies; and hostilities were finally carried so far as to divide the brethren of the same profession. This state of things became quite alarming." In 1839, the Philanthropic Society of the University, feeling itself imposed upon because the faculty had monopolized some of its property (rooms), reported to the faculty that it was much aggrieved because the Dialectic Society had not been treated in a like manner.[91] A heated argument over the question of rooms also developed at Davidson in 1850 with the Philanthropic Society threatening to "secede as a body" from the institution unless justice were granted.[92]

Sometimes breaks came, between members of the same society, usually over the question as to how far the society should go in enforcing the laws of the institution. In 1838, groups of members withdrew from the societies at the University, set up the Delphian Society, and appealed to the faculty for recognition on the grounds that the existing division of the societies promoted sectionalism. An investigation revealed that the members who had withdrawn had done so because of the provisions in the constitutions of the societies which required regular attendance at prayers and at recitations. The plea was not

90. *Minutes of the Dialectic Literary Society*, 1812-1818, p. 195.
91. *Minutes of the Faculty of the University of North Carolina*, 1821-1841, p. 389.
92. Shaw, C. R., *op. cit.*, p. 252.

granted; in fact, no third society was permitted at any of the institutions.

Failure to produce a division in the societies was in part responsible for the organization of many small secret clubs among the more mischievously inclined students. During the year 1838, the University faculty held several meetings in an attempt to cope with a strange society which had been organized secretly by a group of students. It was called the "Ugly Club," and was primarily interested in creating some kind of disturbance on or off the campus during the night hours. There was also the "Boring Club," the principal purpose of which was to enable the members to make themselves familiar "with all the paths of vice, in the college for fun and frolic — to gratify appetite, and to study human nature."[93] In 1850, the "G.A.V." club was organized at the University, and if the "Sons of Temperance" (organized in 1829 to bring about prohibition in the institution) may be believed, its main purposes were drinking and swearing. The situation became so bad by 1855 that the University officials found it necessary to require every entering student to sign a pledge that he would not associate himself with the "Ugly Club" or any similar riotous club. The entrance of the chartered fraternities marked a decreasing interest in these clubs.

In the early spring of 1842, an attempt was made to establish a chapter of the Mystical Seven Fraternity at the University, but the opposition of the societies and the faculty was so strong that the Board of Trustees on December 12, 1842, passed a "regula generalis" on the subject, opposing all secret organizations on the grounds that they were injurious to the societies and detrimental to the cause of good morals and sound learning.[94] For a time there was peace, but April 5, 1851, the Beta Chapter of the Delta Kappa Epsilon, the first national chapter

---

93. Johnson, H. V., "A Sketch of the Fraternities of the University of North Carolina" in *North Carolina University Magazine,* February, 1816, p. 85.

94. *Minutes of the Board of Trustees of University of North Carolina,* 1841-68, p. 35.

212

to enter the University, was organized. By 1861, it had 118 members. Other chapters followed: Epsilon Chapter of Phi Gamma Delta, 1851 (died in 1854); Eta of Beta Theta Pi, 1852 (extinct in 1859); Xi chapter of Delta Psi, 1854 (very popular — but died in 1862); Kappa of Delta Phi and Sigma of Chi Psi, 1855 (both died during the war); Lamda of Phi Kappa Sigma, 1856; Xi (grand) chapter of Sigma Alpha Epsilon, 1857 (extinct in 1861); Mu Chapter of Theta Delta Chi, 1857; Zeta Psi and Alpha Chapter of Chi Phi, 1858 (both lived through the war but died during Reconstruction days).[95] Members of the Delta Kappa Epsilon were best known as polite gentlemen who had a disregard and contempt for dull textbooks, who read the fashionable literature of the day, and who appeared in public adorned with canes, gloves, and "ponderous chains" and walked with painful rigidity. The members of Phi Gamma Delta cultivated "with untiring care and diligence the beauty of their complexions, whiskers and teeth."[96] The members of Eta of Beta Theta Pi were best known for love of pancakes, pies, and ham and eggs. Such organizations were marking the way for the decreasing power of the societies, and during the years from 1856 to 1861, they overshadowed every other student activity at the University. Opposition from the societies was strong and bitter. John Smith, speaking before one of the societies, said that they were "hot beds of faction and small vices."[97] There was also criticism against their initiations which were quite severe and terrorizing. In 1856, the February number of the North Carolina University Magazine was dedicated to the freshman class as a "shield and a buckler against the allurements of the fraternities."

There were still minor organizations of various kinds. A cir-

95. Apparently no fraternities were organized in the denominational schools during the ante-bellum period. An attempt was made to organize the Chi Phi fraternity at Davidson in 1859, "but it was evidently sub rosa." — Shaw, C. R., op. cit., p. 261.
96. Williamson, Gibbon, "The History of ;Clubs in the University of North Carolina" in North Carolina University Magazine, February, 1856, p. 25.
97. Ibid., p. 20.

cular sent out by the University Board of Trustees in 1812 stated that "a society had been lately constituted for the cultivation of sacred music, and an organ is now probably finished in New York for the use of this society."[98] During the period from 1825 to 1860, missionary and temperance clubs were established at all the colleges. There were the "Temperance Club" organized at the University in 1829, the "Anti-Tobacco Society" at Wake Forest in 1835, and the "William Society of Missionary Inquiry" at Davidson in 1833. In 1848, a "Law Club" was organized at the University, which died after only a year's existence. The third of the college Y.M.C.A.'s was organized at the University in 1860, but it came too late to create much interest or to do any effective work before the war.

In the field of student newspapers, little interest was taken and the sole attempt is represented by the publication of the *North Carolina University Magazine*. Begun in March, 1844, by an active group of seniors with the aid of President Swain, it was discontinued after nine issues because of a lack of support. In 1852, the publication of the magazine was taken up again and was continued until May, 1861. Those who had been most instrumental in the publication of the magazine had hoped that it would be of great advantage to the University and to the State, and President Swain thought that it might act as a repository for valuable historical papers. But interest was found wanting. The first issue of the magazine led off with an article on "American Poetry" which was later pronounced "a little too Scotch to be natural" as "Burns himself might have needed a glossary for it."[99] There was much of Revolutionary and Colonial history, some poetry, and eight pages of uninteresting foreign news. Later issues, however, showed a closer connection to student life.

Students found some interest in celebrating the holidays. On Thanksgiving, February 22, and July 4, all exercises at the University were suspended with the exception of morning and eve-

---

98. *Raleigh Register,* December 18, 1812, p. 3.
99. Spencer, C. P., "Old Days in Chapel Hill" in *North Carolina University Magazine,* February, 1888, p. 61.

ning prayers. On February 23, 1801, A. D. Murphey wrote from Chapel Hill to John Scott, Orange County: "Yesterday being the birthday of George Washington was celebrated by the young gentlemen of the University in a way suitable to the occasion of the Day. Agreeable to their request, the Faculty have suspended Business on this day, in order to have a ball in the evening."[100] On July 4, 1804, the students by ballot selected Thomas Brown, a student, to deliver the Independence Day oration. Regaled in his cocked hat and dancing red plume, and followed by the students, he marched by drum and fife up to Davie Poplar, where a platform had been built for him, for the delivery of his speech. This honor was one of the greatest aspirations of a freshman. At Wake Forest, Independence Day of 1835 was celebrated by music, marching, the carrying of banners, oratory, reading of the Declaration of Independence, and prayer. It was reported that after lunch the young people were allowed to feast on raisins and lemonade,[101] and at night there was a vivid display of fire works.

The most attractive of all days to the student was commencement day. Even the Negroes and children put on their best clothes for this gala affair, when belles and "rose bud debutantes" flocked from all parts of the state. As the years passed, attendance at all the college commencements showed an increase. The *Raleigh Register* of May 28, 1833, said of the University commencement: "The houses of the village were thronged and crowded until they would hold no more."[102] To many a student, commencement must have been approached with pleasure and with fear. There was the thought of the oral examinations before the members of the Board of Trustees, faculty and any visitors who might wish to attend. For these who had to give orations and declamations there was the fear of the rostrum. On the other hand, there was the pleasure of seeing the crowd and the "fair damsels," of hearing the speeches, of dancing, and, in the case of seniors, of gradua-

100. *Murphey Papers*, 1797-1817, Vol. I, p. 3.
101. Paschal, G. W., *op. cit.*, p. 47.
102. *Raleigh Register*, May 28, 1833, p. 3.

tion. As the editor of the *Raleigh Register* of June 7, 1837 expressed it:

> It is the first young buddings of fame to a collegian, to see, on Commencement Day, an ocean of bonnets and ribbons and the banks of snowy gauze waving and rustling at his appearance, as if the gentle South had breathed upon a wheat field; but it is the full bloom of popularity, if when he returns, he shall see the ocean toss with emotion that rolls deep beneath its surface.[103]

Preparation for the commencement, which usually lasted at least four days, was started months ahead of time. The literary societies busied themselves securing a band and the commencement speakers. There was also the problem of selecting marshals, ball managers, students for the delivery of the orations and declamations, — the salutatory of which was given in Latin Occasionally, these were Greek and French addresses.[104] But probably the most tiring activity of all was studying for the oral examinations.

With the arrival of commencement, students marched out to meet their guests, having been notified of their coming by a watchman who had been stationed out some distance on the road leading to the campus. On Monday evening, ordinarily the time selected for the opening event, a sermon was delivered before the graduating class, which was followed on Tuesday evening by freshmen competing in oratory. Wednesday morning and afternoon were set aside for the delivery of the addresses before the societies, alumni associations (after 1843 at the University and 1848 at Davidson), and other organizations, such as the Historical Association at the University after 1844.[105] On Wednesday night, there was the usual exhibition

---

103. *Raleigh Register*, June 6, 1837, p. 3.
104. *Reports from the Faculty to the Board of Trustees of the University of North Carolina*, 1809-1829, p. 562.
105. The failure of Judge Mason, University Commencement speaker of 1842, to arrive led to a unique commencement feature which consisted of a series of successful experiments performed by Dr. Mitchell, Professor of Chemistry at the University, with an electro-magnetic ap-

(Footnote 105 continued on next page)

216

of the sophomore class. Thursday was the big day. In the morning, there was sacred music and prayer, followed by the Latin salutatory. There followed declamations and orations, often written and delivered with much skill and frankness. William Bingham, in delivering his senior speech on "The People and Their Common Schools" at the University commencement of 1856, spoke of the North Carolina school teacher as being "some thick-skulled dunderhead who has not sense enough to run off a straight row, or make a horse shoe."[106] W.D. Williamson, Congressman from Maine, who visited the University Commencement of 1843, said, "The compositions exhibited undoubted marks of genius and maturity of style; and the speaking was energetic and graceful."[107] In the afternoon of Thursday following another group of speeches, the annual report of the institution was given, degrees were conferred, and honors and prizes were awarded.[108] Finally, came the valedictory, sacred music, and the benediction.

With other things out of the way, the commencement dance began on Thursday evening at eight o'clock and lasted until past three o'clock in the morning. At the University, the dance was quite an elaborate affair after the building of Smith Hall in 1850. As a rule the orchestra was composed of a group of fiddling Negroes, Frank Johnson's being the most noted at the University. Orders from the ball room came fast and furious.

(Footnote 105 continued from last page)

paratus. "The audience did not retire until they had been gratified by a novel, instructive and entertaining exhibition." — Tarboro Press, June 18, 1842.

106. Senior Speeches of the University of North Carolina, 1856, Manuscript, p. 239.

107. Williamson, W. D., "University of North Carolina" in Hillsboro Recorder, February 1, 1844, p. 2.

108. John B. Jasper, writing from Chapel Hill on July 10, 1804 to his Uncle Mr. James Bryan, Newbern, N.C.; "I received the money which I wrote you for. In the senior class of the preparatory John Brown, Alex Foster, and myself were distinguished. . . . I was distinguished but I do declare that I was deserving of better distinction than that which I obtained." — John H. Bryan Papers, 1773-1825, Vol. I, p. 26.

"Promenade All," "Ladies to the Center," "Turn Corners," etc
In the earlier days of the University, President Caldwell was
said to have "danced in pumps and knee breeches."[109] There
was a flash of "gay equipages, gorgeous sashes, and fine raiment (including tight boots and other agonies."[110] "Dancing
was of the pigeon-wing order with a gravity that was almost
severe,"[111] and the only fear which seems to have obsessed the
male dancers was that of being chained to a "wall-flower."[112]
The editor of the *North Carolina University Magazine* wrote of
the commencement dance at the University in 1853: "Many
were the conquests made by Beauty, under the chandeliers
and corn crested columns of the new library. And we hope
that in some instances at least, captivity was led captive."[113]

Outstanding among the University commencements was that
of 1847 which was attended by President James K. Polk, John
Y. Mason, Secretary of the Navy, and Thomas J. Greene of Virginia. J. Johnston Pettigrew, writing of the occasion to his
friend J. Bryan Grimes, said: "Swain was considerably fright-
ened, and made a rambling speech about the comparative merits of Tennessee and North Carolina."[114] Young Pettigrew also
took special notice of Miss Betty Mason, daughter of the Secretary of Navy, saying that she was "quite beautiful with nice
sparkling eyes," Miss Rucker, niece of the President, appeared
to be "very good looking." Of the dances which took place in
Steward's Hall, he complained of the music as being too martial
(a band had been secured from Richmond, Virginia), and the
pieces too short. Visitors had come from different parts of the
state, at least sixteen from Fayetteville, and Gerrard Hall was
crowded with women, but to young Pettigrew the majority of

---

109. Spencer, C. P., *Pen and Ink Sketches of the University of North
Carolina as It Has Been;* — p. 12.
110. Waddell, A. M., *Ante-bellum University, Oration Delivered at the
Centennial of the University of North Carolina,* June 5, 1895, p. 14.
111. *Ibid.,* p. 13.
112. Battle, K. P., *op. cit.,* p. 571.
113. *North Carolina University Magazine,* August, 1853, p. 300.
114. *Bryan Grimes Papers,* 1844-1863, Vol. I, p. 9.

them were not beautiful.[115] Quite a different report was given by the reporter of the *New York Herald* who was very impressed by the whole commencement. The welcome given to President Polk by student Matt. W. Ranson in the salutatory was pronounced "Superior to anything of the kind throughout the whole expedition . . .while the beauty and the finished elegance of the welcome to the ladies drew down upon his devoted head repeated rounds of applause, the people outside heartily joining in; but the ivory of five hundred of the fair of Old Rip Van Winkle was also unanimously exhibited, a still more flattering testimonial of their approbation. Some of them, indeed, as Sam Slick would say, 'snickered right out.' "[116]

In sum, the *ante-bellum* collegiate interests were many and varied. In the absence of any organized system of athletics, students found the most attractive sports in hunting and the game called bandy. A still smaller group took special delight in playing every possible kind of prank on the faculty. Throughout the whole period, however, there was a tendency for the literary societies to dominate the interests of the more serious students, even to the extent of acting as disciplinary agencies for the faculty. Interest in fraternities failed to develop at any of the denominational schools, and not at the University until the last decade before the war; however, an extreme interest was manifested in the organization of minor clubs throughout the whole period. The art of letter writing had not been lost. Student publications were hardly attempted, as nothing but a religious or a political paper could have prospered. The *North Carolina University Magazine* was published for a brief period, but was never very successful. Independence Day, Thanksgiving, and Washington's birthday were celebrated, but the climax of interest was found in the college commencement with its examinations, orations, graduations, and gorgeous balls.

---

115. *Ibid.*, p. 9.
116. *North Carolina University Magazine*, March, 1907, p. 224, contains all the accounts published in the *New York Herald* on President Polk's visit to the University in 1847.

VII

Manners and Morals

North Carolina in the early *ante-bellum* period was still a frontier community with frontier problems, manners, and modes of living. Life among the students, just as life among the people of the state at large, was crude. Many students at the University and the other colleges in the state doubtless conformed to the laws of these institutions and the ideals of those in authority. But not all were of this kind. Some, to be sure, would have been more or less mannerly without the compulsion of law; but many fell into a laxity of manners and morals and revolted against the requirements of the academic communities in which they were temporarily settled.[1] This condition prevailed in all of the colleges. The "minutes of the faculty" of the various institutions are replete with instances of stealing, cheating, gambling, drinking, fighting, and sexual immorality. T. H Hamilton, a student at Davidson, wrote in a letter dated October 7, 1837:

> There is one thing I can say without any doubt on the subject that under such means of grace as we here enjoy, we shall either grow in grace or increase fearfully in wickedness. A man here who is a Christian must be one indeed. There is no chance for middle ground. There are a number of pious young men here and nearly all the in-

---

1. An interesting discussion of the student's attitude toward the old classical curriculum will be found in Jordan, David Starr, *The Trend of the American University,* pp. 1-10.

fluential students are pious, but there are many here who are growing up the farthest advanced in wickedness according to age that I ever saw. I think there could not be much worse found in the state. They will not work nor study and for mischief they are always ready. They are saucy and impudent and in short the general part of them are destitute of every moral principle.[2]

The *North Carolina Presbyterian* of March 19, 1858 stated: "It is a reproach to our land that it should ever be so with our colleges, that instead of being places of piety, one cannot send a child thither without great danger of his morals." Braxton Craven, president of Normal College and later of Trinity, who was much worried by the questionable habits among the students in his institution, wrote: "It has long been the custom in Southern colleges for students to have a code of regulations and morals peculiar to themselves. According to this code, they may practice all dissipation, depredations, play tricks and then club together for concealment, and if one should divulge anything, he is insulted and scoffed."[3] President Caldwell of the University expressed a similar opinion in a report to the board of trustees in 1830, when he said that rebellious students encouraged and fortified one another. "They naturally become banded together against authority and good order and studious of all secret or open methods of evading or resisting the laws."[4] W. A. Graham stated that intoxication by whiskey had "occasioned more scandal to the University than all other causes combined."[5] But these practices were not confined to the South alone, for Henry Barnard, a visitor to Chapel Hill in 1833, wrote in a letter to his brother on March 25: "It was for a long time doubted in the North whether anything like college discipline could be maintained at the South, but I did not observe any difference be-

2. Shaw, C. R., *Davidson College*, p. 31.
3. Brooks, E. C., "Braxton Craven and Trinity College" in *Trinity Alumni Register*, January, 1916, p. 254.
4. *Reports from the Faculty to the Board of Trustees of the University of North Carolina*, 1830-1839, p. 43.
5. *Journal of the Faculty of the University of North Carolina*, 1856-85, p. 107.

tween the habits of the students here and at Yale — except
that in the boasted land of refinement their manners are more
rough and their dress even vulgarly plain . . . . a more raw set
of fellows you don't see often collected."[6]

There was much of crudeness and conceit in college students
of this period. Often a stranger who was attempting to give a
program of music or a lecture was hissed by the students who
also generally indulged in other expressions of contempt. Much
shouting and yelling always marked their departure from a
building. Students also refused to attend class if the regular
professor did not attend. In 1859, twenty-five students at the
University refused to make up the Bible lesson they "fessed on
Sunday" and were expelled.[7] The seniors in the same institution
in 1835 insisted upon having their commencement ball, not
withstanding the recent death of President Caldwell, and the
trustees, horrified, pained, and mortified by the behavior of
the seniors, were moved to pass a resolution prohibiting the
festivities "for the approaching commencement."[8] Such names
as "Old Bull (Phillips at the University), and "Old Bunk" (Pres
ident Swain) were used by students to describe members of
the faculty. Students chewed their tobacco and spat the juice
in whatever places seemed most convenient, to the annoyance
of college officials, particularly the librarians of the literary societies. The day of the cigarette had not yet arrived, but the
plug was used quite frequently and, on special occasions, the
cigar. Table manners were likewise rough. A charge was
brought against Charles Wright, a student at the University in
1807, for "appropriating a whole fowl to himself" and for carrying off "a portion of victuals from the table."[9] Students also
used their knives often, particularly in their attempts to eat

---

6. Barnard, Henry, "The South Atlantic States in 1833" in *Maryland
Historical Magazine*, September, 1918, pp. 324-326.

7. *Journal of the Faculty of the University of North Carolina*, 1856-85,
p. 182.

8. *Minutes of the Executive Committee of the University of North
Carolina*, 1835-1873, p. 12.

9. *Faculty Record of the University of North Carolina*, 1795-1815, p. 144.

peas. Eating was rapid and generally without conversation. At times, the diet was not appetizing; it consisted generally of corn bread, middling meat, collards, and milk for dinner. Beef was sometimes the meat but it was not always sanitary.[10] The manner of dining was described by D. B. Wood, who wrote from Davidson in 1841: "A tin horn was sounded for the different meals. A blessing was asked, and when *amen* was said not a biscuit was left on the plates."[11]

Although the general appearance of the students was not altogether attractive, the dress of many of them frequently reflected acquaintance with fitness and fashion. Long curly hair, goatee, and moustache were often in evidence.[12] A graduate of Davidson in 1843 wrote: "The students dressed quite commonly on week days — some better on Sundays. Many of them were of limited means and not able to dress in much style."[13] Rough and crudely made shoes were generally worn by those of less wealth and in many cases, particularly in the absence of a village shoemaker, boys found it necessary to go barefooted. Patched pantaloons were not uncommon. In 1804, the faculty of the University expressed much pleasure that all the seniors on commencement day were dressed in uniform suits of homespun cloth.[14] A friend of his gave a description of Zebulon B. Vance when he arrived at the University, "home-made shoes and clothes about three inches between pants and shoes, showing his sturdy ankles."[5] Long trousers with pistol-like legs had come into vogue by 1840 and the long-tailed coat and the bright waistcoast continued to be fashionable. For such students as

10. Weeks, S. B., "The University of North Carolina in 1805" in *North Carolina University Magazine*, April, 1894, p. 333.
11. Shaw, C. R., *op. cit.*, p. 39.
12. At New Garden Boarding School such practices were frowned upon by the faculty, who forbid the boys the right of roaching their hair or wearing whiskers. — Raper, C. L., *Church and Private Schools of North Carolina*, p. 169.
13. Shaw, C. R., *op. cit.*, p. 42.
14. *Reports from the Faculty to the Board of Trustees of the University of North Carolina, 1809-1829*, p. 38.
15. Dowd, Clement, *Life of Zebulon B. Vance*, p. 22.

Vance two suits of clothes became a necessity, one for Sunday or special occasions and the other for the week days. A practice among the University boys was revealed in a comment offered to the ladies in the *Raleigh Register,* May 21, 1828: "A friend of ours suggests, that hereafter if young ladies should discover holes in their black silk stockings just as they are dressed for church, and their mothers should be too conscientious to darn them, they had better adopt the Chapel Hill remedy, i.e. black the shin with ink opposite the hole. This is one of the greatest discoveries of modern times."[16] Carelessness in dress was evident among a large part of the student body, much to the annoyance of the faculty[17] who always favored inexpensiveness, plainness, and neatness of dress.[18] The aristocratic element in the colleges stood out more prominently in bright-colored shirts, large, protruding, and bright-colored bow neckties, broad-brimmed beaver hats and well polished boots.[19] After 1850, the aristocratic tendencies among the University students became more evident. A visitor in Chapel Hill in 1857 saw students wearing luxurious clothes and glittering watch seals. They were well-kept in person and had elegant manners.[21] Sometimes a "jaunty cap" was worn to contrast with a blue jacket decorated with bright buttons. Heavily starched white linen pantaloons, snowy collars, gloves and linen dusters were also common articles of apparel. It was said of the "Chapel Hill boys," when they arrived in a little town on their "elegant steeds," that they attracted the attention of the whole neighborhood, and horrified the minister when they failed to look at him on Sunday at services.[22] The haberdashery and the manners of the students were probably best exhibited at the commencement balls. Dancing

16. *Raleigh Register,* May 21, 1838, p. 3.
17. *Journal of the Faculty of the University of North Carolina,* 1849-55, p. 276.
18. *Raleigh Register,* January 1, 1828.
19. *John H. Bryan Papers,* 1773-1825, Vol. I, p. 32.
20. "A Visit to the University" in *North Carolina University Magazine,* 1857, p. 228.
21. "The Old University and Its Reputation," in *North Carolina University Magazine,* February 1885, p. 216.

without gloves or pumps would have been thought peculiarly vulgar. General Edward J. Mallet, of New York, gave a description of his general appearance when he was graduated at the University in 1818:

My coat was broadcloth, of sea green color, high velvet collar to match, swallow tail, pockets outside, with lapels and large silver plated buttons; white satin damask vest, showing the edge of a blue undervest; a wide opening for bosom ruffles, and no shirt collar. The neck was dressed with a layer of four or five three cornered cravats, artistically laid and surrounded with a cambric stock, pleated and buckled behind. By pantaloons were white canton crepe lined with pink muslin, and showed a peach blossom tint. They were rather short, in order to display flesh colored silk stockings; and this exposure was increased by very low cut pumps, with shiny buckles. My hair was very black, very long and queued.[22]

Little opportunity for social relations of students with women was offered unless it was during vacation or in violation of the rules of the colleges. The dances afforded some of the students an opportunity to learn manners and social graces and to practice forbearance and self-restraint. But the dances were not held very frequently and were not attended by all the students. The etiquette of the time gave a young man the privilege of taking a girl's arm above the elbow and demanded a waist line bow in case of an introduction. The students probably had their own ideas about women's fashions and called feminine ringlets "beau catchers." The extent of sexual immorality among University students is suggested by the many attempts of the college officials to check the lewd practices. A faculty report of 1803 revealed that a group of students, after being warmed up with liquor from a nearby tavern, "entered a house with much violence, disturbing the family in the night, and bent upon committing disorders with a high degree of licentiousness."[23] The University trustees of 1810 saw great evil and essential dis-

---

22. *Memoirs of Edward J. Mallett*, May 1, 1880, p. 39. (not published).
23. *Faculty Record of the University of North Carolina*, 1795-1815, p. 75.

225

advantages arising "to the good morals of youth in the University from the . . . . resorting to disorderly houses" in the neighborhood.[24] So bad did the practice become that students were forbidden to board at any house in the village, unless granted special permission by the president. The faculties of the various colleges also were very worried by students who, after leaving home, spent much of their time in local towns attracting the attention and courting the company of "lewd women." Some members of the sophomore class of the University of 1839 were admonished by the President for "having gone to a house of ill fame in the village during the night."[25] About this time it was also found necessary for President Swain to send a letter to the father of William Lea stating "that his son is the father of an illegitimate child in the village."[26] John A. Turrentine, a member of the senior class in 1850 was admonished for spending the night at a house of ill fame in the suburbs of Chapel Hill and there engaged in a disgraceful fight. The parents were informed of the irregularities of students Bell, Allison, and Blunt "especially in the matter of frequenting houses of ill-fame."[27] On one Sunday morning about three o'clock in 1854, President Swain caught one Gaines, a senior, and other students, careening through the streets with a carriage and with "very improper company for him inside." One of the students on being questioned about being around the carriage said he was there "for the purpose of getting some of his friends away from it."[28] Resolutions for the prosecution of "Lewd women who are known to keep bawdy houses near Chapel Hill" were passed by the faculty in 1856.[29] McClure, a student from Arkansas in 1857,

---

24. *Minutes of the Board of Trustees of the University of North Carolina,* 1801-1810, p. 195.
25. *Minutes of the Faculty of the University of North Carolina,* 1821-41, p. 358.
26. *Ibid.,* p. 359.
27. *Journal of the Faculty of the University of North Carolina,* 1849-55, p. 44.
28. *Ibid.,* p. 260.
29. *Journal of the Faculty of the University of North Carolina,* 1886-85, p. 12.

was dismissed for forcing some females, presiding a few miles from the village, from their homes."[30] Records of the denominational colleges were not kept as completely as those of the University, but there is no reason to believe that the students in those institutions differed from those at Chapel Hill. The records do show that students were often expelled for immorality.[31] There were a few milder forms of improper conduct such as posting pictures of nude women on the walls of the rooms, and writing indecent letters to citizens of the state and members of the faculty. At times such practices were engaged in for purposes of annoyance. An excellent case was portrayed in 1829 when a tutor of the University caught a student, clad only in a shirt, out of his room. The tutor in reporting the case said that the student "returned into his room and placing himself before the window aggravated his conduct with studied attitudes of indecency ... The last thing done was to remove as far as possible the little remaining covering from his person and expose himself to the public area and the front of the other buildings."[32]

It is evident also that there was much drinking. Almost every page of the faculty records of the colleges and the University gave evidence of the expulsion of students for "intoxication," having "ardent spirits" in their rooms, and the use of "spirituous liquors." As early as 1796 at the University, trouble arose between the students and the faculty over the frequent attendance of the former at the local taverns, and there followed an act forbidding attendance at such places except by special permission of the President.[33] Regulations of a similar nature, passed throughout the entire period by the higher institutions,

---

30. *Ibid.*, p. 125.
31. *Minutes of the Faculty of Davidson College,* 1842-1861, p. 213; *Record Book of the Faculty of Wake Forest College,* 1856-1897, p. 13.
32. *Minutes of the Faculty of the University of North Carolina,* 1821-1841, p. 107. Students were probably no more lax in their sexual life than students of today. For a good insight into modern conditions see Wolfe, Thomas, *Look Homeward, Angel,* New York, Scribner's, 1929.
33. *Minutes of the Board of Trustees of the University of North Carolina,* 1790-1797, p. 220.

threats of expulsion, and lectures, all seemed to have little effect in checking the drinking habit. In 1831, Elisha Mitchell, addressing the University students on the topic of *Arguments for Temperance*, spoke of the excessive drinking habit of the time and the evils which always followed it. February 22 and July 4 were pointed out as the days of greatest excesses in drinking. The Bible was pointed to as opposed to the use of distilled liquors, as the process of distillation was not known before its supposed discovery by a French chemist in the thirteenth century.[34] A committee report of the faculty of the University, in June, 1839, expressed deep regret at "the number of cases which have occurred to call for the exercise of correct discipline by that body. On the pages of this journal (Faculty) are to be found so many instances of insolence, dissipation, vices, such vice on the part of some of our students as to inflict the most deadly pain on the hearts of those to whom the interests of the institution and the happiness, and reputation of its success are endued by the strongest ties."[35] Punishments by the faculties of the colleges were often inflicted upon the wrong student, thus aggravating the situation, causing the students to band together in support of their mistreated friend and for the protection of the guilty one. And woe to that student who gave information.

Richard Armistead, of the class of 1804, was one of the first of the University students to stage a drinking party. With his jug of whiskey, he conduucted his company into his own room, and there, as he later confessed to the faculty, "drank fully with his companions."[36] Instances such as that of Robert Somerville,

34. Mitchell, Elisha, *Arguments for Temperance; Address to the Students of the University of North Carolina*, March 13, 1831, p. 17. Serious opposition against the use of wine was not made. Students were allowed the use of wine, though not to an excess, and the faculties always found it quite pleasant after their social meetings.
35. *Reports from the Faculty to the Board of Trustees of the University of North Carolina*, 1830-1839, p. 432.
36. *Faculty Record of the University of North Carolina*, 1795-1815, p. 334.

who was suspended for five months in October, 1810, for intoxication in the public streets, were quite common. The appearance of intoxicated students in the classroom, on the stage, and before the faculty, in body assembled, was not unknown. One student, on being questioned as to why he had appeared on the stage in an intoxicated condition, replied that he was attempting to stimulate himself and had taken a little more than he should.[37] On another occasion a group of University juniors, who had been caught at a nearby spring heavily under the influence of "ardent spirits," replied, when asked as to why they had broken the laws of the University, "they had entered into this revelry, because it was probably the last time they were to be together, and that they wished an opportunity to enjoy one another's company with conviviality, before their separation.[38] Students McDuffie and McKay, who were found in a very drunken state in their room at two o'clock in the morning (1849), replied, when questioned about their drinking, that they were studying for an examination on the following day and had to have something to keep them awake. The practice of "treating" an upper class or classman was an accepted custom and continued in popularity at the University in spite of an opposing ordinance passed by the faculty in 1823.[39] In 1840, a group of freshmen, on being questioned about their activities in a boisterous treat staged the night before, replied "that an individual would be considered mean and niggardly who should refuse to comply, that believing this representation to be true, they subscribed two dollars to defray the expenses of the treat, but remained at their rooms and conducted themselves quietly during the night."[40] Candidates for ball managers in 1850 admitted their purchase of much whiskey and wine for the purpose of a treat, and regretted the fact that these drinks, which

37. *Minutes of the Faculty of the University of North Carolina,* 1821-41, p. 427.
38. *Ibid.,* p. 20.
39. *Ibid.,* p. 21.
40. *Ibid.,* p. 485.

had been stored in a room, had been broken into and had caused a week of great disturbance.[41] Some of the episodes were not lacking in humor. After students Edward B. Dudley and Thomas D. Meares had been tried in 1837 on charges of intoxication, the faculty concluded: "It does not appear that at the time the supper and glasses of egg-nog were called in, any idea was entertained that the meeting was to be protracted until a very late hour of the night, much less that it was to be terminated in boisterous revelry and dissipation." The culprits were admonished.[42] In 1855, student Sellars, who had pledged to join the Temperance Society on being allowed to return to the University, was called before the faculty to answer for his intoxication. His answer was "that he took a drink before sending it in (petition to the society) on that day, and he expected to join the order."[43] Faculty investigation of student Saunder's room on November 25, 1853, at three-thirty in the morning, revealed a bottle of spirits with several tumblers upon the table, "and a man of low character asleep on the settee."[44] In the last week of May, 1856, a rumor reached the faculty that a wagoner, stationed about a mile from the campus, was selling a great deal of liquor to the students. Professor Hedrick was appointed to investigate the situation. Slick as a detective, he came upon his prey at eleven o'clock at night and found the salesmen and his customers all seated around a campfire considerably intoxicated. Seniors, when found guilty of drinking, were suspended until commencement day, at which time they were given a private examination upon "moral science," and, if passed satisfactorily, the diploma was awarded.[45]

Drinking among students at Davidson, Wake Forest, and Trinity was probably not different from those among students

41. *Journal of the Faculty of the University of North Carolina*, 1849-55, p. 38.
42. *Minutes of the Faculty of the University of North Carolina*, 1821-41, p. 284.
43. *Journal of the Faculty of the University of North Carolina*, 1848-55, p. 281.
44. *Ibid.*, p. 219.
45. *Ibid.*, p. 239.

at the University, but the records are not so nearly complete. In 1846, students Joseph A. Gillespie, J. M. Henderson, and R. J. English were suspended indefinitely from Davidson because of intoxication and other crimes.[46] Of these, most notorious for drinking at Davidson in 1850 was J. W. D. Doby who always kept a jog and a flask of whiskey in his room.[47] In 1856, sixty-five Davidson students proved bold enough to send in the following petition: "We the undersigned being Freemen would humbly request of the Faculty the 4th of this month as being the day on which our independence was declared as a holiday to be spent in whatever manner we may deem proper."[48] In 1856, M. L. Fay, of Davidson, wrote his faculty that students Orr and Wiley had threatened him with his life and had used language horrible enough to shock a heathen. So bad were the conditions that the trustees were continually urging the faculty to be more severe and vigilant.[49]

Drinking was also accompanied by fighting in the society halls, in the classrooms, in the dormitories, on the campus, down town, and around the villages. At Davidson in 1843, students R. A. H. Neagle, H. T. McDugald and J. T. Kell got into a fight with a group of Negroes who had refused to take off their hats to them. The students had knocked off the hats of the Negroes with sticks, and after some words and cursing, Kell proceeded to knock his man down with a blow on the head.[50] A quarrel between students Collins and Penick of the Eumenean Society at Davidson, in which Collins had tried to hit Penick with a stick and Penick had retreated, at the same time drawing his pistol, was finally settled by the President's call to order. For weapons, students most frequently used rocks which were sometimes directed at the head of the professor as well as the student.[51] The frequent use of stones was shown by the

46. *Minutes of the Faculty of Davidson College,* 1842-1861, p. 4.
47. *Ibid.,* p. 28. For other references see pages 3, 5, 6, 10, 13, 18, 19, etc.
48. *Ibid.,* p. 450.
49. *Minutes of the Board of Trustees of Davidson College,* 1836-1861, p. 86.
50. *Minutes of the Faculty of Davidson College,* 1842-1861, pp. 65-66.
51. *Ibid.,* p. 108.

great difficulty of keeping window glasses in the society halls and in the college buildings.[52] So many window glasses were broken out at the University that it was found necessary to keep a special record of each student's breakage. A statement of January 25, 1809, showed that fifty-two window panes had been broken out, W. C. Cowen leading the list with eight. As early as 1798, John D. Toomer and Atlas Jones were found guilty of rocking the house of a neighbor, John McCauley, after nine o'clock at night and, "on the protest of McCauley, went into his house and threatened his life, saying they would put him to death."[53] Students, as a result of the monitor act of 1805, beat Mr. Gillespie (tutor), waylaid and stoned Mr. Webb, threatened Mr. Flinn, and made violent threats against Murphey and Caldwell. So bad were the conditions that the Legislature appointed a committee to investigate the situation. Among the disorders charged against the students in 1809 was that of throwing rocks and brick bats, particularly at the heads of the tutors.[54] On a Sunday night in August, 1822, between the hours of nine and eleven, students assaulted the house of William Marbee, a citizen of Chapel Hill, throwing stones, breaking two window panes, and beating in the sashes.[55] A general statement of an occasional group of students quite often found in the minutes of the faculty follows: "In a disorderly assembly on the previous night which at a late hour, paraded the streets, stoned a house in the village, indulged in vociferation and profanity, and it is believed in drinking to excess."[56] Carrying pistols, knives, sword canes, or clubs for protection was a common practice for the students, and those they seemed always ready to use. In 1801, Maurice Jones, of the University, thrust a knife

---

52. *Minutes of the Eumenean Society of Davidson College,* 1852-1858, p. 203.
53. *Faculty Record of the University of North Carolina,* 1795-1815, p. 38
54. *Ibid.,* p. 179.
55. *Minutes of the Faculty of the University of North Carolina,* 1821-41, p. 8.
56. *Ibid.,* p. 427.

deep into the shoulder of Richard Henderson, and for the attack was severely whipped. Anthony Foister and Richard Armistead engaged in a fight because Foister had written a filthy piece of composition about him and had struck it upon one of the college doors. In 1802, Thomas Neeves "was called up for having struck Osborne Jeffers with a stick and cut him over the eye."[57] Reports of the faculty to the trustees in 1810 showed that students had been guilty of firing pistols, of bursting down the doors of tutors, of breaking glass over a professor's head while on recitation, of fighting with rocks, and throwing stones at the faculty, and of using knives too promiscuously.[58] In 1816 Walter Leak, firing a pistol in front of one of the tutor's doors, encouraged the pupils to rise up with him against the rules of the faculty saying, "he for one would not bow."[59] So incensed was Martin Armstrong against student William H. Haywood that he presented himself before Haywood on the Sabbath, "struck him on the head with a club, and knocked him down, repeating his blows as he fell, so that he was deprived of sense for the time."[60] An argument between J. Davis and A. Barbee in 1828, over a secret sophomore organization, finally culminated with Barbee waylaying Davis at the recitation room door and beating him unmercifully with a stick. One of the most interesting student feuds developed on May 31, 1836, and involved Duncan McRae, D. L. Smith, Benjamin Hobson, William F. Brown, and L. Brown. A dispute over some trivial affair between W. Brown and Smith in Smith's room had led to Brown's being hit over the head with a chair and carried out unconscious. On the following day, L. Brown told Smith that he had treated his brother like a rascal and Smith replied by

---

57. *Faculty Record of the University of North Carolina*, 1798-1815, p. 41.
58. *Minutes of the Board of Trustees of the University of North Carolina*, 1801-1810, pp. 190-200.
59. *Reports from the Faculty to the Board of Trustees of the University of North Carolina*, 1809-1829, p. 155.
60. *Ibid.*, p. 307.

striking Brown three times with a hickory walking cane. As L. Brown attempted to grab a chair, Duncan McRae stepped in, and in spite of Smith's choking him, was able to gain possession of the cane. McRae now found it necessary, as a result of Smith's threats, to carry first a pistol and later a sword cane for rotection. Accosting McRae one day, Smith asked him, "Why the cane?" On a closer approach, both students drew in preparation for a fight. Smith aimed a blow, and as McRae dodged, hit Hobson who was trying to make peace between the two boys. McRae then aimed a blow at Smith, and as Smith dodged, the spear penetrated Hobson's thigh.[61] Sometimes the use of pistols proved fatal as it did in the case of Singletary who was mortally wounded by Chapplan White from Tennessee in 1855. After the fracas, White was said to have disappeared through the forest.[62] Sometimes differences between students led to dueling, but such cases appear to have been rare, if judged by the available records. In December, 1802, the board of trustees requested the faculty "to expel from the University, Samuel G. Hopkins, John H. Hawkins, and Hugh Nunn, the two first having been engaged in a duel."[63] J. Bryan Grimes writing from Chapel Hill on October 4, 1847, to J. Johnston Pettigrew at Washington said: "There was a duel to come off between F. Harnes and Smikes Yellowby. I am not informed how it terminated."[64] One other incident connected with the University occurred in 1859 when the father of Thomas Land of Shreveport, Louisiana, sent a challenge to President Swain for expelling his son from the

---

61. *Minutes of the Board of Trustees of the University of North Carolina, 1821-1841,* pp. 254-255.

62. *North Carolina Standard.* December 12, 1855.

63. *Minutes of the Board of Trustees of the University of North Carolina, 1801-1810,* p. 18. Duels were not uncommon outside college in this period. And several were fought in the South Carolina College. See J. Marion Sims, *The Story of My Life,* Chapter V.

64. *Bryan Grimes Papers,* 1844-1863, Vol. I, p. 15. Neither of the names mentioned appear in Grant's *Alumni History of the University of North Carolina.*

University. Swain accepted the proposal as a joke.[65]

Excesses of the students sometimes led them into complete revolt with the faculty. Threats were made with clubs, pistols, and sometimes with gunpowder. Placing gunpowder in the door knob leading to a tutor's room, and timing the load so that it would go off in the tutor's presence, was not unknown.[66] In 1850, a gunpowder explosion before the chemical laboratory of the University, intended to injure the professor within, destroyed much equipment and filled the building with smoke. It was during that year that probably the most serious of the University riots occurred, on the night of August 13, beginning by the ringing of the college bell. Upon the appearance of three members of the faculty, Phillips, Mitchell, and Fetter, in old West dormitory, "They were hailed with opprobrious language, and stones and brick bats were thrown at them whenever it was possible, ... Threats of maltreatment were freely uttered."[67] In terror, the three professors fled to the safe keeping of the laboratory, Fetter being hit twice and Phillips suffering a bruise on the head. Stones and brick bats continued to be thrown; window panes were broken; and attempts were made to burst open the door. After a time, the three professors, thinking that all was quiet and the students had disbanded, returned to Old West for an investigation. Here they were cornered in a student's room where they were again assailed for more than an hour by students, with threats of "kill them" being frequently uttered. So bad was the assault that the light was knocked out and window and door panels were broken in, and

---

65. Of the Peter Dromgoole affair, which tradition says occurred at the University in 1833, there seems to be not a word of truth. Letters written by the young man show that he left the University as a result of a disagreement with his father. — Cotton, Bruce, "Peter Dromgoole" in *North Carolina University Magazine*, November, 1924, p. 509.
66. *Reports from the Faculty to the Board of Trustees of the University of North Carolina.* 1809-1829, p. 287.
67. *Journal of the Faculty of the University of North Carolina*, 1849-55, p. 53.

those who were attacked sought the most recessive corners of the room. Professor Phillips was forced to knock one student out of the window with a chair. Finally, at half past two in the morning, the students agreed to stop the riot if the professors would go home, and the proposal was received with unanimous consent. In 1856, a student by the name of Mobley, a rough and tumble character, was found by President Swain and Professor Mitchell in front of the local hotel in an intoxicated condition. On being accosted, Motley denied that he was subject to the laws of the University, fired three times with a revolver into the street, struck the president with a rock, and later seriously wounded an officer who was trying to arrest him.[68] Often disagreement between the student and the professor developed into nothing more than a heated argument, as was the case between George Terry and Professor Smith at the University in 1859 over a French lesson, which Terry had refused to make up unless he received aid, and this Professor Smith had refused to give.

Terry- You are obliged to tell me. That is what you are here for.

Smith- We are sometimes obliged to answer a fool according to his folly.

Terry- I understand you to call me a fool.

Smith- I called you nothing. I repeated a passage of scripture and you were all free to make your own application.

Terry- You insulted me and if you do it again, I will crack this spit-box over your head.[69]

The fighting tendencies of the time were also revealed in the students' frequent "fighting and brawling with the country people." In February, 1853, students Marrow and Wall were suspended from the University for engaging "in a severe fight with

68. *Journal of the Faculty of the University of North Carolina,* 1856-85, p. 93.
69. *Ibid.,* p. 205.

certain persons of low character at a coal kiln in the neighborhood."[70] Student Miller was suspended in 1857 for drawing a knife on the Mayor of Raleigh and student Williams for difficulties with a railroad conductor in Durham. In 1860, student Foard struck a local citizen with a slug shot and then seriously stabbed him.[71]

Excessive drinking and fighting on the part of the *ante-bellum* college boys was also accompanied by the use of a very strong vocabulary. Professors were often shocked by students using "horrible profanity in the public street,"[72] conducting indecent conversations with someone from their windows, using disrespectful language in their essays,[73] and cursing in time of recitation. Probably the greatest swearer on the University campus in the earlier years was John Witherspoon, of the class of 1810, who was called before the faculty on numerous occasions for "too great an attachment to this immoral and unbecoming practice."[74] At Davidson in 1846, J. L. Miller led his class in his ability to curse the faculty, while many others in the student body were no less outspoken.[75] Students Blount and Conrad at Wake Forest were censured in chapel in 1856 for the use of offensive language to the faculty. Blount received his censuring by an "appeal to higher authority — to the Board of Trustees."[76] In 1852, at the University, student Jones was charged "with disturbing an examination of a candidate for college, by Professor Mitchell, by addressing loud, impertinent, and disrespectful remarks to the professor through the window from the

---

70. *Journal of the Faculty of the University of North Carolina*, 1849-55, p. 186.
71. *Journal of the Faculty of the University of North Carolina*, 1856-85, p. 218.
72. *Ibid.*, p. 142.
73. *Minutes of the Faculty of Davidson College*, 1842-1861, p. 106.
74. *Faculty Record of the University of North Carolina*, 1795-1815, p. 119.
75. *Minutes of the Faculty of Davidson College*, 1842-1861, p. 13.
76. *Record Book of the Faculty of Wake Forest College*, 1856-1897, p. 5.

outside of the building."[77] Students also wrote anonymous, menacing, and scurrilous letters to the people of the state, to their stewards, to former professors at other institutions, and to any one who had offended them in the least manner.

Gambling, lying, and stealing were also common practices among *ante-bellum* college students. Most popular of the gambling games were "loo," a card game which could be played by any number of persons, poker, and dice shooting. The playing of "loo" seems to have been most popular in the earlier years at the University,[78] while poker playing and dice shooting retained their popularity throughout the whole period. These games, which were generally accompanied by drinking parties, were usually played with very low stakes, as the only money which the students had consisted of that small amount which they had been able to slip by the college bursar. Cases like that of Alfred Slade, caught in the act of "gaming" and suspended for a term of five months (1816), appeared quite frequent in the reports of the University faculty. A similar situation existed at Davidson where students T. J. Medley, S. K. Pharr, and A. J. Derr were caught in 1859 playing at the game of cards.[79] The same condition existed also at Wake Forest and Trinity. It appears that the harshness of the by-laws was responsible for some of the lying among the students. When caught in campus riots they would often deny being members of the college. When asked on Monday morning, at the calling of the roll, whether they had attended church services on the previous day, students invariably answered in the affirmative, and apparently without any idea of wrong doing. In fact, they seemed to revel in any successful attempt to deceive a college official. Students also seem to have had no scruples in lying for members of their own "gang" or in falsifying against an enemy when the opportunity offered itself. As for stealing, stu-

---

77. *Journal of the Faculty of the University of North Carolina*, 1849-1855, p. 153.

78. *Faculty Record of the University of North Carolina*, 1795-1815, p. 81.

79. *Minutes of the Faculty of Davidson College*, 1842-1861, p. 17.

dents followed the mythical law of Lycurgus which implied that there was no harm in the private transfer of another's property provided those doing so were not caught in the act. Getting compositions out of books not generally read by members of the faculty and turning them in as "the production of their own genius" was for *ante-bellum* students another form of deception.[80] For the nearby neighbor's chickens, corn, potatoes, and other edibles there was no consideration, especially when students were hungry. The contracting of debts without a knowledge of the parents and without any intention of paying them back was also an accepted practice among many. And sometimes students went into their friends pockets during the night hours in search of a little change.[81] Probably the most interesting of the cases of stealing which occurred at any time during the period was that which was participated in by Thomas H. Benton, later the senior senator from Missouri for more than a quarter of a century. While a student of the University in 1799, young Benton on three occasions admitted stealing money belonging to his fellow students. On the night of March 8, following the disappearance of some money which students Baker and Saunders had placed in Benton's trunk for safe-keeping, eight dollars (one of which was a late federal emission) and a pocket book were stolen out of the pockets of William Cherry, and sixteen dollars and a shilling disappeared from the pockets of student Baker. Baker having marked the stolen shilling and one of the dollar bills with a "B" proceeded to catch the guilty party by informing every merchant in town to watch out for such marked money. A few days later a merchant reported that such a bill was in the hands of Thomas Benton, that he had tried to purchase the bill by an exchange of money but had received a refusal. Student Saunders, in the meantime, through faculty advice, had gained entrance into Benton's room late one night and had found Cherry's stolen money in Ben-

80. *Letters, University of North Carolina,* 1796-1835, (manuscript), p. 145.
81. *Record Book of the Philanthropic Society,* 1847-1853 (university), p. 27.

239

ton's pockets.[82] On being searched on the following day, Benton admitted the stealing of $34 from the three boys, and was thus forced to leave the University. Thomas King, a student who had lost $20 out of his chest on February 22, now suspected Benton of stealing his money. A trip was made to Benton's home where Benton admitted his guilt, saying that he had procured a key which "exactly fitted the lock of the chest and with which he had opened it."[83]

Notwithstanding such behavior, *ante-bellum* students showed a deep religious interest. Revivals were held quite frequently at all of the institutions and frequently there were many conversions. Baptism for candidates into the church was regularly participated in at the Sunday meetings of University students, and Holy Communion was administered twice a year. Following the year 1838, a chaplain served regularly as a member of the University faculty. On December 10, 1858, President Swain reported: "By much the most important occurrence of the past session, is the interest upon the subject of religion, which manifested itself among the students, at an early period, and which after some weeks of continuance resulted in such an accession to various churches, as in number an apparent sincerity of those engaged, is without precedent at the University."[84] To a young man at Davidson, a fond mother wrote: "Do not talk of being tempted to turn back; destruction will most

82. *Faculty Record of the University of North Carolina*, 1794-1815, p. 13.

83. *Ibid.*, p. 18. These incidents were later made use of by Benton's political opponents. The *Raleigh Register*, November 28, 1849, suggested that "that affair at Chapel Hill" was probably the first fatal step Benton had made toward "Locofocracy." Benton's biographers Roosevelt, Rogers, and Meigs do not mention these incidents. As for Benton himself, he seems not to have borne any ill will toward the University or the Philanthropic Society. In 1832, he donated $20 toward a proposed new society hall. — See *Letters to the Philanthropic Society*, 1808-1860, p. 80.

84. *Statement of the President of the University of North Carolina*, December 10, 1858, p. 2.

surely follow if you do; but be more deeply engaged than ever in seeking your salvation."[85] In the first year of the existence of Wake Forest (1834), eight large revivals were held which caused many students to become interested in the ministry as well as being more religious-minded. Student W. T. Brooks (Wake Forest) was so deeply interested in his religious activities that he kept a diary of them while in college. On April 30, 1837, he wrote: "Passed the week pretty much as usual, sometimes encouraged and sometimes discouraged. We must expect such difficulties while in this vale of tears, whilst our souls are locked up in this prison of clay, but by and by if we be faithful we shall reach the sunset of our rest."[86] Of Normal College, J. H. Robbins wrote to the *North Carolina Christian Advocate* in 1857: "We are in the midst of a revival of religion at this place; many souls have been converted to God." The editor added: "A college without revivals is like the Temple when the Shekinah had departed. A college whose whole history is marked with revivals leads the van of civilization, and lights the way to heaven."[87] Many students refrained from shaving and writing letters on Sunday. Others felt that the use of tobacco as well as whiskey was sinful.

The simplicity of life seems to have had much part in determining the manners and morals of *ante-bellum* students. In the absence of bath tubs, students bathed in the nearby streams in warm weather and in small wooden tubs in their rooms during the winter months. Tub bathing, however, was not so frequent, and students often passed through the winter without taking a bath. Sewerage systems were not known during the first quarter of the nineteenth century, and in the absence of such conveniences, University boys often resorted to the practice of throwing slop from the windows. Even during the years before the war, many students showed little tendency toward respect

85. *North Carolina Presbyterian*, February 12, 1859, p. 4.
86. Brooks, W. T., *Diary 1834-1839*, p. 28.
87. *North Carolina Christian Advocate*, June 25, 1857, p. 2.

for the niceties of life. And yet, the students seem to have been remarkably healthy, although in 1824 an epidemic of typhoid broke out at the University and in 1854 Davidson was forced to close for a short period because of a number of cases of scarlet fever. No infirmary was provided for the sick students who either stayed in their rooms and were nursed by others boys or were sent to the hotel where they were cared for by some members of their own families. Study was largely by candles, until about 1850, when they were supplanted by lamps. Camphene (made of spirits of turpentine) was also widely used for lighting purposes, but the carelessness of students made unpopular the use of this means of lighting in the colleges. Writing was done by the use of quill pens and often with home-made ink. Fire places remained popular and, where the trustees failed to provide andirons, students found good use for stones on which to place their logs. Generally students chopped their wood, drew their water, and carried out their waste. Evidence exists, however, to show that some of the students of the University found life easier by having their slaves, who were kept in the basement of the South Building. Morning and afternoon washing of faces and hands at the spring, well, or pump was a common practice. Visitors were scarce and letters were few, as the postage was extremely high; it cost as much as eighteen and three quarters cents to mail a letter from Chapel Hill to Raleigh.[88]

At best, college life in North Carolina during the *ante-bellum* period was marked by the influence of the frontier conditions. Students presented a varied picture in their manners and morals. There were present in the colleges "raw-boned" students with their crude ways as well as sons of the southern aristocracy. Manners of dress as late as 1840 exemplified some of the characteristics of the Revolutionary days, while the bright colored waist coats continued to remain popular. Sexual immoral-

---

88. *Reports From the Faculty to the Board of Trustees of the University of North Carolina,* 1809-1829, p. 277.

ity, drinking of "ardent spirits," gambling, lying, and stealing were common among many students. On the other hand, religious revivals were a frequent occurrence, conversions of students were numerous, and a deep sense of religious obligation and superstition invaded the minds of many. The simplicity of every day life, the frontier-like atmosphere of the college campus, provided for much high emotional and little quiet intellectual activity.

VIII

Higher Education of Women

The ideal of universal education, which led William R. Davie to urge and aid in the establishment of a state university, did not lead him to an acceptance of the state's obligation to educate its women. "By a curious twist of the English language the term 'rising generation,' " in the preamble to the first charter of the University of North Carolina, "was construed to mean boys only, and 102 years passed before the state realized that at least half of each rising generation is composed of the other sex."[1] A few of the eighteenth century rationalists had advocated, as did Daniel Defoe in his *Essay on Projects,* that women should learn something more than to "stitch and sew, and such baubles," but little of this philosophy seems to have spread in North Carolina. During the Colonial days, European tradition, in regard to the education of women, had been followed as a natural policy. Girls were to be maintained rather than prepared to maintain themselves independently, — a universally accepted policy which was to prevail for many years. Sons were to carry the burden, while daughters were to be made as agreeable as possible by reason of their own attractiveness. The education of girls and women rarely, if ever, extended beyond the simplest forms of reading, writing, and arithmetic. The colonial college, with its fixed and unchanged curriculum, was not open to them; and much of the nineteenth century had passed be-

---

1. Connor, R. D. W., *North Carolina,* Vol. I, p. 605.

fore higher educational opportunity was made available to them. Many more years were to pass before such opportunity was provided at public expense. John Baptiste Ashe in his will, dated at Bath, 1734, probably expressed the highest colonial sentiment when he said: "I will that my daughter be taught to read and write and some feminine (*sic*) accomplishments which may render her agreeable; and that she be not kept ignorant as to what appertains to a good house wife in the management of household affairs."[2] As servants and wives, women filled their places well, but "how unambitious, how feeble-minded, they must have been," wrote William Hooper in 1859, "to be contented with occupying no more space in the eyes of the world, and in the eyes of men."[3] Howwever, during the period from 1800 to 1860 a rather significant interest developed among the denominations and a few individuals in the higher education of women.

The period from 1800 to 1860 was a period of considerable controversy, with arguments advanced both for and against the higher education of women. It was pointed out that the instruction of man in his infancy was intrusted to women, and because of this fact the education of women would raise the standards of men. Said the *Hillsboro Recorder* of September 7, 1885: "It is not merely a creature who can paint and play and sing and draw and dance; it is a being who can comfort and counsel him (man), soothe his sorrows, lighten his cares, purify his joys, strengthen his principles, and educate his children." In this relationship of the mother and the child, the movement for the education of women received its strongest lead. Education was to prepare the women for the service of mankind. What mind, it was asked, could better order a family or conduct in harmony the numerous affairs of a household than one

2. Grimes, J. Bryan, *North Carolina Wills and Inventories*, pp. 16-17.

3. Hooper, William, *Fifty Years Since*, p. 9.

Even in the schools of Massachusetts girls were not admitted before 1789, and then only for one-half of the school year. They were taught spelling, reading, and composition. See Thwing, C. F., *A History of Higher Education in America*, p. 334.

well disciplined by severe study?[4] The idea of educating women for the companionship of men rather than for mere services was not widely accepted. Equality of natures was denied by even the advocates of the education of women. The need for the lordship of man over the minds and characters of women was admitted as an organic arrangement of providence and a conservative power in society. Even to Calvin H. Wiley, the place of woman was clearly outlined and defined by the Bible.[5] Although the more radical proponents of the cause insisted that Eve did not spend all her time in making her dwelling beautiful or in spreading food for angels, the education of women for their own sake gained little headway. Probably this was best shown in a trite remark made by the editor of *The Southern Index,* July, 1850: "The warmest defenders of such schools are those prudent mammas whose only care is marriage for their daughters, who are destined upon conquest, and who scruple not to use the graces if Cytherea prove unavailing."[6]

Many arguments were advanced against the education of women. It was argued that library ladies from time immemorial set standards for bad house-keeping; that women would stay in their libraries rather than in their kitchens or behind their looms. Moreover, it was argued that education would undermine the health of women, reveal their innate mental inferiority, rob them of all feminine charm, and lead them to neglect home and children in the feverish pursuit of Greek roots and the intricacies of quadratic equations. Women could not enrich their minds without impoverishing their hearts, argued many.[7] To send girls to college, it was said, would not only deprive many boys of their privileges to attend school, but would subject the future mothers to many evil influences. Mrs. Emma Willard, while urging education for girls in New York state in

---

4. Lucy, N., "Domestic Happiness" in *The Parthenian,* 1852, Vol. I, no. 2, p. 95.

5. *The Greensboro Patriot,* April 22, 1854, p. 2.

6. *The Southern Index,* July, 1850, No. 3, p. 38.

7. Goodsell, Willystine, "The Education of Women", in *Twenty Five Years of American Education* (I. L. Kandel, Ed.), p. 335.

the first quarter of the nineteenth century, filed a protest against the "absurdity of sending ladies to college,"[8] and there were many in North Carolina who appeared to hold a similar opinion.[9]

Among the Moravians, however, this opposition gained no headway. They had drifted into North Carolina as early as 1751, and bought land, and by 1766 had laid out the town of Salem in the form of a square. In general, their leaders were men of education and refinement, John Jacob Fries, an accomplished scholar in Hebrew being one of the most prominent. Education had long been an accepted principle by the Moravian body. Comenius, their eminent bishop, had said in his book, *The Great Didactic*, that women should be allowed to engage in the pursuits of both advanced and elementary knowledge.[10] In accordance with this idea, the Moravians at Salem opened a day school in the "Congregation House" in 1772, which was attended by all the Moravian children.[11] Further immediate progress was delayed by the Revolution but, in 1786, a division of the school was made, the "Single Sisters" being moved to their new home on the south east side of the square. Comments by visitors who attended the girls' day school and who expressed the desire that they might be able to send their girls also, led the governing board of the Moravian congregation in 1802 to decide to open the doors of the school to any Christian girl who desired to enter. Samuel G. Kramsh, a native of Silesia,

8. Stephens, Kate, "Education for Women," in *The Forum*, 1889, Vol. III, p. 43.

9. Young Martin Armstrong, writing from the University to his father, Germantown, March 19, 1891, said in refusing to marry his friend Polly: "Was she educated as I wished her to be she would doubtless make me a lovely and amiable companion. But this she is not, nor has she any prospects that I know of becoming so, for her father has refused to send her to school." In *Reports From the Faculty to the Board of Trustees of the University of North Carolina*, 1809-1829, p. 295.

10. Probably the best translation of this work is that of Keatinge, M. W., London, Black, 1896. John Amos Comenius was born in Moravia, in 1592.

11. Lehman, E. A., "Reminiscences of Fifty Years at Salem" in *The Academy*, November, 1914, p. 6334.

but at that time pastor at Hope, North Carolina, was elected on October 31, 1802, as principal of Salem Academy. This was probably the third of the institutions of similar rating to be established in the country and the first in the South.[12]

From 1802 to 1860, the academy prospered, the enrollment increasing from ten in 1804 to 340 in 1859,[13] with the total enrollment for the period being in excess of 4000. Actual enrolling of outside students did not begin until 1804 when Elizabeth Strudwick, of Hillsborough, Rebecca Carter, of Caswell county, and Anna Stein, of Fayetteville, were among the first pupils to enroll. The first graduates from the academy came in 1807, when certificates of scholarship were issued. Attendants at the institution came from all the southern States and from many of the states to the North. A copy of the circular issued by the school on May 23, 1804, stated the entrance requirements and the general plan of the institution:

> The age of admittance of pupils is between 8 and 12 years. The age of 15 terminated their stay in the school, unless parents choose to order their return home sooner, or their continuance in the school. The Branches taught are Reading, Grammar, Writing, Arithmetic, History, Geography, (German if desired), plain Needlework, etc. Music and fine needlework, including drawing, are two extra branches in which instruction is given if expressly desired. The amount of the yearly expenses collectively may be calculated at the rate of between 160 and 180 Dollars, more or less. . . . It is desirable that such as are applied for, should have had the small of the kine pox and measles.[14]

Advanced work was not done in the academy until 1844 when a select class of ten boarders and two day scholars was organized. French, however, had been taught by the principal for

---

12. No catalogue of Salem Academy was published prior to 1854, and no records outside of those of the church were kept with the exception of an *Account Book* and a register of students titled *Daughters in the Boarding School in Salem*. The academy was not chartered until February, 1866.

13. *Catalogue of Salem Female Academy*, 1860, p. 14.

14. Fries, A. L., *Historical Sketch of Salem Female Academy*, pp. 7-8.

many years prior to this time, at the hour of seven o'clock in the morning.

The growth of the institution is in part reflected in the building program. In 1824, an addition was added to South Hall, the first of the buildings of the boarding school, which had been completed in 1805. Demands for more space in 1835 led to the building of a new chapel, and in 1841 the school took complete possession of Gemein Haus. This latter building was torn down in 1854 and replaced by Main Hall, a brick structure of four stories and of Dorian architecture, one hundred feet front by fifty-two feet deep, and very impressive for its day. In addition to dormitory and class rooms, the building was equipped with a new chapel and a dining hall, suitable for seating more than two hundred and fifty persons.

Administering the academy during these years were seven men, prominent among whom were Gotthold Reichel, who served as principal from 1815 to 1833; and Reverend Robert de Schweinitz who remained in office from 1853 to 1866. The principal had a number of assistants, three in 1815, and an increase to more than ten by 1860.

Manifesting an interest similar to that of the Moravians, Mr. and Mrs. William Falkener opened a young ladies' school in the town of Warrenton as early as 1802. An advertisement published in the *Raleigh Register*, December 17, 1804, stated that young girls would be taught so that they might be accomplished in literature and moral and domestic economy. The subjects to be taught included writing, dancing, music, vocal and instrumental, drawing, English and French. Tuition and board were placed at $105 for each of the two sessions. The work of the school, although not of superior grade, was creditable and students came from several parts of the state. Five or more assistants were engaged at times. After the death of the Falkners in 1819, the school closed its doors.[15]

Another early school of much interest was that of Jacob Mordecai, a Jewish emigrant. In 1809, this school also opened in

15. Montgomery, L. W., *Sketches of Old Warrenton, North Carolina,* p. 131.

Warrenton with a curriculum and prices similar to that of the Falkners'. During the ten years which this school was in operation an annual average attendance of students was eighty, many of whom came from other states. A student, commenting on the school in her memoir, said: "The system of teaching was absolutely thorough as far as it went, and that its moral and practical training was in accordance with Edgeworthian ideas, then much in vogue."[16]

The Fayetteville Academy was opened in January, 1793. Largely an institution for boys, it seems to have paid some attention to the education of girls.[17] The school was in charge of the Rev. David Ker, later the first acting president of the University.

Outside of these efforts, little interest seems to have been taken in the education of women in North Carolina during the first quarter of the nineteenth century. But with the coming of the Jacksonian era a real interest in the betterment of women's position in social and economic life expressed itself. As a part of this betterment program appeared an interest in establishing a college for women. The subject was discussed in social circles and formed an interesting topic for conversation at the annual meetings of the denominations. However, the plans were slow in developing and it is only in the last decade before the Civil War that this interest really materialized.[18]

16. Mordecai, Gratz, *Notice of Jacob Mordecai, Founder and Proprietor from 1809 to 1819 of the Warrenton Female Seminary*, pp. 44-45.
17. Coon, C. L., *North Carolina Schools and Academies*, 1790-1840 (A Documentary History), p. 60.
18. Tocqueville, Alexis De, one of the greatest of the French philosophers, made a visit to America during this period and after returning to France published, in 1845, the impressions which the new country had made on him, in a book called *Democracy In America*. On page 210 of Volume Two, he said the American people "believing that they had little chance of repressing in woman the most vehement passions of the human heart, . . . held that the surer way was to teach her the art of combating those passions for herself. As they could not prevent her virtue from being exposed to frequent danger, they determined that she should know how best to defend it; and more reliance was

In the absence of public interest, it is surprising to note that the Methodists were first in the field, since they delayed so long in establishing a school for boys. In 1838, following an appeal to the Legislature, an act was passed incorporating the trustees of "Greensborough Female College," at least one half of whom were always to be members of the North Carolina Conference of the Methodist Episcopal Church.[19] According to the charter, the trustees were given full control of the proposed institution, to receive and administer funds, to elect a president and a faculty, and to pass whatever laws were deemed necessary, provided they were not in contradiction to the laws and constitution of the state. The faculty of the college, by the consent of the trustees, was granted the power to confer all such degrees or marks of literary distinction as were characteristic of other institutions of learning. Property in possession of the corporation was not to exceed $200,000. Land totaling two hundred and ten acres had already been purchased in 1837 at a cost of $3,350, largely paid for by the sale of building lots from all but forty acres of the original purchase. Extremely adverse financial conditions, however, made immediate action impossible and it was not until the meeting of the North Carolina Conference in 1840 that plans were laid for the raising of $10,-000 with which to erect the first building.[20] In 1843, with the probable assurance of the desired funds, the cornerstone of the first building was laid and by 1845 a three-story brick building with thirty-six rooms was completed at a cost of $20,000. Chief among the gifts to the institution was that of Mrs. Susan Mendenhall who made a bequest of $4,000.[21] Because of the building debt, it was found necessary in 1849 to appeal to the state

placed on the free vigor of her will, than on safeguards which have been shaken or overthrown."

19. *Laws of North Carolina*, 1838, p. 101. This was probably the second of the state chartered colleges for women in the South, the first being Wesleyan Female College, Macon, Georgia.

20. *Minutes of the North Carolina Annual Conference of the Methodist Episcopal Church*, 1840-1848, p. 10.

21. Jones, T. M., "Historical Sketch of Greensboro Female College" in *Centennial of Methodism in North Carolina*, p. 162.

for a loan of $10,000. A loan of seven thousand dollars was granted.[22]

In 1846, the college opened under the presidency of the Rev Solomon Lea, who was also professor of ancient languages. Other members of the faculty included the Rev. Benet T. Blake, chaplain and professor of mental and moral science; the Rev. John C. Blackwell, professor of mathematics and natural science; Mrs. Sophia Lea, principal of the music department; an assistant teacher of music, a principal of the preparatory department, and a governess.[23] In general, the college was prosperous from the first year of its opening, the enrollment increasing from eighty-seven the first year of its opening to 351 in 1859. The classification given for the year 1859 was sixteen seniors, twenty-six juniors, thirty-three sophomores, forty-three first year, thirty-seven preparatory, and extras — twenty-five in Latin, thirty-two in French, one hundred two in piano, and twenty-two in painting. The total number of graduates during the period from 1846 to 1859 was 155; the largest number in any one year was nineteen — in 1851. Financial difficulties continued to obstruct the way of those who were charged with the administration of the affairs of the college, but by an arrangement with the Conference, whereby the daughters of the Methodist ministers could attend the institution free, funds totaling $20,000 were made available in 1859.[24] Wings were added to the old building in 1859 and in 1861. Most prominent among the presidents who served during this period (there were four in all) were the Rev. Charles F. Deems and the Rev. T. M. Jones. Deems served from 1850 to 1854 and Jones filled out the rest of the period. Both were men of scholarship and ability and their efforts served markedly to make the college something more than a preparatory institution.

---

22. *Minutes of the North Carolina Annual Conference of the Methodist Episcopal Church,* 1840-1848, p. 135; *Laws of North Carolina,* 1848-1849, p. 803.
23. *Catalogues, Greensborough Female College,* 1846-1860, p. 3.
24. *Minutes of the North Carolina Annual Conference of the Methodist Episcopal Church,* 1846-1864, p. 101.

In addition to the schools already mentioned, more than a dozen other academies, seminaries, and colleges for girls were chartered and established before 1860; Caldwell Institute (Presbyterian), Greensboro, 1833; Wayne Female College (private), Goldsboro, 1834; Edgeworth Female Seminary (Presbyterian), Greensboro, 1840; Warrenton Female College (Methodist), Warren County, 1841; St. Mary's School (Episcopal), Raleigh, 1842; Asheville Female Seminary (Methodist), 1842; Warrenton Female Collegiate Institute (private), Warren County, 1846; Floral College (Presbyterian), Robeson County, 1847; Chowan Baptist Female Institute, Murfreesborough, 1848; Carolina Female College (Methodist), Ansonville, 1849; Thomasville Female College (Presbyterian), Davidson County, 1849; Oxford Female Seminary (Baptist), Oxford, 1851; Wesleyan Female College (Methodist), Murfreesborough, 1853; Charlotte Female Institute (Presbyterian), 1857; Select Boarding and Day School (private), Hillsborough, 1857; Davenport Female College (Methodist), Lenoir, 1857; Louisburg Female Seminary (Methodist), Louisburg, 1857; Statesville Female College (Presbyterian), 1857; Mt. Pleasant Female Seminary (Lutheran), Cabarrus County, 1858; Wilson Collegiate Institute (Methodist, co-educational), Wilson, 1859.[25] The most successful of these efforts made by the denominations, not already discussed, were the Edgeworth Female Seminary, Greensboro. It was formally opened in 1840 but had begun some thirteen years earlier and, although non-denominational in plan, was operated by the Presbyterians; St. Mary's School founded in 1842, at Raleigh, by the Episcopalians; and the Chowan Baptist Female Institute, Murfreesborough, Chowan County, which opened in October, 1848. The success of Edgeworth was largely due to the efforts of John Motley Morehead[26] who in 1840 bought land in Greensboro and on it built a four-story brick building for the school. With the securing of Gilbert Morgan

25. The best source for an account of these schools is Raper, C. L., *Church and Private Schools of North Carolina.*
26. Governor of North Carolina, 1841-1845, and distinguished for his leadership in railroad building in the state.

in 1845 to administer the school, the course of study was raised
to collegiate rank; such subjects as Latin, Greek, French, English, mental science, natural philosophy, and history were
taught. Expenses were on a par with those of Salem. The school
was probably as well equipped as the average college for wom-
en of the period; it had a small library and meager scientific
equipment. In 1856, the approximately two hundred students
in the school were taught by a faculty of twelve, headed by
Principal Richard Sterling, a very able young man who had
taken charge of the institution upon Morgan's resignation in
1850. Probably the larger number of the pupils enrolled were
at all times in the preparatory department.[27] The success of
the St. Mary's School from 1842 to 1860 was due largely to the
efforts of the Rev. Albert Smedes who remained at its head
during the entire period. The annual average enrollment was
in excess of one hundred and the pupils were classified into
primary, preparatory, and academic departments. Although
there was an absence of high academic standards in the school,
it was nevertheless noted for its cultural training and marks of
refinement. The chief aim of the school was to train "refined,
lady-like, Christian women."[28] The Chowan Baptist Female Institute grew out of a request of the Baptists of the counties of
Bertie, Hertford, and Northampton to establish a girls' high
school in their community. The Chowan Baptist Association accepted the request and appointed trustees who, in 1848, purchased a building lot in Murfreesborough for $1,225. So suc-
cessful was the enterprise that in 1851 a joint stock company
took charge and erected a large brick building, which was completed in the following year. The total value of the property at
this time was $35,000. Among the one hundred or more stu-
dents enrolled annually, there were students from Texas, Mississippi, Georgia, Alabama, North Carolina, Virginia, New

---

27. This school was closed during the War and ceased to exist in 1871.
28. Battlo, K. P., "An Estimate of the Character and Work of Rev.
Albert Smedes" in *North Carolina University Magazine,* November,
1893, p. 82.

York, and the District of Columbia.[29] The most effective leader of the institution during the *ante-bellum* period was the Rev. William Hooper who served from 1854 to 1862. The institution was not officially in the hands of the Baptist Association until 1866.

In general, the administration of all the girls' schools and colleges was characterized by a care even more watchful and suspicious than that of the boys at the University and at denominational schools. Close parental authority was zealously exercised. At the head of each school was the principal or the president, assisted by his wife; they acted as father and mother in the training of "their adopted children." Students were divided into companies of twelve or fifteen and each company was placed under the special care of two women. All mail coming to the girls passed first through the hands of the president and was subject to his inspection and censorship. Some restrictions were laid on receiving visitors, even when parental consent was granted. When a pupil entered the college, she was required to read the by-laws and subscribe to them. Among those things which were positively prohibited were attending parties, balls, or dancing schools, leaving the premises without permission, receiving the attention or visits of young men, or in any way corresponding with them, visiting in town or country unless by the known request of the parent or guardian, wearing rings or bracelets, silks or satins, and contracting debts without consent of the parents.[30] A student was not allowed to trade on her own responsibility, all of her funds being turned over to those in charge who made her necessary purchases. The purpose of this arrangement was to teach the pupil how to use money. At Greensboro Female College, a regulation read: "No system of espionage is maintained. Tri-weekly, each pupil makes to her section teacher a report of her own delinquencies, and a record of this report is preserved. She is thus thrown upon

---

29. *Ibid.*, p. 82.
30. *Eleventh Annual Commencement of Oxford Female College,* 1861 p. 7.

her honor."[31] Attendance at prayers twice a day and at religious services on Sunday was required of all, while every absence from church and recitation was recorded and publicly read at commencement, along with the student's standing in scholarship. A jackonet of white for the summer and a dress of mazarine blue worsted for the winter were the usual prescribed uniforms. In the schools where no uniform was used, the clothes were to be of the greatest simplicity, for showy style of dress was considered peculiarly inappropriate to those who were pursuing their education. Such regulations seem to indicate that something besides study had taken possession of the heart; and as for the Sabbath, a morning spent in decorating the person was considered "poor preparation for the duties of the soul."[32] At Salem, the girls were required to make their own dresses, this being a part of the training which would fit them "for the sober duties and solid realities of life."[33]

The curriculum presented a much greater variety of subjects than that presented by the boys' colleges, such a variety being considered necessary for one who was to manage a family with the greatest ease and efficiency and to know "experimentally the duties of every member of it."[34] The curriculum outlined for Greensboro Female College would probably be a fair example of the courses pursued in all of these institutions. Pupils were divided into three departments — preparatory, English, and classical. In the preparatory department, the work consisted of reading, writing, and spelling, with perhaps a little music and drawing. The English department, which formed the basic work of the college, was divided into three classes, — first year, junior, and senior. During the first year, a student pursued such courses as English, arithmetic, geography, rhetoric, algebra, botany, and physiology. The junior year was devoted to natural philosophy, geometry, mental science, geography of the heavens, chemistry and criticism. In the senior year, sub-

31. *Catalogue of Greensboro Female College*, 1860-1861, pp. 20-21.
32. Sigourney, L. H., *Letters to Young Ladies*, p. 104.
33. *Catalogue of Salem Female Academy*, 1859-1860, p. 17.
34. *The Evergreen*, October, 1851, p. 331.

jects like logic, Butler's *Analogy*, trigonometry, mineralogy, astronomy, and the evidences of Christianity were studied. The classical department, based on a four-year course, included, in addition to all the work of the English department, the Greek, Latin, and French languages. There were also special fields of work in which the student might engage herself — work in wax fruit flowers, ornamental needle work in worsted, chenille, etc., oil painting, Florentine painting, studies in heads, crayon, and pastille, and vocal, piano, guitar, or melodeon music. Plain needle work was required of all, and a part of every week was set aside for such instruction. Among the texts used there were Davie's *Arithmetic*, Bullion's *English*, Latin and Greek grammars, Town's *Spelling Book and Analysis*, Woodbridge and William's *Geography*, Mitchell's *Outline Maps*, Watts's *On the Mind*, Davie's *Algebra*, Legendre's *Geometry*, Newman's *Rhetoric*, Lincoln's *Botany*, Paley's *Natural Theology*, Burritt's *Geography of the Heavens*, Blair's *Lectures*, Maffett's *Natural Philosophy*, Smillie's *Natural History*, Alexander's *Evidences*, Kame's *Elements of Criticism*, Draper's *Chemistry*, Wayland's *Moral Philosophy*, and the works of Milton and Shakespeare.[35] The catalogue of Greensboro Female College for 1858-1859 showed that out of the 351 pupils enrolled, 102 were studying piano, fifteen were studying guitar, twenty were studying painting, and fifty-seven were enrolled in Latin and French and none in Greek. The remaining 155 were enrolled in the preparatory and in the English departments. From these figures, it will be seen that the subject of "piano" was highly important and that the classics were of little significance. Perhaps this fact helps in part to explain some of the criticism against the collegiate curriculum for women of the *ante-bellum* period.

Three chief objects were sought by these schools, said Braxton Craven in the July issue of *The Southern Index*, 1850, — exterior accomplishments, mental culture, and education of character. To him the primary purpose seemed to be exterior

---

35. The titles given to these books are by no means considered complete. They are given as they were found in the catalogues and advertisements, etc.

accomplishments. Satirically, he remarked: "Smiles are graded by the angle, blushes are colored to suit the emotion pretended, lisping is taught with as much system as French, salutation in so many steps, forward-march, and adieu is to show a ring, a pretty hand, and bend whalebone."[36] Such a criticism probably had an element of truth in it, but it must be remembered that those who were concerned with the education of girls were serious about the type of curriculum which was offered. Each course presented had a purpose. Music was studied to soothe the feelings, to build up the spirit, to keep away sadness, and to control the passions. An excellent clergyman, who was said to have possessed great knowledge of human nature, was asked if there were any secret in the mode of educating his daughters. He replied, "When anything disturbs their temper, I say to them sing, and if I hear them speaking against any person, I call them to sing to me, and so they have sung away all causes of discontent, and every disposition to scandal."[37] As for the art of reading aloud, "What simpler repayal than this of the price of nurture to an aged father?" it was asked. "What sweeter solace to the sick, whom it is woman's mission to tend? What surer mode of kindling love of books in young children?"[38] Botany, as a science, was considered especially fitted for the gentler sex "to whose country rambles it gives endless variety, while it inspires them with ever increasing reverence for the author of creation."[39] Chemistry, astronomy, botany, and natural history were supposed to be found useful in every day life, as well as learning to sew and to do those things which made a home attractive. Painting was engaged in both as a means of beautifying the home and of keeping the mind away from evil thoughts. Drawing, it was said, "heightens the admiration of nature by enforcing a closer examination of her exquisite workmanship, from hues of the wild flower, to the grandeur of the forest, and

36. *The Southern Index*, July, 1850, p. 38.
37. Sigourney, L. H., *op. cit.*, p. 111.
38. Orton, J., *The Liberal Education of Women*, p. 125.
39. *Ibid.*, p. 125.

the glowing beauties of the extended landscape."[40] History imparted subjects of lofty contemplation and offered many moral lessons. Mental philosophy was to promote self-knowledge. Critical attitudes were to be avoided, while meekness and reverence were encouraged. Justification for the foreign languages was found in the disciplining of the mind, and for English, its use in society. One reason advanced for the teaching of dancing was, as Addison said, so that a lady would "know how to sit still gracefully."[41] George Davis in delivering an address before the students of Greensboro Female College, in 1856, emphasized the teaching of womanly graces. "The flowing drapery, the speaking attitude, and the graceful fall of limbs; so that the gazer may behold, and wonder, how nature and art, when working lovingly together, may adorn and beautify each other." Yet he would not have the ladies made beautiful "with powders, pomades and patches; nor yet with waltzes, redowas and polkas," but that this beauty should be forthcoming from the heart.[42] There was little thought of physical education.

This philosophy of their education seems to have been accepted with little protest from the students. Yet it must not be expected that collegiate girls of the *ante-bellum* period did not have their interests and activities or that they were always gentle and passive in accepting college laws. The dressing craze of 1850 horrified the editor of *The Southern Index* who said, "In every female school of which we have any knowledge the majority spend more for dressing than the amount of the real school bill." He went on to say that "an internal view would exhibit misses in every condition and humor except agreeable; some pouting because they have out courtesied a rival, some pretending to be sick to avoid study, some swearing (be not alarmed, for it is the truth) that the food is intolerable, some stealing corn dodgers from the table, and some buying nic-

---

40. Sigourney, L. H., *op. cit.*, p. 110.
41. *Ibid.*, p. 113.
42. Davis, George, *Address Delivered Before the Young Ladies of Greensboro Female College*, May, 1856, pp. 11-12.

nacs from the servants."[13] Such an opinion, however, notwithstanding the editor's acquaintance with the girls' colleges of
the period, appears somewhat exaggerated. There were other
interests and activities. Usually, there were two literary societies in each institution, where reading and reciting were participated in once each week. Compositions of honor were also
read on the first Monday of each month by three or more students before the student body assembled. At Salem each girl
was given a garden spot in which she could cultivate flowers.
Picnics were frequently held and a walk every Sunday afternoon, unless the weather were bad, helped to break the monotony of the daily routine. The arrival of a new student or a visitor
aroused the feminine curiosity and provoked the usual feminine
"gossip." Regulations of the colleges usually demanded that
young ladies should be in bed by nine o'clock P.M. but, if some
letters written by a student at Greensboro in 1851 are to be believed, faculty members were often called up in the night hours
by the sound of a "violent noise in the passage."[44] Letter writing and letter receiving had interests as well as the receiving
of April fool notes from the boys at Chapel Hill and from other
colleges. At Salem, Christmas offered an opportunity for an
impressive ceremony with dialogues, singing, and the reciting
of poems. New Year's day and Easter were also celebrated.
Commencement, with its oral examinations, love-making, addresses, concerts, dancing, and graduation, was sufficient for
a climax to the college year.

In summary, no effort was made by the state during the

43. *The Southern Index,* July, 1850, pp. 38-40. The bustle, which was
quite popular among the ladies in the 1850's, gave much opportunity
for funmaking among the men. William Hooper, delivering an address
before the student body of the University in 1859, said of the ladies:
"There is no limit to their inventive genius when it is stimulated by
an encroachment on their rightful domains. They have added to the
dimensions of their fame, as well as to their person, by giving birth
to a new order of architecture." — Hooper, William, *Fifty Years Since,*
p. 9.

44. Weaver, C. C., "Greensboro Female College Before the War" in
The College Message, April, 1897, p. 101.

ante-bellum period to establish schools for its women, although some creditable interest was manifested by the denominations and by private individuals. The principal effort and accomplishment in the education of women appeared in Salem Female Academy, founded by the Moravians in 1802, although they had been active in affording elementary education to their girls as early as 1772. The work of William Falkner and of Jacob Mordecai during the early period was also commendable. Following the era of Jacksonian democracy, more than a dozen academies, seminaries, and colleges for women were established, the most prominent of which seems to have been the Greensboro Female College, chartered by the Methodist in 1838 and opened in 1846. The training offered by these schools was never of a superior kind, but measured by the purpose, which was to make good wives and house-keepers, their work seems to rank quite high. It is to be noticed also that most of these schools were established in the larger towns, while the boys' schools were located in secluded spots. This may be accounted for by the fact that it was believed that girls were not as subject to vicious habits as were the boys. Nevertheless, there is some evidence which shows that many of the fairer sex gave the faculty no little trouble in the administration of the college laws.

IX

Conclusions

During the colonial period no institution of higher education was established in North Carolina, due to geographic, economic, and religious conditions. The coast line of the colony,
which lacked good harbors, was not favorable to the growth of
large cities and the encouragement of European commerce. Settlers, coming largely from Virginia and Pennsylvania, tended
to scatter themselves over wide areas and to lead an extremely frontier life. In time, there grew up a class system which did
not stimulate interest in the establishment of a college. Moreover, denominational interest was strong, particularly among
the Presbyterians and the Episcopalians, but due to theological
differences there was a lack of harmony and no denomination
was strong enough in itself to support an institution of higher
education. Sectionalism, promoted by the control of the eastern
part of the colony over the west; differences between the legislative and executive bodies; disputes with England; and European practices in government were among the forces which
made it impossible for the people of the colony to take an active interest in education.

The American Revolution, fostered by new ideals in government, brought about a new state of conditions and led to the
founding of the University of North Carolina. Democratic ideas
of government also called for a new type of curriculum, one
based on the sciences rather than on the traditional classics
These new ideas in education, first encouraged by the English

262

liberals, were put actively into practice by the French in their scientific academies. In America, these new ideas were first advocated by Benjamin Franklin in his plan of education, published in 1749, and first actively put into practice by the University of Pennsylvania. In North Carolina, the leader for eighteenth century rationalism was William R. Davie who introduced the bill for, and made possible the chartering of, the University in 1789. The institution opened its doors in 1795. But the terrors of the French Revolution, the inability to find teachers who were suitably trained, and the persuasions of a devout and energetic classicist, Joseph Caldwell, who became professor of mathematics at the University in 1796, caused Davie to lose faith in his ideal. By 1804, the University had completely returned to the classical fold.

The election of Caldwell as president of the University in 1804 gave the trustees at least a hope of the continued existence of the institution, for he was already recognized as an able leader. During his presidency, which lasted from 1804 to 1835, with the exception of a brief period from 1812 to 1816, the foundations were laid on which a greater institution could be built. The period was marked particularly by a struggle with financial poverty, strong classical interests, and a close scrutiny of the activities of students. From 1835 to 1860, David Lowry Swain served as president of the University, and under him the institution became the leading college in the Southern States and approached a position of national significance. During these years, the purpose of the institution was the training of politicians and servants of the state. Strong scientific interests again were manifested, but only slight inroads were made into the well established classical curriculum. The leader for this scientific progress was Elisha Mitchell, who stood out above all the other members of the *ante-bellum* university faculty in scholarship and in service to the state.

The answer for the failure of the denominations to found an institution of higher education in North Carolina before the second quarter of the nineteenth century is found in the revolt against theology during the revolutionary period and in the

263

lack of organization among the denominations present within the state. With the passing of the eighteenth century, however, there was a marked revival in denominational interest which brought with it a demand for more trained ministers. But for three more decades poverty and the lack of organization prevented the establishing of denominational colleges. Attempts by the Presbyterians as early as 1820 to found a college finally materialized with the opening of Davidson in 1837. The Baptists were more successful in their first efforts and opened Wake Forest Institute in 1834, which became Wake Forest College in 1838. The institution which grew into Trinity College, now Duke University, did not come under the control of the Methodists until 1859, although it had seen more than three decades of careful nursing, first as an old field school and then as an academy and Normal College. The efforts of Braxton Craven to establish a permanent normal college were commendable. The Quakers, Episcopalians, German Reformed, and Lutherans also made attempts to establish colleges.

The curriculum of all the *ante-bellum* colleges was dominated by the classics. Exceptions to this rule were found in the elective scientific curriculum followed by the University during the first decade of its life and the curriculum prescribed for Normal College. But, in general, Latin and Greek were required of all students. Some attention was given to French, Spanish, and even German. There was little instruction in history and English literature as those subjects are known today. In the field of science such subjects as astronomy, chemistry, and mineralogy were taught. Mathematics occupied a high position because of its supposed powers of mental discipline. The subject of political economy resembled in some aspects modern courses in economics, and that of mental science, present day courses in physiology, psychology, and philosophy. Along with these courses went an attempt to indoctrinate the students into the ideas of revealed religion. Attendance at two Sunday services as well as morning and evening prayers daily was required of all students. Learning was a process of memory rather than reason, and the rule of submission rather than activity was followed. In general, training was for the speaking professions — law and the ministry.

Life on the campus and in the classroom seems not to have been very attractive to students. Amidst the dull routine of every day chores, students found pleasure in letter writing, playing pranks on the professors, engaging in night riots about the village, and in participating in some form of athletics. Hunting, fishing, playing bandy, and skating were particularly interesting in the field of sports. Interest in the literary societies, of which there were two at each institution, was quite dominant. Interest in fraternity organizations failed to develop at any of the institutions, with the exception of the University and there only for a decade prior to the Civil War, but secret clubs were in existence at all times. Independence Day, Thanksgiving, and Washington's Birthday, were celebrated with much gusto, as well as commencement day with its graduation exercises and balls. The only student publication for the period was the *North Carolina University Magazine,* first published in 1844.

In spite of the close scrutiny of the faculty, student morals were probably neither better nor worse than they are today. Within the colleges there were at all times a certain group of students who drank to excess, chewed tobacco and spat in whatever place seemed convenient, gambled, indulged in sexual immorality, fought with pistols and swords, stole money and other valuables, and practiced the art of cheating and lying. But such behavior inside the college campus was not strikingly unlike the behavior outside during the period. Students were merely reflecting the morals and manners which they had learned in the midst of a rapidly growing southern slaveocracy. But in their dress all students did not bear the marks of aristocracy. Many of them wore patched tousers and even went barefooted at times. Long curly hair, quite often a moustache, bright waistcoast, low neck tie, long pistol-like trousers, and homemade shoes were often in evidence in the eighteen forties.

In the field of the higher education of women the quality of the education offered was not altogether unlike that found in the academy of the period. No attempt seems to have been

made at any time during the colonial period toward establishing of a girl's school, and the educational training that was
offered consisted largely of the simple forms of reading, writing,
and arithmetic. The interpretation of the constitution of 1776
and of the charter of the University of North Carolina left girls
out of educational consideration; in fact, the state at no time
during the *ante-bellum* period took an interest in the higher
education of its women. Prominent among the girls' schools established were Salem Academy, founded by the Moravians in
1802, and Greensboro Female College, chartered by the Methodists in 1838 and opened in 1846. The Jacksonian era gave
considerable impetus to the education of women for during the
period from 1840 to 1860 more than a dozen girls' colleges,
seminaries, and academies were established here and there in
the state. In general, the curriculum offered in these schools
had as its sole purpose the training of women for service in the
home. A woman must be prepared for domestic duties. Little
interest was taken in the classics and only a smattering of science was taught. English, music, painting, and sewing were
considered the most useful subjects in the curriculum. Emphasis
in teaching was placed on the obedience and humility of those
taught. The scrutinizing care of the faculty was even more
close than in the boys' colleges. Nevertheless, the work of the
girls' schools seem to have been successful and creditable when
measured by the standards of the time.

BIBLIOGRAPHY

I. *Manuscript sources:*

Accompts for the Hillsborough Academy, Begun 1789 (North Carolina Historical Commission)

Addresses of the Dialectic Society, 1797-1860, 4 Vols. (vault of the University library)

Autographs, (Material concerning the *ante-bellum* University — in the vault of the University library)

Book of the Law Club of the University of North Carolina, July 24, 1847-April 30, 1849 (vault of the University library)

Brooks, W. T., *Diary,* 1834-1849 (vault of the Wake Forest library)

John H. Bryan Papers, 1773-1825, Vol. I (North Carolina Historical Commission)

Bursar's Ledger, 1835-1860 (vault of the University library)

Caldwell, Joseph, *A New System of Geometry,* 1806 (vault of the University library)

Daughters in the Boarding School in Salem, 1802-1860 (Register of the students of Salem Academy — in Moravian Archives)

Demerit Roll of the Students of the University of North Carlina (vault of the University library)

Bryan Grimes Papers, 1844-1863, Vol. I (North Carolina Historical Commission)

History of the University of North Carolina (vault of the University library)

Journal of the Examination Committee of the University of North Carolina, 1795-1809 (vault of the University library)

Journal of the Faculty of the University of North Carolina, 1795-1860 (vault of the University library)

267

Journal of the University of North Carolina, 1789-1859 (Treasurer's reports — vault of the University library)

Letters to the Philanthropic Society, 1808-1860 (vault of the University library)

Letters, University of North Carolina, 1796-1835 (vault of the University library)

Willie P. Mangum Papers, 1847-1849 (North Carolina Historical Commission)

Minutes of the Board of Trustees of Davidson College, 1836-1860, (vault of Davidson College Library)

Minutes of the Board of Trustees of the University of North Carolina, 1789-1860 (vault of the University library)

Minutes of the Dialectic Literary Society, 1795-1860 (vault of the University library)

Minutes of the Eumenean Society of Davidson College, 1838-1860 (vault of Davidson College library)

Minutes of the Euzelian Society of Wake Forest College, 1835-1860 (bursar's office of the college)

Minutes of the Executive Committee of the University of North Carolina, 1835-1860 (vault of the University library)

Minutes of the Faculty of Davidson College, 1842-1861 (vault of Davidson College library)

Minutes of the North Carolina Annual Conference of the Methodist Episcopal Church, 1840-1860 (vault of Duke University library)

Minutes of the Philanthropic Society of Davidson College, 1838-1860 (vault of Davidson College library)

Minutes of the Philanthropic Society of Davidson College, 1838-1860 (vault of Davidson College library)

Minutes of the Philanthropic Society, 1797-1860 (vault of the University library)

Minutes of the Philomathesian Society of Wake Forest College, 1835-1860 (bursar's office of the college)

Mitchell, Elisha, *Notebook* (vault of the University library)

Archibald D. Murphey Papers, 1797-1817, Vol. I (North Carolina Historical Commission)

Pettigrew Letters, 1844-1847, Vol. XI (North Carolina Historical Commission)

Record Book of the Faculty of Wake Forest College, 1856-1897 (bursar's office of the college)

Records of the Fines Imposed by the Philanthropic Society,
1856-1859 (vault of the University library)

*(A) Record of the Proceedings of the Alumni Association of
the University of North Carolina,* 1843-1868 (vault of the
University library)

*(A) Record of the Proceedings of the Board of Trustees of
Wake Forest College,* 1834-1888 (bursar's office of the college)

*Reports From the Faculty to the Board of Trustees of the
University of North Carolina,* 1795-1860 (vault of the University library)

Resolutions and By-laws of the Board of Trustees of Davidson College, 1836-1856 (vault of Davidson College library)

Senior Speeches, University of North Carolina, 1856 (vault of
the University library)

Statutes Relative to the University of North Carolina, 1788-1824 (vault of the University library)

Swain Papers (North Carolina Historical Commission)

Zebulon B. Vance Papers, 1827-1863, Vol. I (North Carolina
Historical Commission)

Calvin H. Wiley Papers, 1835-1852 (North Carolina Historical Commission)

II. *Printed sources:*

Abercrombie, John, *Inquiries Concerning the Intellectual Powers and the Investigation of Truth,* New York, Collins, 1859.

Adams, Hannah, *A Summary History of New England,* 1608-1787, Dedham. Mann, 1799.

(The) American Speaker, Boston. Cummings, 1826.

Asbury, Francis, *The Journal of the Reverend Francis Asbury, Bishop of the Methodist Episcopal Church, from August 7, 1771, to December 7, 1815,* New York. Bangs, 1821, 3 Vols.

Autobiography and Biography of Rev. Joseph Caldwell, D.D., Ll.D., Chapel Hill. Neathery, 1860.

Battle, K. P., "The DeRosset Papers" in *The James Sprunt Historical Studies,* 1903, No. 4.

Beattie, James, *Evidences of the Christian Religion*, London. Strahan, 1788.

Bischof, Gustav, *Elements of Chemical and Physical Geology*, London, Cavendish, 1854.

Blair, Hugh, *Lectures on Rhetoric and Belles Lettres*, London. Strahan, 1787.

Brickell, John, *The Natural History of North Carolina*, Dublin, Carson, 1737.

Brown, Thomas, *Lectures on the Philosophy of the Human Mind*, Philadelphia, Gregg, 1824, 3 Vols.

Burkitt, L. and Read, j., *A Concise History of the Kehukee Baptist Association*, Halifax. Hodge, 1803.

Burlamqui, J. J., *The Principles of Natural Law*, Dublin, Rice, 1791.

Butler, Frederick, *A Complete History of the United States of America*, Hartford, Author, 1821.

Byrd, William, *The Westover Manuscripts: Containing the History of the Dividing Line Betwixt Virginia and North Carolina*, Petersburg. Ruffin, 1841.

Caldwell, Joseph, *A Compendium System of Elementary Geometry*, Philadelphia. Fry, 1822.

Caldwell, Joseph, *Letters on Popular Education*, Hillsborough. Heartt, 1832.

Campbell, George, *The Philosophy of Rhetoric*, Boston. Ewer, 1833.

Carey, H. C., *Principles of Political Economy*, Philadelphia. Carey, 1837, 3 Vols.

Catalogues, Greensborough Female College, 1846-1860.

Catalogue of Normal College, 1854.

Catalogues of Salem Female Academy, 1854-1860.

Catalogue of Trinity College, 1859-1860.

Catalogue of the Trustees, Faculty, and Students of Davidson College, 1842-1860.

Catalogue of the Trustees, Faculty, and Students of Wake Forest (Institute) College, 1836-1860.

Catalogues of the University of North Carolina, 1817-1860.

Cavallo, Tiberius, *The Elements of Natural or Experimental Philosophy*, Philadelphia. Fry, 1813, 2 Vols.

Coon, C. L., *North Carolina Schools and Academies, 1790-1840* (a Documentary History), Raleigh. Edwards and

Broughton, 1915.

Defoe, Daniel, "Augusta Triumphans" in *The Complete English Tradesman*, Oxford, Talboys, 1841, Vol. II,

Eleventh Annual Announcement of Oxford Female College, 1861.

Enfield, William, *The History of Philosophy*, Dublin, Wogan, 1792, 2 Vols.

The Speaker or Miscellaneous Pieces, Hudson, Stoddard, 1798.

Ferguson, James, *Astronomy Explained Upon Sir Isaac Newton's Principles*, London. Johnson, 1799 .

Greek Grammar, Boston, Hilliard, 1828.

Fordyce, David, *Dialogues Concerning Education*, London. (no publisher) 1745, 2 Vols.

Franklin, Benjamin, *Proposals For the Education of Youth in Pennsylvania*, Ann Arbor. Clements Library, 1927.

Fuller, Edwin W., *Sea Gift*, New York. Hale, 1873.

Garland, Langdon C., *An Elementary Treatise on Plane Trigonometry*, Philadelphia. Hogan, 1842.

Gough, John, *Practical Arithmetick*, Dublin. (no publisher), 1810.

Grant, Daniel L., *Alumni History of the University of North Carolina*, Chapel Hill. General Alumni Association, 1924.

Grimes, J. Bryan, *North Carolina Wills and Inventories*, Raleigh. Edwards & Broughton, 1912.

Gummere, John, *A Treatise on Surveying*, Philadelphia, Kimber, 1825.

Gutherie, William, *The Orations of Cicero*, London. Whieldon, 1778.

Hamilton, J. G. deR., "Letters of John Rust Eaton" in *The James Sprunt Historical Studies*, Vol. XI, No. 1.

"The Political and Professional Career of Bartlett Yancey" in *The James Sprunt Historical Studies*, Vol. X, No. 2.

"William Richardson Davie; a Memoir" in *The James Sprung Historical Studies*, Vol. VII, No. 1.

Hedge, Levi, *Elements of Logick*, Boston. Cummings, 1824.

Heron, Robert, *A New and Complete System of Universal Geography*, Edinburg. Morrison, 1796.

Hooper, William, *A Short System of Latin Prosody*, Raleigh. Author, 1819.

Horne, T. H., *An Introduction to the Critical Study and*

Knowledge of the Holy Scriptures, Philadelphia. Littell, 1825, 4 Vols.

Hoyt, W. H., *The Papers of Archibald D. Murphey,* Raleigh. Uzzell, 1914, 2 vols.

Hume, David, *The History of England From Julius Caesar to 1688,* Edinburg, Mudie, 1792, 8 Vols.

Hutton, Charles, *A Treatise on Mensuration,* London. Glendinning, 1802.

Jones, E. Alfred, *American Members of the Inns of Court,* London. Saint Catharine Press, 1924.

Knox, Vicesimus, *Liberal Education,* London (no publisher) 1785, 2 Vols.

Kuhner, Raphael, *Grammar of the Greek Language,* Andover. Allen, 1844.

Laws of the University of North Carolina, 1799-1860.

Lowth, Robert, *A Short Introduction to English Grammar,* Philadelphia. Aitken, 1775.

Lyell, Charles, *Elements of Geology,* Philadelphia. Kay, 1839.

Lyttleton, George, *The History of the Life of King Henry II,* London. Dodsley, 1769.

Mackay, Andrew, *The Complete Navigator,* London. Longman, 1810.

Mair, John, *Introduction to Latin Syntax,* Baltimore. Lucas, 1820.

Mavor, William, *Historical Account of the Most Celebrated Voyages, Travels and Discoveries From the Time of Columbus to the Present Period,* London. Newbery, 1796, 24 Vols.

McCorkle, S. E., *A Discourse on the General First Principles of Deism and Revelation Contrasted,* Salisbury. Coupee, 1797.

Melmoth, Courtney, *The Sublime and Beautiful of Scripture,* New York. Tiebout & O'Brien, 1795.

Memoirs of Edward J. Mallett, May 1, 1880 (not published)

Minutes of the Baptist State Convention, 1832-1860.

Mitchell, Elisha, *Elements of Geology,* University of North Carolina, 1842.

Mitchell, Elisha, *Manual of Chemistry,* (no place, no publisher, no date).

Notes on Natural History (no place, no publisher, no date).

Montesquieu, Charles Louis de Secondat, *The Spirit of Laws,*

London. Bell, 1900-1902, 2 Vols. (Translated by Thomas Mugent).

Morse, Jedediah, *The American Universal Geography*, Boston. Andrews, 1793.

Murray, Lindley, *An English Grammar*, New York. Collins, 1814.

Neilson, William, *Greek Exercises*, New York. Swords, 1810.

Olmsted, W. D., *Outlines of the Lectures on Chemistry, Mineralogy, and Geology*, Raleigh. Gales, 1819.

Prideaux, Humphrey. *The Old and New Testaments Connected*, London. Baynes, 1815.

Priestley, Joseph, *Discourses Relating to the Evidences of Revealed Religion*, Philadelphia. Dobson, 1796.

Lectures on History and General Policy, London. Johnson, 1793, 2 Vols.

Ramsay, David, *History of the United States, 1492-1816*, Philadelphia. Skerrett, 1816, 3 Vols.

Raynal, Abbe, *A Philosophical and Political History*, Edinburg. Godon, 1782, 3 Vols.

Reid, Thomas, *Essays on the Intellectual and Active Powers of Man*, Philadelphia. Young, 1793, 2 Vols.

Rollin, Charles, *The Method of Teaching and Studying the Belles Lettres*, London. Lackington, 1798, 4 Vols.

The Roman History from the Foundation of Rome to the Battle of Actium, London, Knapton, 1750, 15 Vols.

Rosenmuller, E. F. C., *The Biblical Geography of Asia Minor, Phoenicia, and Arabia*, Edinburg. Clark, 1841.

Ruddiman, Thomas, *The Rudiments of the Latin Tongue*, Raleigh. Star, 1809.

Schaw, Janet, *The Journal of a Lady of Quality* (Ed. E. W. and C. M. Andrews), New Haven. Yale University Press, 1921.

(The) Sem-Centennial Catalogue of Davidson College, 1837-1887, Raleigh. Uzzell, 1881.

Sheridan, Thomas, *A Plan of Education for the Young Nobility of Great Britain*, London. Dilly, 1769.

Sigourney, L. H., *Letters to Young Ladies*, New York. Harper's & Bros., 1837.

Simpson, Thomas, *A Treatise on Algebra*, Philadelphia. Palmer, 1809.

Smollett, T., *The History of England from 1688 to the Death of George II*, London. Cadell, 1793.

Stewart, Dugall, *Elements of the Philosophy of the Human Mind*, New York. Eastburn, 1818, 2 Vols.

Strahan, W., *Political Essays Concerning the Present State of the British Empire*, London. Strand, 1772.

Sykes, A. A., *The Principle and Connexion of Natural and Revealed Religion*, London, Knapton, 1740.

Tocqueville, Alexis de, *Democracy in America*, New York. Langley, 1840.

Trimmer, Joshua, *Practical Geology and Mineralogy*, Philadelphia. Lea & Blanchard, 1842.

Upshur, Abel Parker, *A Brief Inquiry into the True Nature and Character of Our Federal Government*, Petersburg, Va., 1840.

Valpy, R., *The Elements of Greek Grammar*, New York. Collins, 1825.

Vattell, Monsieur de, *The Law of Nations*, Philadelphia Small, 1817.

Volney, C. F., *Lectures on History*, Philadelphia. Bioren, 1801.

Voltaire, Monsieur de, *An Essay on Universal History, The Manners and Spirit of Nations*, London. Nourse, 1759, 4 Vols.

Wagstaff, H. M., "The Harris Letters" in *The James Sprunt Historical Studies*, Vol. 14, No. 1.

Wake Forest College, (The) Charter and Laws, 1839.

Wayland, D. S., *The Works of William Paley*, London, Cowie, 1787, 5 Vols.

Wayland, Francis, *The Elements of Moral Science*, Boston. Gould, 1884.

The Elements of Political Economy, New York. Leavitt, 1837.

Webster, Noah, *An American Selection of Lessons in Reading and Speaking*, Boston. Thomas & Andrews, 1803.

Dissertation on the English Language, Boston. Thomas, 1789.

West, Gilbert, *A Defense of the Christian Revelation*, London. Printed by Subscription, 1748.

Whatley, R., *Elements of Logic*, Boston. Munroe, 1843.

Elements of Rhetoric, Boston, Monroe, 1858.

Williamson, Hugh, *The History of North Carolina*, Philadelphia. Dobson, 1812, 2 Vols.

Witherspoon, John, *Lectures on Moral Philosophy and Eloquence*, Philadelphia, Woodward, 1810.

Wood, Thomas, *Germs of Thought; or Rudiments of Knowledge Intended to Promote the Mental and Religious Improvement of Youth*, New York, Mercian, 1821.

Young, J. R., *An Elementary Treatise on Algebra*, Philadelphia. Carey, 1832.

III. *Public Documents*

Annals of the Congress of the United States.

(The) Colonial Records of North Carolina, (Ed. W. L. Saunders) Raleigh. Daniels, 1890, 10 Vols.

Constitution of the United States and of the State of North Carolina, Raleigh. Gales, 1842 (Contains references)

Executive Documents (North Carolina)

House Journal (North Carolina).

Journal of the Legislature (North Carolina).

Laws of North Carolina.

Martin, F. X., *A Collection of the Private Acts of the General Assembly of the State of North Carolina*, Newbern Martin, 1794.

Proceedings and Debates of the North Carolina Convention of 1835, Raleigh. Gales, 1836.

Senate Journal (North Carolina).

(The) State Records of North Carolina (Ed. Walter Clark), Goldsboro, Nash, 1905, 16 Vols.

IV. *Newspapers, periodicals, etc.*

(The) Biblical Recorder, 1835-1860 (Baptist publication).

(The) Evergreen, October, 1851 (Ed. Braxton Craven).

Fayetteville Gazette 1792-

Fayetteville Observer, 1825-1860.

Harbinger, 1833- (Published under the supervision of the University faculty).

Hillsborough Recorder, 1820-1860.

North Carolina Christian Advocate, 1856 (Methodist publication).

North Carolina Chronicle, 1826-

North Carolina Gazette, 1752-
North Carolina Journal, 1792-
(The) North Carolina Journal of Education, 1858-1860 (Ed.
    Calvin H. Wiley).
North Carolina Presbyterian, 1857-1860.
North Carolina Standard, 1835-1860.
North Carolina University Magazine, 1844-1860.
(The) Primitive Baptist, 1836-1847.
Raleigh Register, 1799-1860.
(The) Southern Index, July, 1850 (Ed. Braxton Craven).
Tarborough Free Press, 1824-1851.
Western Carolinian, 1820-1844.

V. *Pamphlets, Articles, etc.*

Badger, George E., *A View of the Question in Controversy Be-
    tween the University of North Carolina and the Claimants
    of Her Western Lands,* Raleigh. Lawerence, 1826.
Baker, Archibald, *The Science of the Mind, Address Deliv-
    ered Before the Two Literary Societies of Davidson Col-
    lege,* July 31, 1845, Raleigh. Gales, 1845.
Barnard, Henry, "The South Atlantic States in 1833" in *Mary-
    land Historical Magazine,* September, 1918.
Berkeley, William, "An Official Report on Virginia" in *Ameri-
    can History Told by Contemporairies* (Ed. A. B. Hart).
    New York. MacMillan, 1901, Vol. I.
Caldwell, Joseph, *Address to the Senior Class and Before the
    Audience Assembled at the Annual Commencement,* June
    28, 1827, Raleigh, Gales, 1827.
Davis, George, *Address Delivered Before the Young Ladies
    of Greensboro Female College, May, 1856,* Greensboro
    Times, 1856.
Dow, Lorenzo, *Extracts from the Original Letters to the Meth-
    odist Bishops,* Liverpool, Forshaw, 1806.
Gaston, William, *Address Delivered Before the Dialectic and
    Philanthropic Societies at Chapel Hill, N.C., June, 1832,*
    Chapel Hill. Henderson, 1858.
Hooper, William, *Fifty Years Since, An Address Delivered Be-
    fore the Alumni Association of the University of North
    Carolina,* June 7, 1879, Chapel Hill. Neathery, 1861.

The Force of Habit, Gorman, Raleigh. 1851.

A Valedictory Address Delivered to the Students of the University of North Carolina, January 21, 1838, Raleigh. Register, 1838.

Howard, George, *Miscellaneous Publications Printed at the Office of the Press at Tarboro, N. C.,* 1833-1837.

Ives, L. S., *The Importance of Christian Education,* Fayetteville. Hale, 1833.

Manly, Charles, *An Address Delivered Before the Alumni and the Senior Class of the University of North Carolina,* June, 1838, Raleigh. Loring, 1838.

Micklejohn, George, "A Sermon" in *The North Carolina Booklet,* Vol. 8.

Mitchell, Elisha, *Arguments for Temperance, Address to the Students of the University of North Carolina,* March 13, 1831, Raleigh. Gales, 1831.

Moore, B. F., *Report on Escheats to the Trustees of the University of North Carolina,* Raleigh. Gales, 1851.

Mordecai, Gratz, *Notice of Jacob Mordecai, Founder, and Proprietor from 1809 to 1819 of the Warrenton (N.C.) Female Seminary,* Philadelphia. American Jewish Historical Society, 1897.

Morrison R. H., *The Inaugural Address, Davidson College, August 2, 1838,* Philadelphia. Martien, 1838.

Palmer, B. M., *Baconianism and the Bible,* Columbia, S. C., Johnston, 1852.

Report of the State of the Episcopal School of North Carolina, November, 1834, Raleigh. Gales, 1834.

Saunders, R. M., *Address Delivered Before the Two Literary Societies of Wake Forest College, June 9, 1852,* Raleigh. Rolden, 1852.

Sparrow, P. M., *Inaugural Address at Davidson Collge, August 2, 1838,* Philadelphia. Martien, 1838.

Statement of the President of the University of North Carolina, December, 19, 1858.

Statistics, Facts, and Dates, for the Sunday Recitations of the Junior Class in the University, Raleigh. Gales, 1843

Thacher, Moses, *An Address Delivered Before the Members of the Anti-Masonic State Convention, Augusta, Maine, July 4, 1832,* Hallowell. Merrick, 1832.

Vance, Z. B., *Life and Character of Honorable David L. Swain*, Durham. Blackwell, 1878.

Vistor, "The First College in North Carolina" in *Hillsborough Recorder* February 24, 1842.

Williamson, Gibbon, "The History of Clubs in the University of North Carolina" in *North Carolina University Magazine*, February, 1856.

I. *General Works*

Ashe, S. A., *History of North Carolina*, Greensboro. Van Noppen, 1908, Vol. I.

Boyd, W. K., *History of North Carolina* (The Federal Period), New York. Lewis, 1919, Vol. II.

Cole, James R., *Miscellany*, Dallas. Bedford, 1897.

Connor, R. D. W., *North Carolina*, New York. The American Historical Society, 1929, Vol. I.

Foote, W. H., *Sketches of North Carolina Historical and Biographical*, New York. Carter, 1846.

Hawks, Francis, *History of North Carolina, 1663-1729*, Fayetteville. Hale, Hale, 1858, 2 Vols.

Knight, E. W., *Education in the United States*, New York Ginn, 1929.

Public Education in the South, New York. Ginn, 1922.

Public School Education in North Carolina, New York Houghton Mifflin, 1916.

Raper, C. L., *The Church and Private Schools of North Carolina*, Greensboro. Stone, 1893.

Smith, C. L., *History of Education in North Carolina*, Washington. Government Printing Office, 1888.

Thwing, C. F., *A History of Higher Education in America*, New York. Appleton, 1906.

II. *Special Works*

Battle, K. P., *History of the University of North Carolina*, Raleigh. Edwards & Broughton,1907-1912, Vol. 1.

Bernheim, G. D., & Cox, G. H., *The History of the Evangelical Lutheran Synod and Ministerium of North Carolina*, Philadelphia. Lutheran Synod Pub. Society, 1902.

278

Blandin, I. M. E., *History of Higher Education of Women in the South Prior to 1860*, New York. Neale, 1909.

Burkhead, L. S., *Centennial of Methodism in North Carolina*, Raleigh. Nichols, 1876.

Chamberlain, H. S., *Old Days in Chapel Hill, Being the Life and Letters of Cornelia Phillips Spencer*, Chapel Hill University Press, 1926.

Connor, R. D. W., *Ante-Bellum Builders of North Carolina*, Greensboro. (North Carolina State Normal and Industrial College Historical Publication No. 3), 1914.

Coulter, E. M., *College Life in the Old South*, New York. Macmillan, 1928.

Crittendon, C. C., "North Carolina Newspapers Before 1790" in *The James Sprunt Historical Studies*, Vol. 20, No. 1.

Dowd, Clement, *Life of Zebulon Baird Vance*, Charlotte. Observer Press, 1897.

Dowd, Jerome, *Life of Braxton Craven, D.D., LL.D.*, Raleigh. Edwards, 1896.

Fay, Bernard, *The Revolutionary Spirit in France and America*, New York. Harcourt, Brace & Co., 1927.

Grissom, W. L., *History of Methodism in North Carolina from 1772 to the Present Time*, Nashville. Smith & Lamar, 1908.

Hansen, A. O., *Liberalism and American Education in the Eighteenth Century*, New York. MacMillan, 1826.

Historical Sketch of the Reformed Church in North Carolina, (Board of Editors) Philadelphia. Reformed Church, 1908.

Huxley, Thomas H., *Science and Culture*, New York. Appleton, 1884.

Jordan, David S., *The Trend of the American University* California. Stanford Press, 1928.

Klain, Zora, *Quaker Contributions to Education in North Carolina*, Philadelphia. Westbrook, 1925.

Konkle, B. A., *John Motley Morehead and the Development of North Carolina, 1796-1866*, Philadelphia. Campbell, 1922.

Leonard, J. C., *History of Catawba College*, (no place,) Trustees of College, 1927.

Macaulay, Thomas B., *Lord Bacon"*, in *Critical and Historical Essays*. London, Longman's, 1866, Vol. II.

Montgomery, L. W., *Sketches of Old Warrenton North Carolina*, Raleigh. Edwards & Broughton, 1924.

Oliver, David D., "The Society for the Propagation of the Gospel in North Carolina" in *The James Sprunt Historical Studies*, Vol. IX, No. 1.

Orton, Jr., *The Liberal Education of Women*, New York Barnes, 1873.

Parrington, V. S., *The Colonial Mind, 1620-1800*, New York Harcourt Brace & Co. 1927.

Randall, J. H., *The Making of the Modern Mind*, New York Houghton Miffling Co., 1926.

Schmidt, G. P., *The Old Time College President*, Columbia University Press, 1929.

Shaw, C. R., *Davidson College*, New York. Revell, 1928.

Slosson, E. E., *The American Spirit in Education*, New Haven. Yale University Press, 1921.

Snow, A. J., *Matter and Gravity in Newton's Physical Philosophy*, London, Oxford, 1926.

Sparks, Jared, "Lives of William Richardson Davie and Samuel Kirkland" in *The Library of Ameircan Biography*, Boston. Little & Brown, 1848, Vol. XV.

Spencer, C. P., *Pen and Ink Sketches of the University of North Carolina*, (not published)

Taylor, C. E., *General Catalogue of Wake Forest College*. 1834-1892, Raleigh. Edwards, 1892.

Thwing, C. F., *The American and the German University*, New York. MacMillan, 1928. ,

Weeks, S. B., *Libraries and Literature in North Carolina in the Eighteenth Century*, Washington. Government, 1896.

The Press of North Carolina in the Eighteenth Century, Brooklyn, Hist. Printing Club, 1891.

Welker, G. W., *Historical Sketch of the Reformed Church in North Carolina*, Philadelphia. (Board of Editors), 1908.

Williams, Charles B., *A History of the Baptists of North Carolina*, Raleigh. Edwards & Broughton, 1901.

III. *Newspapers, Periodicals, etc.*

(The) Academy, 1876- (Official publication of the Salem Female Academy)

Alumni Register of Duke University, 1925-1930.

(The) Alumni Review, 1912-1930 (University).

Chapel Hill Weekly, 1923-1930.

(The) College Message (Official publication of the Greensboro Female College)

Davidson College Magazine, 1870-1930.

(The) James Sprunt Historical Studies, University of North Carolina, 1900-1930.

(The) North Carolina University Magazine, 1860-1930.

(The) North Carolina Booklet, Raleigh. The North Carolina Society Daughters of the Revolution, 1903-1926.

Trinity Alumni Register, 1115-1924...

(The) University of North Carolina Record, 1896-1929.

(The) Wake Forest Student, 1882-1930.

IV. *Pamphlets, Articles, etc.*

Ashe, S. A., "Social Conditions in North Carolina in 1783" in *The North Carolina Booklet,* Vol. X, April, 1911.

Baldwin, J. A., "History of Methodism in North Carolina, 1800-1837" in *Raleigh Christian Advocate,* February 7, 1894.

Barnard, W., "The Columbian Literary Society" in *Trinity Alumni Register,* October, 1915.

Bassett, J. S., "Some Phases of Early Plantation Life in North Carolina" in *The Trinity Archive,* 1892, Vol. 6.

Battle, R. H., "Memoir of Reverend Charles Phillips" in the *North Carolina University Magazine,* 1890, No. 1.

"The Dialectic Society of the University of North Carolina From 1850-1854" in *Catalogue of the Members of the Dialectic Society,* Baltimore. Friedenwall, 1890.

Brooks, E. C., "The First State Normal Becomes Trinity College" in *Trinity Alumni Register,* July, 1915.

"Braxton Craven and Trinity College" in *Trinity Alumni Register,* January, 1916.

Brown, E. E., "The Origin of the American State University" in *University of California Publications,* Vol. #, April, 1903.

Cheshire, J. B., "Decay and Revival" in Sketches of *Church History in North Carolina,* Wilmington. De Rosset, 1892.

Cobb, Collier, "Some Beginnings in Science" in *Popular Science Monthly,* October, 1896.

Cole, James R., "Trinity College Ante-bellum" in *Trinity Alumni Register,* April, 1915.

Craven, Braxton, "Historical Sketch of Trinity College" in *Centennial of Methodism in North Carolina* (Ed. L. S Burkhead) Raleigh. Nichols, 1876.

Drake, W. E., "Benjamin Franklin and the University of North Carolina" in *The High School Journal,* February, 1929.

Drane, R. B., "Colonial Parishes and Church Schools" in *Sketches of Church History in North Carolina,* Wilmington. DeRosset, 1892.

Fries, A. L., *Historical Sketch of Salem Female Academy.* Salem. Keehin, 1902.

Goodsell, Willystine, "The Education of Women" in *Twenty-Five Years of American Education* (Ed. I. L. Kandel) New York. Macmillan, 1924.

Haywood, M. D., "The Story of Queens College or Liberty Hall in the Province of North Carolina" in *The North Carolina Booklet,* Vol. 11, No. 3.

Holden, W. W., *Address on the History of Journalism in North Carolina,* Raleigh. News and Observer, 1881.

Holton, Holland, "The Beginnings of the Hesperian Literary Society" in *Trinity Alumni Register,* January, 1916.

Hooper, A. M., "The Life of William Hooper" in *The North Carolina Booklet,* 1905, Vol. 5.

Johnson, H. V., "A Sketch of the Fraternities of the University of North Carolina" in *North Carolina University Magazine,* February, 1916.

Johnston, R. Z., "The Administration of Reverend Drury Lacy, D.D." in *First Semi-Centenary of Davidson College,* June 13, 1887, Raleigh, Uzzell, 1888.

Lewis, McDaniel, "Early Athletics" in *North Carolina University Magazine,* May, 1914.

Lewis, R. H., "Athletics in the University, Muscular and Vocal Forty Years Ago" in *North Carolina University Magazine,* 1894-1895.

Lewis, R. H., "A Brief Sketch of the Dialectic Society, 1848-1852" in *Catalogue of the Members of the Dialectic Society,* Baltimore. Friedenwall, 1890.

Nash, Francis, "The History of Orange County" in *The North Carolina Booklet,* October, 1910.

Orr, J. L., "A Log College and Its President" in *North Carolina University Magazine,* March, 1912.

Paschal, G. W., "History of Wake Forest College" in *Wake Forest College Bulletin*, Vols. XIX-XXII.

Peacock, Dred, "Some Things Not Generally Known About Trinity College" in *Greensboro Daily News*, October 23, 1929.

"President Polk's Visit to the University of North Carolina" in *North Carolina University Magazine*, March, 1907.

Pritchard, D. D., "Brief History of the Literary Society" in *The Wake Forest Student*, 1882, Vol. 1, No. 2.

Purefoy, James, "Wake Forest College — Its Birth" in *The Wake Forest Student*, 1886, Vol. V, No. 5.

Pugh, J. F., "The History of the University of North Carolina Library" in *North Carolina University Magazine*, March, 1914.

Ramsay, J. G., "The Administration of the Reverend Robert Hall Morrison" in *First Semi-Centenary Celebration of Davidson College, June 13, 1887*, Raleigh. Uzzell, 1888.

Raper, C. L., "Social Life in Colonial North Carolina" in *The North Carolina Booklet*, 1903, Vol. 1.

Spencer, C. P., "Old Days in Chapel Hill" in *North Carolina University Magazine*, 1884-1889.

Waddell, A. M., *The Ante-bellum University, Oration Delivered at the Celebration of the Centennial of the University of North Carolina*, Wilmington. Bell, 1895.

Wait, Rev. Samuel, "The Origin and Early History of Wake Forest College" in *The Wake Forest Student*, October, 1882.

White, A., "The Administration of Reverend Samuel Williamson's in *First Semi-Centenary Celebration of Davidson College, June 13, 1887*, Raleigh. Uzzell, 1888.

Woolicott, Philip, "Fifty Four Years of the Y.M.C.A." in *North Carolina University Magazine*, April, 1914.